THE SNOW **W9-CSM-181**

In 1973, Peter Matthiessen and field biologist George Schaller traveled high into the remote mountains of Nepal to study the Himalayan blue sheep and possibly glimpse the rare and beautiful snow leopard. Matthiessen, a student of Zen Buddhism, was also on a spiritual quest to find the Lama of Shey at the ancient shrine on Crystal Mountain. As the climb proceeds, Matthiessen charts his inner path as well as his outer one, with a deepening Buddhist understanding of reality, suffering, impermanence, and beauty. An unforgettable spiritual journey through the Himalayas, *The Snow Leopard* is perhaps the crowning achievement of Peter Matthiessen's remarkable body of writing.

"One of the most wonderful accounts I know of journeying in our time."

—W. S. Merwin

"You could well school yourself as a young American writer, in the early 21st century, by reading and then rereading the works of Peter Matthiessen. But of course he wasn't just a writer's writer; he was for all readers. He was for the world."

—*National Geographic*

PENGUIN CLASSICS

THE SNOW LEOPARD

PETER MATTHIESSEN (1927–2014) is the only writer who has ever won the National Book Award in both fiction and nonfiction. His travels as a naturalist and explorer have resulted in more than a dozen books on natural history and the environment, including *The Snow Leopard*, his first NBA winner. Matthiessen's equally important career in fiction has produced a collection of stories and nine novels, among them *At Play in the Fields of the Lord* (an NBA finalist) and the Everglades trilogy (*Killing Mister Watson, Lost Man's River,* and *Bone by Bone*), which, rewritten and distilled, were published in one volume in 2008 under the title *Shadow Country*, winner of the NBA in fiction. *Shadow Country* was also the 2010 recipient of the William Dean Howells Medal, given by the American Academy of Arts and Letters for the most distinguished American novel published during the previous five years. Matthiessen was a member of the American Academy of Arts and Letters. His final novel, *In Paradise*, was published just after his death in 2014.

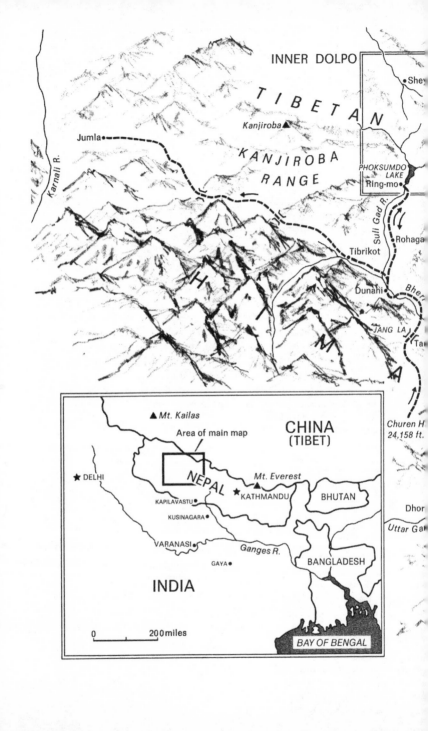

INNER DOLPO

T I B E T A N

Shey

Kanjiroba ▲

Jumla ●

KANJIROBA RANGE

PHOKSUMDO LAKE

Ring-mo ●

Karnali R.

Suli Gad R.

Rohaga ●

Tibrikot ●

Dunahi ●

Bheri

JANG LA

Ta

Churen H. 24,158 ft.

▲ Mt. Kailas

Area of main map

CHINA (TIBET)

★ DELHI

NEPAL

Mt. Everest ▲

★ KATHMANDU

BHUTAN

KAPILAVASTU ●

KUSINAGARA ●

VARANASI ●

Ganges R.

BANGLADESH

GAYA ●

INDIA

Dhor

Uttar Ga

0   200 miles

BAY OF BENGAL

CHINA
(TIBET)

PLATEAU

LO

• Mustang

• Tarap

Tarap R.

• Tscharka

• Muktinath

Kali Gandaki R.

• Jamoson

Dhaulagiri
26,810 ft.

DHAULAGIRI

Annapurna
26,504 ft.

Putha Hiunchuli
23,800 ft.

ANNAPURNA

Magyandi R.

Beni

Kusma

▲ Machhapuchare
22,958 ft.

• Pokhara

0   10   20 miles

Kali Gandaki R.

Samling

Yelu-Kanju R.

SALDANG PASS

Dölma-Jang

Tsakang

Somdo Mt.

Crystal Mt.

Shey Gompa
(Crystal Monastery

Yeju (White) R.

Kanju (Black) R.

Phoksumdo R.

Black Pond Camp

KANG LA

Snowfields
Camp

Cave Camp

Kang Geralba

SCHALLER'S
ROUTE

Silver Birch Camp

Snow leopard
seen here

PHOKSUMDO
LAKE

Ring-mo

Pung-mo

BUGU LA

Murwa

Camp

Saldang 卐

amgung 卐

卐 Namdo

SCHALLER'S
ROUTE

Tcha ●
● Raka

NAM-KHONG VALLEY

Nam-Khong R.

*Cairn of
argali skulls*

)(*NAMDO LA*

○ Camp

INNER
DOLPO

卐	Buddhist monasteries
卍	B'on monasteries
)(	High pass

PETER MATTHIESSEN

The Snow Leopard

PENGUIN BOOKS

For
Nakagawa Soen Roshi
Shimano Eido Roshi
Taizan Maezumi Roshi
GASSHO
in gratitude, affection,
and respect

PENGUIN BOOKS

An imprint of Penguin Random House LLC
375 Hudson Street
New York, New York 10014
penguin.com

First published in the United States of America by The Viking Press 1978
Published in Penguin Books 1987
This edition published 2016

A portion of this book originally appeared in *The New Yorker.*

ISBN 9780143129523

Printed in the United States of America
1   3   5   7   9   10   8   6   4   2

Set in Sabon

Contents

This is at bottom the only courage that is demanded of us: to have courage for the most strange, the most singular and the most inexplicable that we may encounter. That mankind has in this sense been cowardly has done life endless harm; the experiences that are called "visions," the whole so-called "spirit-world," death, all those things that are so closely akin to us, have by daily parrying been so crowded out of life that the senses with which we could have grasped them are atrophied. To say nothing of God.

RAINER MARIA RILKE

Acknowledgments

Especially I wish to thank George Schaller for inviting me to accompany him to Dolpo in the first place, for his excellent company during our journey, and for his assistance and good counsel ever since. Dr. Schaller has furnished the striking photograph that appears on the book's dust jacket and frontispiece, and has been kind enough to review the manuscript for errors of emphasis as well as of fact. Warm thanks are also due to Donald Hall, who was generous, painstaking, and inspiring in his comments at an early stage when candid opinion was crucial, to Maria Eckhart, who made sensible and constructive suggestions throughout the several drafts; and to Elisabeth Sifton, the book's editor at The Viking Press, whose dedication and warm, tough-minded, and incisive defense of the book against its author's meddling in the later stages made a great difference.

In their unfailing good humor, loyalty, and generosity, our excellent sherpas and good friends Jang-bu, Tukten, and Phu-Tsering, Dawa and Gyaltsen, as well as our young Tamang porters, made a hard journey a very happy one—not an easy task. To Tukten Sherpa I owe a special debt that is more meaningfully expressed in the book itself.

Dr. Robert Fleming, Sr., was very hospitable in Kathmandu, and helpful as well with bird identifications and sound advice. Ashok Kuenar Hamal of the Nepal Panchat kindly expedited matters in Dunahi, and Dr. Eiji Kawamura of the Kitasato Himalayan Expedition was generous in his aid to Dawa Sherpa on our return journey. John Harrison of the Sterling Library at Yale University offered generous assistance with research materials; John Blower (F.A.O. Wildlife Adviser to the Nepal Government), Robert Fleming, Jr., Michael Cheney, Joel Ziskin, and Rodney Jackson contributed valuable information.

The patient guidance of the three Zen masters to whom this book is dedicated and the various writings of such Tibetan scholars as Lama Anagarika Govinda, Dr. David Snellgrove, John Blofeld, and the late Dr. W. Y. Evans-Wentz have been drawn upon without restraint. Since I am no authority on Buddhism, I owe gratitude and thanks to Lama Govinda and to Tetsugen Sensei (with Taizan Maezumi Roshi) for generous and helpful comment on the manuscript, and to Robin Kornman, a student of Chögyam Trungpa, Rinpoche, who inspected it for technical transgressions—fine doctrinal points, transliteration of Sanskrit and Tibetan terms, and other matters on which no two scholars seem able to agree. A number of inconsistencies doubtless remain, but I like to think these will not matter very much to those who understand why this book was written.

Finally, I should like to thank the many writers, poets, and explorers of the mind whose words have contributed to my understanding, whether or not they are identified here or in the Notes.

P.M.
Sagaponack, New York
Winter, 1978

prologue

In late September of 1973, I set out with GS on a journey to the Crystal Mountain, walking west under Annapurna and north along the Kali Gandaki River, then west and north again, around the Dhaulagiri peaks and across the Kanjiroba, two hundred and fifty miles or more to the Land of Dolpo, on the Tibetan Plateau.

GS is the zoologist George Schaller. I knew him first in 1969, in the Serengeti Plain of East Africa, where he was working on his celebrated study of the lion.[1]* When I saw him next, in New York City in the spring of 1972, he had started a survey of wild sheep and goats and their near relatives the goat-antelopes. He wondered if I might like to join him the following year on an expedition to northwest Nepal, near the frontier of Tibet, to study the bharal, or Himalayan blue sheep; it was his feeling, which he meant to confirm, that this strange "sheep" of remote ranges was actually less sheep than goat, and perhaps quite close to the archetypal ancestor of both. We would go in the autumn to observe the animals in rut, since the eating and sleeping that occupied them throughout the remainder of the year gave almost no clue to evolution and comparative behavior. Near Shey Gompa, "Crystal Monastery," where the Buddhist lama had forbidden people to molest them, the bharal were said to be numerous and easily observed. And where bharal were numerous, there was bound to appear that rarest and most beautiful of the great cats, the snow leopard. GS knew of only two Westerners—he was one—who had laid eyes

*Superior numbers refer to the Notes that begin on page 319.

on the Himalayan snow leopard in the past twenty-five years; the hope of glimpsing this near-mythic beast in the snow mountains was reason enough for the entire journey.

Twelve years before, on a visit to Nepal, I had seen those astonishing snow peaks to the north; to close that distance, to go step by step across the greatest range on earth to somewhere called the Crystal Mountain, was a true pilgrimage, a journey of the heart. Since the usurpation of Tibet by the Chinese, the Land of Dolpo, all but unknown to Westerners even today, was said to be the last enclave of pure Tibetan culture left on earth, and Tibetan culture was the last citadel of "all that present-day humanity is longing for, either because it has been lost or not yet been realized or because it is in danger of disappearing from human sight: the stability of a tradition, which has its roots not only in a historical or cultural past, but within the innermost being of man. . . ."[2] The Lama of Shey, the most revered of all the *rinpoches,* the "precious ones," in Dolpo, had remained in seclusion when a scholar of Tibetan religions[3] reached the Crystal Monastery seventeen years ago, but surely our own luck would be better.

On the way to Nepal, I stopped at Varanasi, the holy city on the Ganges, and visited the Buddhist shrines at Bodh Gaya and Sarnath. In those monsoon days of mid-September, the brown heat of India was awesome, and after a few days on the Ganges Plain, I was glad to fly north to Kathmandu, in the green foothills of the Himalayan wall. That day was clear, and among the temple spires and tiered pagodas, black kites and red veered on the wind. The dry air at 4000 feet was a great relief from the humidity of India, but in the north the peaks were hidden by thick clouds of the monsoon, and by evening it was raining.

I found GS at the hotel. We had not met in a year or more, our last correspondence had been in midsummer, and he was relieved that I had turned up without mishap. For the next two hours we talked so intensely that I wondered later if there was anything left to speak about in the months ahead; we shall have no company but each other, and we do not know each other very well. (Of GS, I had written earlier that "he is single-minded, not easy to know," and "a stern pragmatist, unable to muster up much grace in the face of unscientific attitudes; he takes a hard-eyed look at almost everything." He was also described as a "lean, intent young man,"[4] and I find him as lean and as intent as ever.)

The rains prevailed throughout the last three days in Kathmandu. GS was desperate to get under way, not only because he loathes all cities but because winter comes early to the Himalaya, and these rains of the monsoon would bring heavy snow to the high passes between this place and our destination. (We later learned that the October rains set an all-time record.) Months before, he had applied for permission to enter Dolpo, but only now, on the final day, were permits granted. Last letters were written and sent off; there would be no mail where we were going. All excess gear and clothing were discarded, and traveler's checks exchanged for small rupee notes by the dirty packet, since large bills have no currency among the hill peoples. With our Sherpa camp assistants, we packed tents and pots, and bargained for last-minute supplies in the Oriental rumpus of the Asan Bazaar, where in 1961 I had bought a small bronze Buddha, green with age. My wife and I were to become students of Zen Buddhism, and the green bronze Buddha from Kathmandu was the one I chose for a small altar in Deborah's room in the New York hospital where she died last year of cancer, in the winter.

In the early morning of September 26, in a hard rain, with a driver, two Sherpas, and all expedition gear, we packed ourselves into the Land Rover that would carry us as far as Pokhara; two more Sherpas and five Tamang porters were to come next day by bus, in time for departure from Pokhara on the twenty-eighth. But all arrivals and departures were in doubt; it had rained without relent for thirty hours. In the calamitous weather, the journey was losing all reality, and the warm smile of a pretty tourist at the hotel desk unsettled me; where did I imagine I was going, where and why?

From Kathmandu there is a road through Gorkha country to Pokhara, in the central foothills; farther west, no roads exist at all. The road winds through steep gorges of the Trisuli River, now in torrent; dirty whitecaps filled the rapids, and the brown flood was thickened every little while by thunderous rockslides down the walls of the ravine. Repeatedly the rocks fell on the road: the driver would wait for the slide to ease, then snake his way through the debris, while all heads peered at the boulders poised overhead. In raining mountains, a group of shrouded figures passed, bearing a corpse, and the sight aroused a dim, restless foreboding.

After midday, the rain eased, and the Land Rover rode into Pokhara on a shaft of storm light. Next day there was humid sun and shifting southern skies, but to the north a deep tumult of swirling grays was all that could be seen of the Himalaya. At dusk, white egrets flapped across the sunken clouds, now black with rain; on earth, the dark had come. Then, four miles above these mud streets of the lowlands, at a point so high as to seem overhead, a luminous whiteness shone—the light of snows. Glaciers loomed and vanished in the grays, and the sky parted, and the snow cone of Machhapuchare glistened like a spire of a higher kingdom.

In the night, the stars convened, and the vast ghost of Machhapuchare radiated light, although there was no moon. In the shed where we lay down, behind a sort of inn, there were mosquitoes. My friend, dreaming, cried out in his sleep. Restless, I went out at daybreak and saw three peaks of Annapurna, soaring clear of low, soft clouds. This day we would depart for the northwest.

westward

Just as a white summer cloud, in harmony with heaven and earth freely floats in the blue sky from horizon to horizon following the breath of the atmosphere—in the same way the pilgrim abandons himself to the breath of the greater life that . . . leads him beyond the farthest horizons to an aim which is already present within him, though yet hidden from his sight.

LAMA GOVINDA
The Way of the White Clouds

All other creatures look down toward the earth, but man was given a face so that he might turn his eyes toward the stars and his gaze upon the sky.

OVID
Metamorphoses

SEPTEMBER 28

At sunrise the small expedition meets beneath a giant fig beyond Pokhara—two white sahibs, four Sherpas, fourteen porters. The Sherpas are of the famous mountain tribe of northeast Nepal, near Namche Bazaar, whose men accompany the ascents of the great peaks; they are Buddhist herders who have come down in recent centuries out of eastern Tibet—*sherpa* is a Tibetan word for "easterner"—and their language, culture, and appearance all reflect Tibetan origin. One of the porters is also a Sherpa, and two are refugee Tibetans; the rest are of mixed Aryan and Mongol stock. Mostly barefoot, in ragged shorts or the big-seated, jodhpur-legged pants of India, wearing all manner of old vests and shawls and headgear, the porters pick over the tall wicker baskets. In addition to their own food and blankets, they must carry a load of up to eighty pounds that is braced on their bent backs by a tump line around the forehead, and there is much hefting and denunciation of the loads, together with shrill bargaining, before any journey in these mountains can begin. Porters are mostly local men of uncertain occupation and unsteadfast habit, notorious for giving trouble. But it is also true that their toil is hard and wretchedly rewarded—about one dollar a day. As a rule, they accompany an expedition for no more than a week away from home, after which they are re-placed by others, and the hefting and denunciation start anew. Today nearly two hours pass, and clouds have gathered, before all fourteen are mollified, and the tattered line sets off toward the west.

We are glad to go. These edges of Pokhara might be tropical outskirts anywhere—vacant children, listless adults, bent dogs and thin chickens in a litter of sagging shacks and rubble, mud, weeds, stagnant ditches, bad sweet smells, vivid bright broken plastic bits, and dirty fruit peelings awaiting the carrion pig; for want of better fare, both pigs and dogs consume the human excrement that lies everywhere along the paths. In fair weather, all this flux is tolerable, but now at the dreg end of the rainy season, the mire of life seems leached into the sallow skins of these thin beings, who squat and soap themselves and wring their clothes each morning in the rain puddles.

Brown eyes observe us as we pass. Confronted with the pain of Asia, one cannot look and cannot turn away. In India, human misery seems so pervasive that one takes in only stray details: a warped leg or a dead eye, a sick pariah dog eating withered grass, an ancient woman lifting her sari to move her shrunken bowels by the road. Yet in Varanasi there is hope of life that has been abandoned in such cities as Calcutta, which seems resigned to the dead and dying in its gutters. Shiva dances in the spicy foods, in the exhilarated bells of the swarming bicycles, the angry bus horns, the chatter of the temple monkeys, the vermilion tikka dot on the women's foreheads, even in the scent of charred human flesh that pervades the ghats. The people smile—that is the greatest miracle of all. In the heat and stench and shriek of Varanasi, where in fiery sunrise swallows fly like departing spirits over the vast silent river, one delights in the smile of a blind girl being led, of a Hindu gentleman in white turban gazing benignly at the bus driver who reviles him, of a flute-playing beggar boy, of a slow old woman pouring holy water from Ganga, the River, onto a stone elephant daubed red.

Near the burning ghats, and the industry of death, a river palace has been painted with huge candy-striped tigers.

No doubt Varanasi is the destination of this ancient Hindu at the outskirts of Pokhara, propped up on a basket borne on poles across the shoulders of four servants—off, it appears, on his last pilgrimage to the Mother Ganges, to the dark temples that surround the ghats, to those hostels where the pilgrim waits his turn to join the company of white-shrouded cadavers by the river edge, waits again to be laid upon the stacks of fired wood: the attendants will push this yellow foot, that shriveled elbow, back into the fire, and rake his remains off the burning platform into the swift river. And still enough scraps will remain to sustain life in the long-headed cadaverous dogs that haunt the ashes, while sacred kine—huge white silent things— devour the straw thongs that had bound this worn-out body to its stretcher.

The old man has been ravened from within. That blind and greedy stare of his, that caved-in look, and the mouth working, reveal who now inhabits him, who now stares out.

I nod to Death in passing, aware of the sound of my own feet upon my path. The ancient is lost in a shadow world, and gives no sign.

Gray river road, gray sky. From rock to torrent rock flits a pied wagtail.

Wayfarers: a delicate woman bears a hamper of small silver fishes, and another bends low beneath a basket of rocks that puts my own light pack to shame; her rocks will be hammered to gravel by other women of Pokhara, in the labor of the myriad brown hands that will surface a new road south to India.

Through a shaft of sun moves a band of Magar women, scarlet-shawled; they wear heavy brass ornaments in the left nostril. In the new sun, a red-combed rooster clambers quickly to the roof matting of a roadside hut, and fitfully a little girl starts singing. The light irradiates white peaks of Annapurna marching down the sky, in the great rampart that spreads east and west for eighteen hundred miles, the Himalaya—the *alaya* (abode, or home) of *hima* (snow).

Hibiscus, frangipani, bougainvillea: seen under snow peaks, these tropical blossoms become the flowers of heroic landscapes. Macaques scamper in green meadow, and a turquoise roller spins in a golden light. Drongos, rollers, barbets, and the white Egyptian vulture are the common birds, and all have close relatives in East Africa, where GS and I first met; he wonders how this vulture would react if confronted with the egg of an ostrich, which was also a common Asian bird during the Pleistocene. In Africa, the Egyptian vulture is recognized as a tool-using species, due to its knack of cracking the huge ostrich eggs by slinging rocks at them with its beak.

Until quite recently, these Nepal lowlands were broadleaf evergreen *sal* forest *(Shorea robusta),* the haunt of elephant and tiger and the great Indian rhinoceros. Forest-cutting and poaching cleared them out; except in last retreats such as the Rapti Valley, to the southeast, the saintly tread of elephants is gone. The last wild Indian cheetah was sighted in central India in 1952, the Asian lion is reduced to a single small population in the Gir Forest, northwest of Bombay, and the tiger becomes legendary almost everywhere. Especially in India and Pakistan, the hoofed animals are rapidly disappearing, due to destruction of habitat by subsistence agriculture, overcutting of the forests, overgrazing by the scraggy hordes of domestic animals, erosion, flood—the whole dismal cycle of events that accompanies overcrowding by human beings. In Asia more than all places on earth, it is crucial to establish wildlife sanctuaries at once, before the last animals are overwhelmed. As GS has written, "Man is modifying the world so fast and so drastically that most animals cannot adapt to the new conditions. In the Himalaya as elsewhere there is a great dying, one infinitely sadder than the Pleistocene extinctions, for man now has the knowledge and the need to save these remnants of his past."[1]

The track along the Yamdi River is a main trading route, passing through rice paddies and villages on its way west to the Kali Gandaki River, where it turns north to Mustang and Tibet. Green village compounds, set about with giant banyans and old stone pools and walls, are cropped to lawn by water buffalo and cattle; the fresh water and soft shade give them the harmony of parks. These village folk own even less than those of Pokhara, yet they are spared by their old economies from modern poverty: one understands why "village life" has been celebrated as the natural, happy domain of man by many thinkers, from Lao-tzu to Gandhi. In a warm sun children play, and women roll clothes on rocks at the village fountain and pound grain in stone mortars, and from all sides come reassuring dung smells and chicken clatter and wafts of fire smoke from the low hearths. In tidy yards, behind strong stiles and walls, the clay huts are of warm earthen red, with thatched roofs, hand-carved sills and shutters, and yellow-flowered pumpkin vines. Maize is stacked in narrow cribs, and rice is spread to dry on broad straw mats, and between the banana and papaya trees big calm spiders hang against the sky.

A canal bridged here and there by ten-foot granite slabs runs through a hamlet, pouring slowly over shining pebbles. It is midday, the sun melts the air, and we sit on a stone wall in the cool shade. By the canal is the village tea house, a simple open-fronted hut with makeshift benches and a clay oven in the form of a rounded mound on the clay floor. The mound has a side opening for inserting twigs and two holes on the top for boiling water, which is poured through a strainer of cheap tea dust into a glass containing coarse sugar and buffalo milk. With this *chiya* we take plain bread and a fresh cucumber, while children playing on the shining stones pretend to splash us, and a collared dove sways on a tall stalk of bamboo.

One by one the porters come, turning around to lower their loads onto the wall. A porter of shy face and childlike smile, who looks too slight for his load, is playing comb music on a fig leaf. "Too many hot," says another, smiling. This is the Sherpa porter, Tukten, a wiry small man with Mongol eyes and outsized ears and a disconcerting smile—I wonder why this Tukten is a porter.

I set off ahead, walking alone in the cool breeze of the valley. In the bright September light and mountain shadow—steep foothills are closing in as the valley narrows, and the snow peaks to the north are no longer seen—the path follows a dike between the reedy canal and the green terraces of rice that descend in steps to the margins of the river. Across the canal, more terraces ascend to the crests of the high hills, and a blue sky.

At a rest wall, two figs of different species were planted long ago; one is a banyan, or nigrodha *(Ficus indica),* the other a pipal *(F. religiosa),* sacred to both the Hindus and the Buddhists. Wild flowers and painted stones are set among the buttressed roots, to bring the traveler good fortune, and stone terraces are built up around the trunks in such a way that the shade-seeking traveler may back up and set down his load while standing almost straight. These resting places are everywhere along the trading routes, some of them so ancient that the great trees have long since died, leaving two round holes in a stonework oval platform. Like the tea houses and the broad stepping-stones that are built into the hills, the rest walls impart a blessedness to this landscape, as if we had wandered into a lost country of the golden age.

Awaiting the line of porters that winds through the paddies, I sit on the top level of the wall, my feet on the step on which the loads are set and my back against a tree. In dry sunshine and the limpid breeze down from the mountains, two black cows are threshing rice, flanks gleaming in the light of afternoon. First the paddy is drained and the rice sickled, then the yoked animals, tied by a long line to a stake in the middle of the rice, are driven round and round in a slowly decreasing circle while children fling the stalks beneath their hooves. Then the stalks are tossed into the air, and the grains beneath swept into baskets to be taken home and winnowed. The fire-colored dragonflies in the early autumn air, the bent backs in bright reds and yellows, the gleam on the black cattle and grain stubble, the fresh green of the paddies and the sparkling river—over everything lies an immortal light, like transparent silver.

In the clean air and absence of all sound, of even the simplest machinery—for the track is often tortuous and steep, and fords too many streams, to permit bicycles—in the warmth and harmony and seeming plenty, come whispers of a paradisal age. Apparently the grove of *sal* trees called Lumbini, only thirty miles south of this same tree, in fertile lands north of the Rapti River, has changed little since the sixth century B.C. when Siddhartha Gautama was born there to a rich clan of the Sakya tribe in a kingdom of elephants and tigers. Gautama forsook a life of ease to become a holy mendicant, or "wanderer"—a common practice in northern India even today. Later he was known as Sakyamuni (Sage of the Sakyas), and afterward, the Buddha— the Awakened One. Fig trees and the smoke of peasant fires, the greensward and gaunt cattle, white egrets and jungle crows are still seen on the Ganges Plain where Sakyamuni passed his life, from Lumbini south and east to Varanasi (an ancient city even when Gautama came there) and Rajgir and Gaya. Tradition says that he traveled as far north as Kathmandu (even then a prosperous city of the Newars) and preached on the hill of Swayambhunath, among the monkeys and the pines.

In Sakyamuni's time, the disciplines called yogas were already well evolved. Perhaps a thousand years before, the dark-skinned Dravidians of lowland India had been overcome by nomad Aryans from the Asian steppes who were bearing their creed of sky gods, wind, and light across Eurasia.[2] Aryan concepts were contained in their Sanskrit Vedas, or knowledge— ancient texts of unknown origin which include the Rig Veda and the Upanishads and were to become the base of the Hindu religion. To the wandering ascetic named Sakyamuni, such epic preachments on the nature of the Universe and Man were useless as a cure for human suffering. In what became known as the Four Noble Truths, Sakyamuni perceived that man's existence is inseparable from sorrow; that the cause of suffering is craving; that peace is attained by extinguishing craving; that this liberation may be brought about by following the Eightfold Path: right attention to one's understanding, intentions, speech, and actions; right livelihood, effort, mindfulness; right concentration, by which is meant the unification of the self through sitting yoga.

The Vedas already included the idea that mortal desire— since it implies lack—had no place in the highest state of being; that what was needed was that death-in-life and spiritual rebirth sought by all teachers, from the early shamans to the existentialists. Sakyamuni's creed was less a rejection of Vedic philosophy than an effort to apply it, and his intense practice of meditation does not content itself with the serenity of yoga states (which in his view falls sort of ultimate truth) but goes beyond, until the transparent radiance of stilled mind opens out in *prajna,* or transcendent *knowing,* that higher consciousness or "Mind" which is inherent in all sentient beings, and which depends on the unsentimental embrace of all existence. A true experience of *prajna* corresponds to "enlightenment" or liberation—not change, but transformation—a profound vision of his identity with universal life, past, present, and future, that keeps man from doing harm to others and sets him free from fear of birth-and-death.

In the fifth century B.C., near the town of Gaya, south and east of Varanasi, Sakyamuni attained enlightenment in the deep experience that his own "true nature," his Buddha-nature, was no different from the nature of the universe. For half a century thereafter, at such places as the Deer Park in Sarnath, and Nalanda, and the Vulture's Peak near present-day Rajgir, he taught a doctrine based upon the impermanence of individual existence, the eternal continuity of becoming, as in the morning river that appears the same as the river of the night before, now passed away. (Though he preached to women and weakened the caste system by admitting low-born brethren to his order, Sakyamuni never involved himself in social justice, far less government; his way holds that self-realization is the greatest contribution one can make to one's fellow man.) At the age of eighty, he ended his days at Kusinagara (the modern Kusinara), forty miles east of Gorakhpur and just west of the Kali Gandaki River.

This much is true; all else is part of the great Buddha legend, which is truth of a different order. In regard to his enlightenment, it is related that this wanderer was in his thirties when he gave up the rigors of the yogi and embraced the "Middle Path" between sensuality and mortification, accepting food in a golden bowl from the daughter of the village headman. Thereupon, he was renounced by his disciples. At dusk he sat himself beneath a pipal tree with his face toward the East, vowing that though his skin and nerves and bones should waste away and his life-blood dry, he would not leave this seat until he had attained Supreme Enlightenment. All that night, beset by demons, Sakyamuni sat in meditation. And in that golden daybreak, it is told, the Self-Awakened One truly perceived the Morning Star, as if seeing it for the first time in his life.

In what is now known as Bodh Gaya—still a pastoral land of cattle savanna, shimmering water, rice paddies, palms, and red-clay hamlets without paved roads or wires—a Buddhist temple stands beside an ancient pipal, descended from that *bodhi* tree, or "Enlightenment Tree," beneath which this man sat. Here in a warm dawn, ten days ago, with three Tibetan monks in maroon robes, I watched the rising of the Morning Star and came away no wiser than before. But later I wondered if the Tibetans were aware that the *bodhi* tree was murmuring with gusts of birds, while another large pipal, so close by that it touched the holy tree with many branches, was without life. I make no claim for this event: I simply declare what I saw there at Bodh Gaya.

Already the Yamdi Khola narrows; soon it will vanish among mountains. In a village on the northern slope, the huts are round or oval rather than rectangular, and Jang-bu, the head Sherpa, says that this is a village of the Gurung, a people who came down long ago out of Tibet. In this region of southern Nepal live various hill peoples of Mongol and Aryan mix, most of them Paharis, or hill Hindus. For centuries, the Hindus have come up along the river valleys from the great plain of the Ganges, while Tibetans crossed the mountain passes from the north: the Tibetan-speaking Buddhist tribes, which include the Sherpas, are called Bhotes, or southern Tibetans. (Bhot or B'od is Tibet; Bhutan, which lies at the southern edge of Tibet, means "End of Bhot.") Of the tribes represented by the porters, the Gurungs and Tamangs tend toward Buddhism, while the Chetris and Magars are Hindus. Whether Hindu or Buddhist, most of these tribes—and the Gurung especially—pay respect to the animist deities of the old religions that persist in remote corners of the Asian mountains.

Some long-haired Tibetans, buttery flat faces red with ocher sheen, descend the river barefoot on the silver stones. (Ocher is a traditional protection against cold and insects, and before the civilizing influence of Buddhism, Tibet was known as the Land of the Red-faced Devils.) These people are bound for Pokhara from Dhorpatan, a week away. When crops are harvested, the Tibetans, Mustang Bhotes, and other hill peoples follow the ridges and valleys south and east to Pokhara and Kathmandu, trading wool and salt for grain and paper, knives, tobacco, rice, and tea. One Tibetan boy has caught a rockfish in the shallows;

he runs to show me, almond eyes agleam. The children all along the way are friendly and playful, even gay; though they beg a little, they are not serious about it, as are the grim Hindu children of the towns. More likely they will take your hand and walk along a little, or do a somersault, or tag and run away.

Where the valley narrows to a canyon, there is a tea house and some huts, and here a pack train of shaggy Mongol ponies descends from the mountain in a melody of bells and splashes across the swift green water at the ford. From the tea house, a trail climbs steeply toward the southwest sky. In this land, the subsistence economies have always depended upon travel, and in its decades—centuries, perhaps—as a trade route for the hill peoples, broad steps have been worn into the mountain path. Wild chestnut trees overhang the trail; we pull down branches to pick the spiny nuts.

At sunset, the trail arrives at the hill village called Naudanda. Here I try out my new home, a one-man mountain tent, in poor condition. Phu-Tsering, our merry cook, in bright red cap, brings supper of lentils and rice, and afterward I sit outside on a wicker stool acquired at the tea house at the ford, and listen to cicadas and a jackal. This east-west ridge falls steeply on both sides to the Yandi Valley in the north, the Marsa in the south; from Naudanda, the Yamdi Khola is no more than a white ribbon rushing down between dark walls of conifers into its gorge. Far away eastward, far below, the Marsa River opens out into Lake Phewa, near Pokhara, which glints in the sunset of the foothills. There are no roads west of Pokhara, which is the last outpost of the modern world; in one day's walk we are a century away.

SEPTEMBER 29

A luminous mountain morning. Mist and fire smoke, sun shafts and dark ravines: a peak of Annapurna poises on soft clouds. In fresh light, to the peeping of baby chickens, we take breakfast in the village tea house, and are under way well before seven.

A child dragging bent useless legs is crawling up the hill outside the village. Nose to the stones, goat dung, and muddy trickles, she pulls herself along like a broken cricket. We falter, ashamed of our strong step, and noticing this, she gazes up, clear-eyed, without resentment—it seems much worse that she is pretty. In Bengal, GS says stiffly, beggars will break their children's knees to achieve this pitiable effect for business purposes: this is his way of expressing his distress. But the child that lies here at our boots is not a beggar; she is merely a child, staring in curiosity at tall, white strangers. I long to give her something—a new life?—yet am afraid to tamper with such dignity. And so I smile as best I can, and say *"Namas-te!"* "Good morning!" How absurd! And her voice follows as we go away, a small clear smiling voice—*"Namas-te!"*—a Sanskrit word for greeting and parting that means, "I salute you."

We are subdued by this reminder of mortality. I think of the corpse in Gorkha Country, borne on thin shoulders in the mountain rain, the black cloths blowing; I see the ancient dying man outside Pokhara; I hear again my own wife's final breath. Such sights caused Sakyamuni to forsake Lumbini and go in search of the secret of existence that would free men from the pain of this sensory world, known as samsara.

Grieve not for me, but mourn for those who stay behind, bound by longings to which the fruit is sorrow . . . for what confidence have we in life when death is ever at hand? . . . Even were I to return to my kindred by reason of affection, yet we should be divided in the end by death. The meeting and parting of living things is as when clouds having come together drift apart again, or as when the leaves are parted from the trees. There is nothing we may call our own in a union that is but a dream. . . .[3]

And yet, as his own death drew near, Sakyamuni turned again toward the north ("Come, Ananda, let us go to Kusinagara"). Like the rest of us, perhaps he longed for home.

The path tends west around small mountains, then climbs toward a village in the pass. Where a white vulture sails in the sunny mist, a high forest comes in view, threaded by waterfalls. We are escorted through the village by a boy playing a tom-tom; he wears a saucy hat, short shirt, and vest, and nothing more. One day this boy and others will destroy that forest, and their steep fields will erode in rain, and the thin soil will wash away into the torrents, clogging the river channels farther down so that monsoon floods will spread across the land. With its rapidly increasing population, primitive agriculture, and steep terrain, Nepal has the most serious erosion problem of any country in the world, and the problem worsens as more forests disappear in the scouring of the land for food and fuel; in eastern Nepal, and especially the Kathmandu Valley, firewood for cooking (not to speak of heat) is already precious, brought in by peasants who have walked for many miles to sell the meager faggots on their backs. The country folk cook their own food by burning cakes of livestock dung, depriving the soil of the precious manure that would nourish it and permit it to hold water. Without wood humus or manure, the soil deteriorates, compacts, and turns to dust, to be washed away in the rush of the monsoon.

In GS's view, Asia is fifteen to twenty years behind East Africa in its attitudes toward conservation, and the gap may well prove fatal. All of the region from western India to Turkey, and all of northern Africa as well, has turned to desert in historic times, and yet a country such as Pakistan, with but 3 percent of its territories left in forest, is doing nothing at all about the impending disaster, despite a huge idle standing army—sponsored, of course, by military-industrial interests in the United States—that could just as well be out in the weary countryside planting new trees.

Pine, rhododendron, barberry. Down mountain fields, a path of stones flows like mercury in the sunlight; even the huts have roofs of silver slates. The path winds around the mountain to the bottom of the pine forest, where a shady hamlet overlooks the confluence of the Modir River with its tributary from the north. This is the way of foot travel in Nepal, steeply up and steeply down the labyrinthine valleys. The down is hardest on the legs and feet, which jam at the knees and into the toe of the boot. In Kathmandu, our youngest Sherpa, Gyaltsen, had taken my mountain boots to a cobbler to have them stretched; unstretched, the boots came back with neat round patches of bright leather sewn onto the outside surfaces at the indicated points. The patches were removed in Pokhara, but the cobbler there had no tool to stretch the boots, and so they are just as narrow and—due to perforations—less rainworthy than before.

Today we have been walking for ten hours; there are signs of blisters. Gyaltsen, who is carrying my backpack, is somewhere far behind, and since I have no sneakers in my rucksack, I walk barefoot. My feet are still tough from the past summer, and the paths are mostly rain-softened, for we have descended once again into a lowland. Eyes to the ground, alert for sticks and stones, I can admire a cocoa-colored wood frog and the pale lavender-blue winged blossoms of the orchid tree *(Bauhinia)* and the warm loaf left by a buffalo, deposited calmly from the look of it and even, perhaps, in contemplation.

But since the encounter with the crawling child, I look at paradise askance. Along the Modir, my feet are hurt by sharp rock shale, and where we make camp in the village of Gijan, we pick off leeches: while taking rice supper in a local hut, GS investigates wetness in his sneaker and finds it full of his own blood.

It relieves me that GS is mortal, prey to the afflictions of the common pilgrim. I am an inspired walker, but he is formidable; were it not for the slow pace of the porters, he would run me into the ground. GS's strong legs are so crucial to his work in the high mountains of the world that he will not ski or play rough sports for fear he might do them damage. I tease him now about his bloody shoe, quoting a letter from the curator of mammals at the American Museum of Natural History in New York City (in regard to a set of mousetraps for collecting purposes that I would bring to GS from America): "I look forward to learning what you and George see, hear, and accomplish in a march through Nepal. I should warn you, the last friend I had who went walking with George in Asia came back—or more properly, *turned* back—when his boots were full of blood. . . ."

"That chap was out of shape," GS says shortly.

SEPTEMBER 30

Yesterday we walked for eleven hours of rough up-and-down, and this morning the delicate porter who plays fig-leaf music has disappeared. Jang-bu, the head Sherpa, replaces him in Gijan with an old Magar named Bimbahadur, a crook-legged veteran of the Gurkha regiments who goes barefoot, in huge shorts. (Whether Hindu or Buddhist, a Nepalese who joins the regiments is called a "Gurkha." The legend of these soldiers had its start in 1769, when the armies of the King of Gorkha spread out from the central valleys, absorbing the small tribal kingdoms and creating the Hindu state now called Nepal; in their great ferocity, they rushed into Tibet, only to be thrown back by the Chinese, who considered Tibet to be part of China even then. In the mid-nineteenth century, brandishing the wicked hatchet-knife known as the *kukri*, Gurkha troops were sent to aid the British raj during the Indian mutiny, and Gurkha regiments were later supported by both India and Britain.)

Our Sherpa porter, Tukten, is also a Gurkha veteran, and he and Bimbahadur are soon companions, since Tukten—perhaps because he took a porter's job, or for other reasons not yet clear—is kept at a subtle distance by the younger Sherpas. Tukten might be thirty-five or fifty-three—his face is ageless—whereas Jang-bu, Phu-Tsering the cook, and the two camp assistants Gyaltsen and Dawa are all in their early twenties. In his knickers and high sneakers, Gyaltsen looks like a schoolboy and has in fact brought tattered schoolbooks with him.

The route from Gijan goes west along a mountain ridge to a high point with a view of four deep valleys. Below, in the village where the Modir meets the Jare, a woman sits in a window frame of old carved birds. The Modir is crossed on a wooden bridge with chain rail; the bridge sways and creaks over gray torrents that rush down from the Annapurna glaciers to the north.

A rice-field path follows narrow dikes worn to grease by human feet. A mist along the mountains: heavy heat. The green rice, red huts, the red clothes of the women point up the darkness of these valleys. Away from the rivers, a rooster's cry cracks the still air, or an outraged human voice—a woman ranting at her buffalo, gone brooding in the pines, or the vacant laugh of a crazy man echoing outward toward the mountains.

Sun in the wings of dragonflies, over a meadow still in shadow: a dove calls from the secrets of the mountains. Now Machhapuchare rises, a halo of cloud wisps spun in a tight whorl around the pinnacle. (Unlike the other peaks of the Annapurna massif, Machhapuchare remains pristine, not because it is impregnable—it was climbed to within fifty feet of the summit in 1957—but because to set foot on the peak is forbidden; the Gurung revere it as a holy mountain, and the Nepal government wisely preserves it *in mysterium tremendum*.) Soon all Annapurna is high and clear, turning minutely all day long as the trail moves westward. In 1950, the westernmost summit, known as Annapurna One, became the first peak of 25,000 feet or more that man had climbed.

How easy it feels to be superfluous on this expedition, in no haste and without gainful destination—*gnaskor*, or "going around places," as pilgrimages are described in Tibet. GS is back there harrying the porters, who overlook no opportunity to rest; the Sherpas pretend to help him, but they know that the porters will not walk more than seven hours if they can help it and, lacking tents, are usually aware before they set out in the morning of the hut or cave where they will spend the night. GS knows this, too, but he also knows that the season is against him, and he will not really be at ease until he reaches the land of the blue sheep and the snow leopard. "Once the data start coming in," he said in Kathmandu, "I don't care about much else; I feel I'm justifying my existence." (This single-mindedness helps to account for his reputation: I have heard GS referred to by a peer as "the finest field biologist working today.") Also, he dislikes all these small villages; we are still too close to civilization to suit him. "The fewer people, the better," he says often. Originally he wished to fly this small expedition to the strip at Dhorpatan, a settlement of Tibetan refugees to the west, where all the porters that we needed might be found. But no plane was available until the second week of October, and with the weather still uncertain, it seemed best to make the trek to Dhorpatan on foot. Now he overtakes me, fretting: "It would take us four days to Dhorpatan instead of eight or nine if we didn't have to wait for these damned porters."

GS sighs, for he knows that there is nothing to be done to speed the pace. "I wish we were up there at eight thousand feet right now—I like crisp air." I do not answer. The porters' pace just suits me, not less so because my boots feel stiff and small. I enjoy crisp air myself, but I am happy in this moment; we shall be up there in cold weather soon enough.

Glowing with nut grease, a squirrel observes our passing from its perch in a cotton tree *(Bombax)* in immense red blossom. This relative of the African baobab is often the one wild tree left standing, contributing to the village commons the deer-park aspect that calms this southern countryside. Now the air is struck by the shrill of a single cicada, brilliant, eerie, a sound as fierce as a sword blade shrieking on a lathe, yet subtle, bell-like, with a ring that causes the spider webs to shimmer in the sunlight. I stand transfixed by this unearthly sound that radiates from all the world at once, as Tukten, passing, smiles. In this enigmatic smile there is something of Kasapa. Seeking among his disciples for a successor, Sakyamuni held up a single lotus flower and was silent. Perceiving in this emblematic gesture the unified nature of existence, Kasapa smiled.

Kusma, a large Hindu village near the Kali Gandaki River, lies at about 3000 feet, nearly the lowest point of altitude on this journey. Phu-Tsering replenishes our supplies with fresh cucumbers and guavas, and by noon we are under way once more, moving north along the eastern bank. In the first village on the river is a small wood temple, with two stone cows decked out in red hibiscus; on a stone head in the temple wall is another unfathomable smile. The village creaks to the soft rhythm of an ancient rice treadle, and under the windows babies sway in wicker baskets. In the serene and indiscriminate domesticity of these sunny villages, sow and piglet, cow and calf, mother and infant, hen and chicks, nanny and kid commingle in a common pulse of being. We eat a papaya at the tea house, and afterward bathe in the deep pools of a mountain torrent that comes foaming down over pale rocks beyond the village. On this last day of September I linger for a while in a warm waterfall, in the moist sun, while my washed clothes bake dry upon the stones.

All afternoon the trail continues up the Kali Gandaki, which rushes down from Mustang and Tibet onto the Ganges Plain; because it flows between the soaring massifs of Annapurna and Dhaulagiri, both more than 26,000 feet in altitude,[4] the Kali Gandaki has the deepest canyon of any river in the world. Kali signifies "black female" or "dark woman," and it is true that its steep walls, gray torrent, and black boulders give a hellish darkness to this river. Fierce Kali the Black, the female aspect of Time and Death, and the Devourer of All Things, is the consort of the Hindu god of the Himalaya, Great Shiva the Re-Creator and Destroyer; her black image, with its necklace of human skulls, is the emblem of this dark river that, rumbling down out of hidden peaks and vast clouds of unknowing, has filled the traveler with dread since the first human tried to cross and was borne away.

A far cicada rings high and clear over the river's heavy wash. Morning glory, a lone dandelion, cassia, orchids. So far from the nearest sea, I am taken aback by the sight of a purple land crab, like a relict of the ancient days when the Indian subcontinent, adrift on the earth's mantle, moved northward to collide with the Asian land mass, driving these marine rocks, inch by inch, five miles into the skies: the Kali Gandaki is a famous source of the black sacred stones called saligrams, which contain the spiral fossil forms of marine univalves. The rise of the Himalaya, begun in the Eocene, some fifty million years ago, is still continuing: an earthquake in 1959 caused mountains to fall into the rivers and changed the course of the great Brahmaputra, which comes down out of Tibet through northeastern

India to join the Ganges near its delta at the Bay of Bengal. All the great rivers of southern Asia fall from the highest country in the world, from the Indus that empties into the Arabian Sea east to the Ganges and the Brahmaputra, the Mekong and the Yangtze, and even the great Hwang Ho that pours eastward across all of China into the Yellow Sea; since they come from the Tibetan Plateau, these rivers are much older than the mountains, and the Kali Gandaki forged its great abysses as the mountains rose.

At Paniavas, which has a brass cow head on its village font, a bridge crosses the roaring river, and camp is made on the far side in sudden rain. At twilight, I walk beneath the dripping trees. From the hill above, in their bird voices, the Pahari children cry out their few phrases of schoolbook English, laughing at my answers.

Good-a morning!
What it is you-a name?
What time it is by you-a watch?
Where are you-a going?

OCTOBER 1

The monsoon rains continue all night long, and in the morning it is cool and cloudy. Along the trail up the Gandaki, there are fewer settlements, fewer stone huts in which travelers may take shelter, and with the north wind comes the uneasy feeling that, in this autumn season, we are bound into the wind, against the weather. Down the river comes a common sandpiper, the Eurasian kin of the spotted sandpiper of home: it teeters and flits from boulder to black boulder, bound for warm mud margins to the south. I have seen this jaunty bird in many places, from Galway to New Guinea, and am cheered a little when I meet it again here.

Under the clouds, the lower flanks of great Dhaulagiri, 26,810 feet high, are white from last night's storm; the snow line is much lower than the altitudes that we must cross to get to Dolpo. This track continues northward to Jamoson and Mustang, and originally we planned to trek as far as Jamoson, then head west into Dolpo by way of Tscharka. But permits to travel beyond Jamoson are difficult to obtain from the Nepal government, which is very sensitive about all of the wild region on the northwest border. Before the Gorkha wars in the late eighteenth century, Dolpo and Mustang were kingdoms of Tibet, a historical fact that might tempt Chinese encroachment. And both regions are hideouts of the fierce Tibetan nomads known as Kham-pa, who still actively resist the Chinese occupation and retreat to Dolpo and Mustang after their raids. Even in Marco Polo's time, the Kham-pa were renowned bandits, and from all reports[5] are fond of their old habits. Our present route, approaching from the south, lessens the chances of encountering

Kham-pa and drawing attention to a situation that Nepal, for the sake of good relations with its tremendous neighbor, is anxious to ignore.

A bridge crosses the river to the trade center at Beni, from where another track heads west, under Dhaulagiri. We shall travel in this direction for six days, then round the western end of the Dhaulagiri massif on a route north across the Himalaya. Here at Beni Bazaar, the police are suspicious and aggressive, checking us out with exaggerated care; our permit for Dolpo is uncommon. But at last the papers are returned, and we leave this place as soon as possible.

The path follows the northern bank of a tributary river, the Magyandi, where the valley sides are too steep for farming, and the few poor hamlets lack even a tea stall. It is October now; the orchids disappear. Across the river, ghostly waterfalls— sometimes six or seven may be seen at once—flow down out of the clouds. A stone millhouse spans the white water of a stream where a ravine strikes into the river; there is no bridge, no sign of life, and the hermit, if he has not died, shares his solitudes with the macaques that perch like sentinels about the silent dwelling.

A Tibetan with two women overtakes us; he stops short, cocking his head, to look us over, then invites us to accompany him to Dhorpatan. GS and I love to travel light, and would be happy to go with him, but we merely point in the direction of the porters who, as usual, are an hour or more behind.

We camp by the river at Tatopani, in a heavy rain.

OCTOBER 2

Long ago, some traveler brought poinsettia and oleander to Tatopani, and there is a tea stall in this village. Across from the tea stall, on a thatch roof, grows a cucumber with yellow-flowered vine; under the eaves, on the clay windowsill, a flute, a wood comb, and a bright red pepper lie in happy composition. Beneath the windowsill, small children tumble, and one little girl, sedate and serious, changes her clothes from top to bottom. In the mud street, in the rain, three small boys hunching knee to knee play cards beneath a black umbrella.

At midmorning, we set out in a light rain. The Magyandi is rising, and over the thick rush and leaping of the torrent, the rumble of boulders, southbound swallows fly away down the gray river. Rain comes and goes. At midafternoon, the track arrives at this region's main village, called Darbang, where the slate-roofed houses are strongly built of red and white clay bricks, with carved wood windows.

On the school veranda, Jang-bu and Phu-Tsering build a fire to dry sleeping bags, which are turned each little while by Dawa and Gyaltsen. Like all Sherpa work, this is offered and accomplished cheerfully, and usually Tukten lends a hand, although such help is not expected of the porters and he is not paid for it. The Sherpas are alert for ways in which to be of use, yet are never insistent, far less servile; since they are paid to perform a service, why not do it as well as possible? "Here, sir! I will wash the mud!" "I carry that, sir!" As GS says, "When the going gets rough, they take care of you first." Yet their dignity is unassailable, for the service is rendered for its own sake—it is the task, not the employer, that is served. As Buddhists, they know that the doing matters more than the attainment or reward, that to serve in this selfless way is to be free. Because of their belief in karma—the principle of cause and effect that permeates Buddhism and Hinduism (and Christianity, for that matter: as ye sow, so shall ye reap)—they are tolerant and unjudgmental, knowing that bad acts will receive their due without the intervention of the victim. The generous and open outlook of the Sherpas, a kind of merry defenselessness, is by no means common, even among unsophisticated peoples; I have never encountered it before except among the Eskimos. And since, in prehistory, the nomadic Mongol ancestors of both Tibetans and native Americans are thought to have spread from the same region of northern Asia, I wonder if this sense of life is not a common heritage from the far past.

These simple and uneducated men comport themselves with the wise calm of monks, and their well-being is in no way separable from their religion. And of course they are all incipient Buddhas—we are, too—according to the Mahayana texts compiled several centuries after Sakyamuni's death. Since Mahayana insists on the interdependence of all life and aspires to the salvation of all beings, not just those who follow monastic orders, it does not demand renunciation of ordinary life (though it is expected that renunciation will later come about of its own accord) and is less narrow in all respects than the Hinayana of Ceylon and Southeast Asia, which adheres closely to the early Buddhism of Sakyamuni. As in the Hebrew and Christian traditions, which were developing in the same period, Mahayana suggests that spiritual attainment will be limited in him who seeks God only for himself: "Hast thou attuned thy being to humanity's great pain, O Candidate for Light?"[6] Thus there developed the ideal of the Bodhisattva (roughly, Buddha-Being) who has deferred his own entry into the eternal peace of nirvana, remaining here in the samsara state until all of us become enlightened; in this way Mahayana answered man's need for a personal god and a divine savior, which early Buddhism and Hinayana lack. Mahayana lies at the foundation of the Tantric Buddhism of the Himalaya, Tibet, and Central Asia, as well as that extraordinary sect that developed in China, traveled eastward to Korea and Japan, and is now established in the United States.

The traditional founder of Ch'an Buddhism (in Japan, Zen) was Bodhidharma, a great teacher in the apostolic line of Sakyamuni, who carried the teaching from India to China in A.D. 527. Perhaps influenced by the simplicity of the Chinese philosophy called Tao (the Way), the fierce "blue-eyed monk," or "wall-gazer," exhorted his followers to ignore the sectarian disputes, ponderous scriptures, proliferating icons, and priestly trappings of organized religion and return to the intense meditation that had opened the Buddha's Path. Led by a succession of great masters, Zen Buddhism (of which Bodhidharma was First Patriarch in China) infused all of Oriental art and culture with the spare clarity of its vision. In Zen thought, even attachment to the Buddha's "golden words" may get in the way of ultimate perception; hence the Zen expression "Kill the Buddha!" The Universe itself is the scripture of Zen, for which religion is no more and no less than the apprehension of the infinite in every moment.

> How wondrous, how mysterious!
> I carry fuel, I draw water.[7]

OCTOBER 3

From the river above Darbang comes evil thunder. The cliffs are falling, and three wet dogs that scavenge in the schoolyard turn to listen. Rocks tremble and bound into the river, which after two days of heavy rain is rushing, roaring, lunging through the canyon.

The daily rain is nagging at our nerves, and mine especially, since my cramped and ratty tent leaks very badly. Hunched in a cold and soggy sleeping bag amongst the puddles, I have envied the owner of the crisp blue tent next door, and perhaps these base feelings fired our first argument, this dark morning, when GS tossed used cans and papers into the schoolyard. He asserted that he did so because the local people are always avid for containers, which is true. But why not set the cans upon the wall instead of littering the place, and making the people pick them up out of the mud?

Beneath GS's stern control are gleams of anger, it appears, although he talks little of himself—there isn't much to go on. Essentially, I think, he is a solitary; a certain shy warmth is most apparent when he speaks of crows and pigs. Last year in New York, he said, "Perhaps you can teach me how to write about *people;* I don't know how to go about it." This sort of open and lonely remark redeems his sternness and an occasional lack of proportion brought about by sheer intensity. "When Kay is typing up my notes, and I don't hear the typewriter," he says, "I go and ask her what's the matter: she gets wild at me." He often says this—"Kay gets wild at me"—as if to remind himself that his wife may have good reason.

In the Serengeti, GS was much respected and well liked, and

he has fine, old-fashioned qualities in abundance. His mix of brains, strength, and integrity is not so common, and counts for a lot on an expedition such as ours: how many of one's friends, these days, could be entrusted with one's life?

When the rain relents a bit, we straggle out, but soon a man coming from the west warns Phu-Tsering about danger on the trails. Phu-Tsering, who is never serious if he can help it, murmurs, "Two day rain—very bad," making a sliding motion with his brown hand. In places the ledge trail has collapsed into the river, and elsewhere slides have buried it in an avalanche of shale. Crossing these places, the porters stare upward through the restless mists at the overhanging rocks. The young Tamang porter Pirim has a scrap of English, and as he passes me, remarks, "Today, tomorrow, trail no good." To assure me that he is serious, he swings with his heavy load to gaze at me from beneath the tump line around his forehead, then hobbles on along the path that climbs up this steep canyon. Such warnings, according to GS, are apt to precede threats to quit or demands for higher pay, but later, commanding the porters to stay closer together, he acknowledges the perilous conditions: "If one of these chaps slips," he says, "we'll never miss him until the end of the day." Not long afterward we must clamber up through bushes, since a whole traverse has fallen down the mountain.

Beyond a bridge over the Danga stream is a steep slippery ascent; soon the worst of the climb is past. A pine forest drifts by in breaths of mist, and on the mountain face just opposite, seen through shifting clouds, ribbons of water turn from white to brown as they gather up soil in the fall to the roaring rivers. On a corner of the trail is a weird shrine where horns of many slaughtered goats are piled in a kind of altar, with red ribbons tied to branches of the trees. At this time of year, people pay homage to Durga, a dread demoness of ancient origin, who emerged again in the first centuries A.D. as the black Kali, the dreadful female aspect of Lord Shiva and embodiment of all horrors of the mortal mind.

A bird note and the water rush command the stillness. Even in rain, this landscape is hallucinatory—gorges and waterfalls, the pines and clouds that come and go, fire-colored dwellings painted with odd flowers and bizarre designs, the cloud-mirrors of the rice paddies in steps down the steep mountainside, a flock of vermilion minivets, blown through a wind-tossed tumult of bamboo.

We walk on in mud and gloom and cold. At the mountain village called Sibang, to the beat of tom-toms, a buffalo is slowly killed for Durga Puja and its fresh blood drunk, while children stand in a circle in the rain. These mountain children have the big bellies of malnutrition, and though they seem no less content than the children of the valleys, they are quiet, and do not sing out to us; one of the blood-drinkers has the loveliest face of any child that I have ever seen.

OCTOBER 4

The rain increases by the early morning, and with trails impassable, we shall remain in this old cowshed. Good Dawa in his
orange knee socks—he is a big strong fellow but so shy that he
cannot look a sahib in the face—has scraped the bulk of the
manure against one wall and bridged the deepest pools in the
mud floor with stepping stones. We live on an isle of canvas
tenting spread between the lines of leak, and spend most of a
dark day in sleeping bags, propped up against the wall.

Recently we have lived almost exclusively on a white diet
of rice or chapatis (unleavened bread) accompanied by dhal
(small lentils) and cracked corn or potatoes. A few guavas, pa-
payas, cucumbers, and plantains were available in the villages
along the rivers, but as the train climbs north and west, and autumn deepens, these are seen no more. Yesterday, Phu-Tsering
bought some silver fish caught in wicker traps in the stream ed-
dies, as well as fresh meat from the slaughtered buffalo, and so
we celebrate the Durga Puja. Some arak, or raki—white spirits
distilled from rice or maize or millet—has been located, and an
old one-eyed porter dances to the harmonies of Jang-bu, whose
hands gleam with finger rings as he plays. The head Sherpa is
boyish, even for twenty-four, but he is intelligent and person-
able, and commands respect.

We are not really in the mood for celebration. GS is off somewhere in his own head, and I am wondering about my children.
Rue, Sara, and Luke are away at school and college; only the
youngest is at home. Last summer, GS sent word from Pakistan
that if Alex were of happy and adaptable turn of mind—he was
and is—Kay Schaller would be glad to take him into her house-

hold in Lahore, where the two Schaller boys attend an American school. But since he is only eight it seemed better in the end to forego this generous invitation and leave him in our own house, which had been lent to a family of his friends. And for the moment, at least, all was well. Just before leaving Kathmandu, I received the following communication:

Dear Dad,

How are you. I am fine. I was very sad, I was even crying, because I didn't write to you. But I feel a lot better since I'm writing to you now. The cat and the dog are great, but I'm going to be sad when they die. School is doing pretty well. I hope you can make it back for Thanksgiving. Did I spell that right. Yes ☐ No ☐

I hope your mountain boots are still good. I hope you are having a very good time.

Love,
Alex

Save my letters and bring them home so I can see if they got to you. Hugs and kisses. By By a millyon times for now. Love

Your sun
Alex

I think of the parting with my sun on the day that school had opened, just a month before, a clear morning of September, of monarch butterflies and goldenrod, late roses, shining pine needles, of flights of cormorant headed south along the coast in a dry east wind. Alex asked how long I would be gone, and when I told him, blurted out, "Too long!" I had driven him to school, and he was upset that he might be seen in tears. "That's much too long," he wept, and this was true. Hugging him, I promised to be home before Thanksgiving.

OCTOBER 5

We set off at daybreak in light intermittent rain that lasts all morning. The monsoon's end is now long overdue.

At Muna, the path turns away from the Magyandi torrent, far below, and follows a ridge for several miles above the valley of the Dara Khola. At this altitude, near 7000 feet, the trail passes among oaks. The mountain lacks all sign of people or planting, and GS is ecstatic. We look for sign of forest animals, such as the Asiatic black bear (called the moon bear) and the yellow-throated marten and the beautiful red panda. This cloud forest—who knows?—may hide a yeti. At the wood edge, alder and ilex, viburnum, barberry, and rhododendron, daisies and everlasting, wild strawberry, sphagnum moss and bracken all appear, and pale lavender asters much like those that would be abundant now in woods and fields at home. In the autumn trees, the flicker-like cry of a woodpecker, the chickadee voices of the tits seem wistful, and bring back my uneasiness about my children.

In a dark grove of mossy oaks, wet camp is made at 9000 feet. Through the ragged treetops, skies are clearing. There is a moon, and cold.

How strange everything seems. How strange everything is. One "I" feels like an observer of this man who lies here in this sleeping bag in Asian mountains; another "I" is thinking about Alex; a third is the tired man who tries to sleep.

In his first summers, forsaking all his toys, my son would stand rapt for near an hour in his sandbox in the orchard, as doves and redwings came and went on the warm wind, the leaves dancing, the clouds flying, birdsong and sweet smell of privet and rose. The child was not observing; he was at rest in the very center of the universe, a part of things, unaware of endings and beginnings, still in unison with the primordial nature of creation, letting all light and phenomena pour through. Ecstasy is identity with all existence, and ecstasy showed in his bright paintings; like the Aurignacian hunter, who became the deer he drew on the cave wall, there was no "self" to separate him from the bird or flower. The same spontaneous identity with the object is achieved in the bold sumi painting of Japan— a strong expression of Zen culture, since to become one with whatever one does is a true realization of the Way.

Amazingly, we take for granted that instinct for survival, fear of death, must separate us from the happiness of pure and uninterpreted experience, in which body, mind, and nature are the same. And this debasement of our vision, the retreat from wonder, the backing away like lobsters from free-swimming life into safe crannies, the desperate instinct that our life passes unlived, is reflected in proliferation without joy, corrosive money rot, the gross befouling of the earth and air and water from which we came.

Compare the wild, free paintings of the child with the stiff, pinched "pictures" these become as the painter notices the painting and tries to portray "reality" as others see it; self-conscious now, he steps out of his own painting and, finding himself apart from things, notices the silence all around and becomes alarmed by the vast significations of Creation. The armor of the "I" begins to form, the construction and desperate assertion of separate identity, the loneliness: "Man has closed himself up, till he sees all things through the narrow chinks of his cavern."[8]

Alex is eight, and already he has shut away the wildness of the world. I lost it, too, in early childhood. But memories would come on wings of light—a shining bird, high pines and sun, the fire in a floating leaf, the autumn heat in weathered wood, wood smell, a child, soft lichen on a stone—a light-filled immanence, shimmering and breathing, and yet so fleeting that it left me breathless and in pain. One night in 1945, on a Navy vessel in a Pacific storm, my relief on bow watch, seasick, failed to appear, and I was alone for eight hours in a maelstrom of wind and water, noise and iron; again and again, waves crashed across the deck, until water, air, and iron became one. Overwhelmed, exhausted, all thought and emotion beaten out of me, I lost my sense of self, the heartbeat I heard was the heart of the world, I breathed with the mighty risings and declines of earth, and this evanescence seemed less frightening than exalting. Afterward, there was pain of loss—loss of *what,* I wondered, understanding nothing.

Most poets know about these pangs of loss, and here and there in my prose readings, strange passages would leap like unicorns out of the page. "The Piper at the Gates of Dawn"[9] was an early example, and a description of singing fishes in a novel by Hamsun, and a passage in Borges, and another in Thoreau, and many in Hesse, who wrote of little else. Hamsun's characters tend to destroy themselves, and Hamsun and Hesse, with the authority of failure, warned of the fatal spell of the mystical search—so did Kierkegaard, who declared that too much "possibility" led to the madhouse. But when I came upon these cautionary words, I already had what Kierkegaard called "the sickness of infinitude," wandering from one path to another with no real recognition that I was embarked upon a search, and scarcely a clue as to what I might be after. I only knew that at the bottom of each breath there was a hollow place that needed to be filled.

In 1948 in Paris, a disciple of the late mystic-philosopher George Gurdjieff introduced me to "the Work," in which (as in so many disciplines) great emphasis is placed on "self-remembering"—paying attention to the present moment instead of wandering the ephemeral worlds of past and future. I continued in this work after returning to America, though briefly; it seemed to me that Gurdjieff's methods were too esoteric, that despite an evident deep strength among the leaders, too few among the rest of us were meant to follow. I went back to reading and began to write, and my confused state is plain in my first books.

In 1959, in the jungles of Peru, I would experiment with *yajé,* or *ayahuasca,* a hallucinogen of morbid effect used by shamans of the Amazon tribes to induce states that we call "supernatural," not because they transcend the laws of nature but because they still elude the grasp of formal science. (Most hallucinogens are derivatives of wild plants—mushrooms, cactus, a morning glory, many others—used for sacred purposes the world over; the ancients' soma may have been made from a poisonous mushroom of the genus *Amanita*.) Though frightening, the experience made clear that this family of chemicals (the phenol alkaloids) might lead to another way of seeing, and not in the slow labor of ascetic discipline but in cool efficiency and speed, as in flight through air. I never saw drugs as a path, far less as a way of life, but for the next ten years, I used them regularly—mostly LSD but also mescaline and psilocybin. The journeys were all scaring, often beautiful, often grotesque, and here and there a blissful passage was attained that in my ignorance I took for religious experience: I was a true believer in my magic carpet, ready to fly as far as it would take me. In 1961, in Thailand and Cambodia, on my way to an expedition in New Guinea, I experimented with a raw peasant form of heroin (sold to me as "opium") that frightened me to death, or a point close to it, one hollow night in an ancient hotel at the edge of black jungle and the silhouetted ruins of Angkor Wat. After a first ecstatic rush, I was stricken, paralyzed, unable to get my breath; with no one to call to, unable to call, I imagined that the End had come in this dead silent room under slow fans. Returning home a few months later, I treated drugs with more respect, working seriously with a renegade psychiatrist who was making bold, early experiments in the use of the hallucinogens in therapy. My companion was a girl named Deborah Love, who was adrift on the same instinctive search.

The search may begin with a restless feeling, as if one were being watched. One turns in all directions and sees nothing. Yet one senses that there is a source for this deep restlessness; and the path that leads there is not a path to a strange place, but the path home. ("But you *are* home," cries the Witch of the North. "All you have to do is wake up!") The journey is hard, for the secret place *where we have always been* is overgrown with thorns and thickets of "ideas," of fears and defenses, prejudices and repressions. The holy grail is what Zen Buddhists call our own "true nature"; each man is his own savior after all.

> The fact that many a man who goes his own way ends in ruin means nothing. . . . He *must* obey his own law, as if it were a daemon whispering to him of new and wonderful paths. . . . There are not a few who are called awake by the summons of the voice, whereupon they are at once set apart from the others, feeling themselves confronted with a problem about which the others know nothing. In most cases it is impossible to explain to the others what has happened, for any understanding is walled off by impenetrable prejudices. "You are no different from anybody else," they will chorus, or, "there's no such thing," and even if there is such a thing, it is immediately branded as "morbid." . . . He is at once set apart and isolated, as he has resolved to obey the law that commands him from within. "His *own* law!" everybody will cry. But he knows better: it is *the* law. . . . The only meaningful life is a life that strives for the individual realization—absolute and unconditional—of its own particular law. . . . To the extent that a man is untrue to the law of his being . . . he has failed to realize his life's meaning.
>
> The undiscovered vein within us is a living part of the psyche; classical Chinese philosophy names this interior way "Tao," and likens it to a flow of water that moves irresistibly towards its goal. To rest in Tao means fulfillment, wholeness, one's destination reached, one's mission done; the beginning, end, and perfect realization of the meaning of existence innate in all things.[10]

This passage from Jung was the first hard clue to the nature of my distemper. I was sitting in a garden in the mountains of Italy when I read it, and I was so excited that for the first and only time in all my life I actually yelled and jumped out of my chair: this searching was not morbid after all!

Not that D and I considered ourselves "seekers": we were embarrassed by such terms, and shied from people who employed them. We read and talked and read again, but what we needed was a teacher and a discipline. In those days, instant gurus were turning up as thick as bean sprouts, but true teachers were very hard to find. Finally D asked me to introduce her to the hallucinogens. I gave her mescaline on an autumn night of wind and rain.

On her first drug trip, D freaked out; that is the drug term, and there is no better. She started to laugh, and her mouth opened wide and she could not close it; her armor had cracked, and all the night winds of the world went howling through. Turning to me, she saw my flesh dissolve, my head become a skull—the whole night went like that. Yet she later saw that she might free herself by living out the fear of death, the demoniac rage at one's own helplessness that drug hallucinations seem to represent, and in that way let go of a life-killing accumulation of defenses. And she accepted the one danger of the mystical search: there is no way back without doing oneself harm. Many paths appear, but once the way is taken, it must be followed to the end.

And so, with great courage, D tried again, and sometimes things went better. I remember an April afternoon in 1962, when we had taken LSD together. She came out onto the terrace of a country house and drifted toward me, down across the lawn. D had black hair and beautiful wide eyes; in the spring breeze and light of flowers, she looked bewitched. We had been quarreling in recent days, and recriminations rose, tumbling all over one another in the rush to be spoken, yet as we drew near, the arguments aired so often in the past rose one by one and passed away in silence. There was no need to speak, the other knew to the last word what would be said. Struck dumb by this telepathy, our mouths snapped shut at the same instant, then burst into smiles at the precise timing of this comic mime of our old fights; delighted, we embraced and laughed and laughed. And still not one word had been spoken; only later did we discover that all thoughts, laughter, and emotions had been not similar but *just the same, one mind, one Mind,* even to this: that as we held each other, both bodies turned into sapling trees that flowed into each other, grew together in one strong trunk that pushed a taproot deeper and deeper into the ground.

And yet, and yet . . . an "I" remained, aware that something-was-happening, aware even that something-was-happening because of drugs. At no time did the "I" dissolve into the miracle.

Mostly D went on long, gray journeys, plagued by fear of death. I had bad trips, too, but they were rare; most were magic shows, mysterious, enthralling. After each—even the bad ones—I seemed to go more lightly on my way, leaving behind old residues of rage and pain. Whether joyful or dark, the drug vision can be astonishing, but eventually this vision will repeat itself, until even the magic show grows boring; for me, this occurred in the late 1960s, by which time D had already turned toward Zen.

Now those psychedelic years seem far away; I neither miss them nor regret them. Drugs can clear away the past, enhance the present; toward the inner garden, they can only point the way. Lacking the temper of ascetic discipline, the drug vision remains a sort of dream that cannot be brought over into daily life. Old mists may be banished, that is true, but the alien chemical agent forms another mist, maintaining the separation of the "I" from true experience of the One.

OCTOBER 6

Daybreak brings pink-copper glow to aerial ferns along the oak limbs, but as we climb, the ferns give way to graybeard lichens. Near 10,000 feet, the oaks die out, and clouds close in again, with fitful rain.

At Jaljala Ridge, GS's altimeter reads 11,200 feet. The dark foundations of Annapurna and Dhaulgiri are both visible, and a shadow between them is the gorge of the Kali Gandaki, far away eastward and below. All peaks are cloud-hidden, and just beneath the swirling clouds is a white stillness; the descending snow line is no more than a thousand feet above the ridge where we now stand, and far below the high passes we must cross. Unless the monsoon ends while the weather is still warm enough to melt high snows, there will be trouble in the weeks to come.

The trail moves westward over Jaljala, crossing wet tundra set about with purple gentians and a pink-belled heath. Then the first ray of sun in days strikes the harlequin feathers of a hoopoe, and I smile. Like many of the foothills birds, *Upupa* is also a bird of Africa, but I saw one much more recently—last month, in fact—in the mountains of Umbria, in Italy. Because of its sun-ray crest, the hoopoe is a "solar bird"—doubtless an omen of a change in weather—and in Sufi mythology its breast mark is a sign that it has entered the way of spiritual knowledge:

> I [the hoopoe] am a messenger of the world invisible. . . . For years I have travelled by sea and land, over mountains and valleys. . . .

> We have a true king, he lives behind the mountains. . . . He is
> close to us, but we are far from him. The place where he dwells
> is inaccessible, and no tongue is able to utter his name. Before
> him hang a hundred thousand veils of light and darkness. . . .
>
> Do not imagine that the journey is short; and one must have
> the heart of a lion to follow this unusual road, for it is very
> long. . . . One plods along in a state of amazement, sometimes
> smiling, sometimes weeping.[11]

The snow cone of Great Dhaulagiri, five miles high, rises
from the clouds behind and is quickly misted over; though far
away, it fills the whole northeast. Ahead, a valley of yellow
maples descends gently to the west, on one side a wall of firs,
on the other a rampart of bare rock; the valley stream sparkles
with shifting storm light, attracting three species of the superb
Asian redstarts *(Phoenicurus),* which are related to the nightin-
gale. "This is the first day since we've left that I feel I've gotten
out into the open," GS says.

This wilderness will certainly be gone by the century's end.
Already, as the valley widens, signs of slash-and-burn appear
("Fire very bad, sah!" Tukten says), and rockslides caused by
destruction of the forests block the river with huge fallen trees.
The water turns brown and torrential, diverted farther down the
valley into channels between pale strands of deadwood and silted
stones—this is the Uttar Ganga (Northern River) pouring away
between the western mountains to its meeting with the Bheri
and the great Karnali, which will carry it southward into India.

The trail, flooded by monsoon torrents, is lost among the
river islands, oxbows, and incoming streams. Here and there
the drifted trees serve us as bridges, and GS, slowly but steadily,
walks almost all of them upright. But I have lost that steady
step and feel unbalanced by my rucksack, and must hitch ignominiously across the worst of them on my backside. Finally I
cut myself a heavy stick of my own length, as probe and balance; it will be useful later as a stave.

The woodlands open out onto the only broad flat valley in
these mountains, used as summer pasture by the Magars from

the south. In recent years, Dhorpatan has become a great encampment of Tibetans, who came here in the flight from the
Chinese that began in 1950. They raise horses and potatoes,
making journeys in winter to Pokhara and Kathmandu to trade
their last turquoise, silver, and religious artifacts in the bazaars
and visit with countrymen from other settlements, for Tibetans
have a nomad heritage and love to travel.

In Tibet, where wolves and brigands prosper, the nomads'
camps and remote villages are guarded by big black or brindle
mastiffs. Such dogs are also found in northern Nepal, and last
year in the Bhote Khosi region GS was set upon by two of them
that were guarding some Bhote packs left on the trail; he nar-
rowly escaped serious injury. The mastiffs are so fierce that Tibetan travelers carry a charm portraying a savage dog fettered
in chain: the chain is clasped by the mystical "thunderbolt," or
dorje, and an inscription reads, "The mouth of the blue dog is
bound beforehand."[12] During the day the dogs are chained; at
night they roam as sentinels and guards. In the first of the
Dhorpatan encampments, we walked the center of the mud
thoroughfares to avoid the snarling, straining animals on both
sides. Then one of these broke or slipped its chain and came for
us from behind, without a bark.

Since GS was several yards ahead, I was selected for attack,
which was thwarted only in the last split second. Luckily, I
heard it coming, and swung around upon it with my heavy
stick: the beast tumbled back and then came on again, snarling
now in a low, ugly way. Searching in vain for a heavy rock, I
did my best to crack its skull, while the dog lunged back and
forth at the tip of my stick in horrid fury. Meanwhile, GS had
located a heavy split of wood; he hurled it at the dog with all
his force. The brute dodged, then sprang after it, sinking its
teeth deep into the wood. Finally, it was driven off by a Tibetan, who until now had watched calmly from the doorway of
his hut to see how I might fare. From Dhorpatan north across
the Himalaya, it was said, such dogs were common, and I never
walked without my stave again. If I had not cut it in the hour
before (after eight days of getting by without one), I might have
been hurt badly, and I marvel to this day at the precise timing.

Dhorpatan has no bazaar and no real center, being strung out in scattered hut clusters all along the northern side of the broad valley. There are a few low-caste Magars here, but otherwise the people are Tibetan. Buddhist prayer flags fly from every hut, and heaps of prayer stones rise like gigantic cairns from the valley floor.

When the porters appear, our supplies are stored in the cold back room of a dank earthen house set against the open hillside. We shall sleep here, too, to guard things, for as in most refugee settlements, morale is low and theft endemic. Across the passage is a common room where villagers come and go, and beyond that room, at the heart of the house, is a simple altar. Here the day ends with the low murmuring of OM MANI PADME HUM. As she chants, the old woman kneads dark ivory beads with one dried hand and with the other twirls an ancient prayer wheel of silver and copper. The prayer wheel is inscribed with the same mantra, and so is the tight-rolled scroll inside it, spinning out the invocation that calls the universe to attention:

OM!

OCTOBER 7

Half of our porters left this morning, returning over Jaljala Ridge to the Kali Gandaki, and the Tibetans who might have replaced them are busy digging their potatoes for trade across the mountains. GS is understandably upset: why wasn't he warned of this potato harvest by the trekking outfitters in Kathmandu, who had assured him that porters were abundant in Dhorpatan? Jang-bu says there is not one porter to be found—"maybe tomorrow."

The five young Tamangs brought from Kathmandu, Tukten the Sherpa, and old Bimbahadur the Magar are still with us. The Tamangs, or Lamas, are hill people of Mongol origins from the Trisuli River region, west of Kathmandu; like the Gurungs and Magars, the Tamangs are ancient inhabitants of Nepal, and followed some form of the old B'on religion. These days they incline toward Buddhism, and they get on well with the Sherpas, whom they much resemble in their cheerful, willing ways. Pirim and his brother Tulo Kansha, Karsung, Danbahadur, and Ram Tarang are lean, barefoot youths whose heavy work does not spoil the adventure of new places, and they will go as far as we will take them, although they have no boots or clothes for the deep snows. As for the old Magar, he had said goodbye, and was on the point of heading off with the rest, but Tukten charmed him out of it, this Tukten with his disconcerting smile.

Tukten has elf's ears and a thin neck, a yellow face, and the wild wise eyes of a *naljorpa,* or Tibetan yogi. He radiates that inner quiet which is often associated with spiritual attainment, but perhaps his attainment is a dark one. The other Sherpas are uneasy with him; they mutter that he drinks too much, uses foul language, is not to be trusted. Apparently he has demeaned himself by taking this job as a porter. Yet they defer to him as if he possessed some sort of magic, and sometimes I think I feel his power, too.

This disreputable fellow is somehow known to me, like a dim figure from another life. Tukten himself seems aware that we are in some sort of relation, which he accepts in a way that I cannot; that he is not here by accident is, for me, a restless instinct, whereas he takes our peculiar bond for granted. More often than I like, I feel that gaze of his, as if he were here to watch over me, as if it were he who had made me cut that stick: the gaze is open, calm, benign, without judgment of any kind, and yet, confronted with it, as with a mirror, I am aware of all that is hollow in myself, all that is greedy, angry, and unwise.

I am grateful for a day of rest. My knees and feet and back are sore, and all my gear is wet. I wear my last dry socks upside down so that the hole in the heel sits on the top of my foot; these underpants, ripped, must be worn backward; my broken glasses' frame is taped; my hair is tangled. Dawa brings hot water for laundry and a wash—Dawa and I are the only members of this expedition who enjoy bathing—and I put on clean damp clothes, after which, at my behest, GS crops my long hair to the skull. For years I have worn a wristband of heavy braided cord, first because it was a gift, and latterly as an affectation; this is cut off, too. Finally, I remove my watch, as the time it tells is losing all significance.

In the rain, all day, the Tibetans come to look at us, and again I am struck by the resemblances between our native Americans and these Mongol peoples. Most Dhorpatan Tibetans have the small stature, small hands and feet and noses of the Eskimo, the Mongoloid eye-fold, dark copper skin, and crow-black hair: even the low red-trimmed boots of hide and wool are very similar in appearance and design to the Eskimo mukluks. Their ornaments of turquoise and silver, on the other hand, suggest the Pueblo Indians and the Navajo, while the beads, braids, and striped blankets flung over bare shoulders evoke nothing so much as old pictures of the Plains tribes, an effect enhanced by the squalor of their encampments and the quarrelsome dogs. When traveling, these people use hide tents, children are carried papoose-fashion, and the basis of their diet is a barley or maize meal known as *tsampa;* no real kinship has been demonstrated between native American and Asiatic tongues, yet a similar farina of the Algonkian tribes of my own region is called "samp."

Such similarities are doubtless superficial, but others are more than remarkable in cultures so widely separated in time and space. The animistic kinship with the world around that permeates the life of the Gurung and other tribes in the corners of these mountains (including some that have taken up modern religions), as well as that of the Chukchi Eskimos and other remnant hunter-gatherers of eastern Asia, differs little in its spirit among most of the Eskimos and Indians of the Americas. The great thunderbird of North America is known to the forest Tungus of Siberia; and the sun symbols and sacred eyes, the thread-crosses, cosmic trees, and swastikas that symbolize esoteric teachings of the Old World from ancient Egypt to present-day Tibet have been widespread in the New World since very early times—so early, in fact, that present estimates of dates for nomadic waves of Asian hunters across the Bering land bridge into the New World do not seem to account for them. (Such dates are regularly set back, and may be meaningless; on a clear day one can actually see one continent from the offshore islands of the other, and for all we know people were traveling *in both directions* on the sea and ice even when Beringia was under water.)

Ignoring that body of peculiar lore based on vanished continents and cosmic Masters[13]—and putting aside the current speculation about ocean travel by such atypical Indians as the Inca, the many cultural similarities between the pre-Aryan Dravidians and the Maya, and accounts seeming to indicate that Buddhist missionaries reached the Aleutians and traveled as far south as California by the fourteenth century[14]—one remains faced with an uneasy choice between eerily precise archetypal symbols and the existence and perpetuation of a body of pro-

found intuitive knowledge that antedates all known religions
of man's history.

Asian traditions refer to a hidden kingdom—Shambala, the
Center—in an unknown part of Inner Asia. (The Gobi Desert,
formerly fertile, now a repository of old bones, is often cited;
the desiccation of Central Asia, as broad lakes vanished in dry
pans and grasslands turned into shifting sands, might have
turned an ancient city into a legend. The death of a civilization
can come quickly: the change in climate that dried up rivers
and destroyed the savannas of the central Sahara scattered the
great pastoral civilizations of Fessan and Tassili in just a few
centuries after 2500 B.C.) More likely, Shambala is a symbol
for the Aryan cultures that emerged in that vast region between
6000 and 5000 B.C.—the apparent source of esoteric mystery-
cults throughout Eurasia, which have echoes to this day in the
Tantric Buddhism of Tibet. According to one Tibetan lama,
these mysteries "are the faint echoes of teaching that existed
from time immemorial in Central and North Asia."[15] Another
believes that "no people since the beginning . . . has ever been
without some fragment of this secret lore."[16] This view is supported by ethnologists,[17] who find the same pattern of shaman-
istic practice not only in Asia and the Americas but in Africa,
Australia, Oceania, and Europe. The historical diffusion of such
teachings—and perhaps the prehistorical as well—is supported
by striking consistencies in the practice of what Westerners, having lost the secrets, refer to with mixed fascination and contempt
as "mysticism" or "the occult" but which for the less alienated
cultures, past and present, is only another aspect of reality.

The native American traditions are Eastern cultures, thousands of miles and perhaps thousands of years from their
source. Anyone familiar with Zen thought or the teachings of
Tibetan Buddhism will not be astonished by the insights attributed in recent years to a Yaqui Indian sorcerer of northern
Mexico.[18] In content, attitude, and especially in that cryptic
manner of expression which the inexpressible requires, there is
nothing in the comments of this shaman that might not have
been spoken by a Kagyu-pa lama or Zen roshi. Innumerable parallels to Eastern teachings among native American traditions

might be cited, such as the Aztec concept of existence as a dream state, or the great awe of wind and sky that the Ojibwa of our northern prairies share with the vanished Aryans of the Asian steppes.[19]

Tibetan oracle-priests and Siberian shamans practice dream-travel, telepathy, mystical heat, speed-running, death prediction, and metempsychosis, all of which are known to New World shamans: the Algonkian medicine man who travels as a bird to the spirit world, the jaguar-shamans of the Amazon would be impressed but not surprised by the powers attributed to yogis and *naljorpas*. The energy or essence or breath of being that is called *prana* by Hindu yogins and *chi* by the Chinese is known as *orenda* to the Cree.[20] Such concepts as karma and circular time are taken for granted by almost all native American traditions; time as space and death as becoming are implicit in the earth view of the Hopi, who avoid all linear constructions, knowing as well as any Buddhist that Everything is Right Here Now. As in the great religions of the East, the native American makes small distinction between religious activity and the acts of every day: the religious ceremony is life itself.

Like the Atman of the Vedas, like the Buddhist Mind, like Tao, the Great Spirit of the American Indian is everywhere and in all things, unchanging. Even the Australian aborigines—considered to be the most ancient race on earth—distinguish between linear time and a "Great Time" of dreams, myths, and heroes, in which all is present in this moment. It stirs me that this primordial intuition has been perpetuated by voice and act across countless horizons and for centuries on end, illuminating the dream-life of primitives, the early Indo-European civilizations of the Sumerians and Hittites, the ancient Greeks and the Egyptians, guarded by hidden cults in the Dark Ages, emerging in Christian, Hasidic, and Muslim mysticism (Sufism) as well as in all the splendorous religions of the East. And it is a profound consolation, perhaps the only one, to this haunted animal that wastes most of a long and ghostly life wandering the future and the past on its hind legs, looking for meanings, only to see in the eyes of others of its kind that it must die.

OCTOBER 8

An emissary to the Tibetans from the Dalai Lama's exiled court at Dharmsala, in India, has lately come by way of Tarakot, which lies across the mountains to the north. He says the trail is "very hard, very steep and slippery, too many ups and downs." Since this describes most Himalayan trails, especially in time of snow, it is not to be taken seriously. But another Tibetan, come south in recent days, says that at Jang Pass between here and Tarakot the snow is higher than the knees, and this bad news will make it hard to conscript porters. Also, the police at the Tarakot checkpost are said to be very arbitrary, paying little attention to documents issued by colleagues far away in Kathmandu; they may refuse to let us enter Dolpo, even though our trekking permits authorize us to go as far north as Phoksumdo Lake. Last year an anthropologist had a permit to go to Tarap, in Dolpo, but was forbidden to continue beyond Tarakot, where he was stranded for the winter by a late October blizzard that shut off the Jang Pass. And that blizzard is bad news, too, since the pass between Tarakot and Shey is much higher than this first one at the Jang, and we must cross and then recross it before winter.

Dhorpatan is a sort of purgatory. The dungeon atmosphere of these cold quarters, the merciless rain that drips to the mud floor through the slat roof, the heinous din of the dogfights under the window—at least four last night—deepen the depression caused by all these tales of obstacles and hazards, of icy streams and heavy snows between here and our destination.

Last night, the eerie, clear song of a Tibetan boy disturbed me, not because it was so strange but because it seemed familiar; I realized at last that what it recalled were the sad Quechua *huainus* of the Andes. Later I dreamed about my beautiful eight-year-old boy, whose mother died of cancer just last year. In the dream, I paid a visit to a dark cagelike shelter, where he was being kept with other children. He came to me, smiling, and together we petted a little fox that was also in the cage. Now the cage was seen as an animal pen with a tattered collection of poor creatures in the corners, and I noticed that the little fox was uncared for, and covered with grime. Looking bewildered, it took such shelter as it could find beneath a big and bossy hen that was preoccupied with its own chicks. Realizing that the little fox was Alex, I woke up stricken.

It now seems certain that my promise to be home by Thanksgiving will be broken. Originally we had planned to arrive at Shey Gompa, Crystal Monastery, by October 15. There is no longer any chance of this, nor any real hope of returning home before December.

That we might be trapped at Shey by blizzards is also a grim prospect for GS, who promised his wife that he would have Christmas with the family; Kay and the children are to meet him in Kathmandu. And so he is in low spirits, too, though he discounts the gloom-ridden reports of northward travel: "If you took people seriously in this part of the world," he says, "you would never leave home." And it is true that everywhere dangers and difficulties are exaggerated by the local people, if only as a good excuse for extortion or malingering: one must go oneself to know the truth.

We are desperate to leave this half-civilized hole and get over the high passes while we can. Last March, GS's preliminary expedition to eastern Nepal produced inconclusive data on the blue sheep; if the rut is missed due to the snows, his second blue-sheep expedition will have been wasted. Considering all that he has at stake, he is remarkably patient and resilient, and we manage to get on very well, despite our cold, close quarters.

GS has already devoured all of his books (he devours his last ration of chocolate in the same way, which I rather admire, being too provident myself, too untrustful of "the future") and so he is reading my *Bardo Thodol* (the Tibetan "Book of the

Dead") out of desperation, and taking notes on it, what's more. He is even writing haiku, pursuing it with skill and vigor, and this poem seems to me much better than those I have written here myself:

> On cloud-trails I go
> Alone, with the chatting porters.
> There is a crow.

OCTOBER 9

This morning the rain is lighter, with long lulls, but we are stuck another day. At least we know that planes cannot fly the mountains in this weather; had we counted on coming to Dhorpatan by air, we would still be languishing in Kathmandu. Meanwhile, the season and the snows are gaining, and the new porters, such as they are, are getting restive: Jang-bu, the head Sherpa, fears that if the rain persists another day, they may drift away. They are in here now, hefting the baskets under the whimsical gaze of Phu-Tsering, who pantomimes them comically, taking no trouble to conceal his view that they are low fellows, and light fingered. Phu-Tsering accompanied GS last spring on the first blue-sheep expedition, and it was his high-spirits, rather more than his cuisine, that recommended him for this one.

Our speculations about the Crystal Monastery have led inevitably to talk of Buddhism and Zen. Last year, as a way of alerting GS to my unscientific preoccupations, I sent him a small book entitled *Zen Mind, Beginner's Mind*. Very politely, he had written, "Many thanks for the Zen book, which Kay brought with her to Pakistan. I've only browsed a bit so far. A lot of it seems most sensible, some of it less so, but I have to ponder things some more." GS refuses to believe that the Western mind can truly absorb nonlinear Eastern perceptions; he shares the view of many in the West that Eastern thought evades "reality" and therefore lacks the courage of existence. But the courage-to-be, right here and now and nowhere else, is precisely what Zen, at least, demands: eat when you eat, sleep when you sleep! Zen has no patience with "mysticism," far less the occult, although its emphasis on the enlightenment experience (called *kensho* or *satori*) is what sets it apart from other religions and philosophies.

I remind GS of the Christian mystics such as Meister Eckhardt and Saint Francis, Saint Augustine, and Saint Catherine of Siena, who spent three years in silent meditation: "All the way to Heaven is Heaven," Saint Catherine said, and that is the very breath of Zen, which does not elevate divinity above the common miracles of every day. GS counters by saying that all these people lived before the scientific revolution had changed the very nature of Western thought, which of course is true, but it is also true that in recent years, Western scientists have turned with new respect toward the intuitive sciences of the East. Einstein repeatedly expressed suspicion of the restrictions of linear thought, concluding that propositions arrived at by purely logical means were completely empty of reality even if one could properly explain what "reality" means; it was intuition, he declared, that had been crucial to his thinking. And there are close parallels in the theory of relativity to the Buddhist concept of the identity of time and space, which, like Hindu cosmology, derives from the ancient teachings of the Vedas. Somewhere, Einstein remarks that his theory could be readily explained to Indians of the Uto-Aztecan languages, which include the Pueblo and the Hopi. ("The Hopi does not say 'the light flashed' but merely '*flash*,' without subject or time element; time cannot move because it is also space. The two are never separated; there are no words or expressions referring to time or space as separate from each other. This is close to the 'field' concept of modern physics. Furthermore, there is no temporal future; it is already with us, eventuating or 'manifesting.' What are in English differences of time are in Hopi differences of *validity*.")[21]

The progress of the sciences toward theories of fundamental unity, cosmic symmetry (as in the unified field theory)—how do such theories differ, in the end, from that unity which Plato called "unspeakable" and "indiscribable," the holistic knowledge shared by so many peoples of the earth, Christians included, before the advent of the industrial revolution made new barbarians of the peoples of the West? In the United States, before spiritualist foolishness at the end of the last century confused mysticism with "the occult" and tarnished both, William James wrote a master work of metaphysics; Emerson spoke of "the wise silence, the universal beauty, to which every part and particle is equally related, the eternal One . . ."; Melville referred to "that profound silence, that only voice of God"; Walt Whitman celebrated the most ancient secret, that no God could be found "more divine than yourself." And then, almost everywhere, a clear and subtle illumination that lent magnificence to life and peace to death was overwhelmed in the hard glare of technology. Yet that light is always present, like the stars of noon. Man must perceive it if he is to transcend his fear of meaningless, for no amount of "progress" can take its place. We have outsmarted ourselves, like greedy monkeys, and now we are full of dread.

Not long ago in the Western world, the argument was whether sun or earth lay at the center of the Universe. Even in this century it was believed that ours was the only galaxy, whereas Asian sages long before the time of Christ had intuited correctly that the galaxies numbered in the billions, and that universal time was beyond all apprehension: more than four billion years was but one day in the existence of their Creator, and His night was of equal length, and all of this was no more than "a twinkling of the eye of the immutable, immortal, beginningless Lord, the god of the Universe." In the Rig Veda, an oscillating universe is conceived to be expanding from a center—this is consistent with the "Big Bang" theory, which only in the last decade has met general acceptance among astronomers. In a Hindu myth, the "Fire-Mist," like a sea of milk, is churned by the Creator, and out of this churning come the solidifying forms of stars and planets—in effect, the nebular theory of modern astronomy, with the Fire-Mist composed of the primordial hydrogen atoms from which all matter is thought to derive.

"Nothing exists but atoms and the void"—so wrote Democritus. And it is "void" that underlies the Eastern teachings—not emptiness or absence, but the Uncreated that preceded all creation, the beginningless potential of all things.

> Before heaven and earth
> There was something nebulous
>> silent isolated
>> unchanging and alone
>> eternal
>> the Mother of All Things
> I do not know its name
> I call it Tao[22]

Darkness there was, wrapped in yet more Darkness. . . . The incipient lay covered by the Void. That One Thing . . . was born through the power of heat from its austerity. . . . Where this Creation came from, He who has ordained it from the highest heaven, He indeed knows; or He knows not.[23]

The mystical perception (which is only "mystical" if reality is limited to what can be measured by the intellect and senses) is remarkably consistent in all ages and all places, East and West, a point that has not been ignored by modern science. The physicist seeks to understand reality, while the mystic is trained to experience it directly. Both agree that human mechanisms of perception, stunted as they are by screens of social training that close out all but the practical elements in the sensory barrage, give a very limited picture of existence, which certainly transcends mere physical evidence. Furthermore, both groups agree that appearances are illusory. A great physicist extends this idea: "Modern science classifies the world . . . not into different groups of objects but into different groups of connections. . . . The world thus appears to be a complicated tissue of events, in which connections of different kinds alternate or overlap or combine and thereby determine the texture of the whole."[24] All phenomena are processes, connections, all is in flux, and at moments this flux is actually visible: one has only to open the mind in meditation or have the mind screens knocked awry by drugs or dreams to see that there is no real edge to anything, that in the endless interpenetration of the universe, a molecular flow, a cosmic energy shimmers in all stone and steel as well as flesh.

The ancient intuition that all matter, all "reality," is energy, that all phenomena, including time and space, are mere crystallizations of mind, is an idea with which few physicists have quarreled since the theory of relativity first called into question the separate identities of energy and matter. Today most scientists would agree with the ancient Hindus that nothing exists or is destroyed, things merely change shape or form; that matter is insubstantial in origin, a temporary aggregate of the pervasive energy that animates the electron. And what is this infinitesimal non-thing—to a speck of dust what the dust speck is to the whole earth? "Do we really know what electricity is? By knowing the laws according to which it acts and by making use of them, we still do not know the origin or the real nature of this force, which ultimately may be the very source of life, and consciousness, the divine power and mover of all that exists."[25]

The cosmic radiation that is thought to come from the explosion of creation strikes the earth with equal intensity from all directions, which suggests either that the earth is at the center of the universe, as in our innocence we once supposed, or that the known universe has no center. Such an idea holds no terror for mystics; in the mystical vision, the universe, its center, and its origins are simultaneous, all around us, all within us, and all One.

> I am everywhere and in everything: I am the sun and stars. I am time and space and I am He. When I am everywhere, where can I move? When there is no past and no future, and I am eternal existence, then where is time?[26]

In the Book of Job, the Lord demands, "Where wast thou when I laid the foundations of the earth? Declare, if thou hath understanding! Who laid the cornerstones thereof, when the morning stars sang together, and all the sons of God shouted for joy?"

"I was *there*!"—surely that is the answer to God's question. For no matter how the universe came into being, most of the atoms in these fleeting assemblies that we think of as our bodies have been in existence since the beginning. What the Buddha perceived was his identity with the Universe; to experience existence in this way is to be the Buddha. Even the brilliant "white light" that may accompany mystical experience (the "inner light" attested to by Eskimo shamans) might be perceived as a primordial memory of Creation. "Man is the matter of the cosmos, contemplating itself," a modern astronomer has said;[27] another points out that each breath we take contains hundreds of thousands of the inert, pervasive argon atoms that were actually breathed in his lifetime by the Buddha, and indeed contain parts of the "snorts, sighs, bellows, shrieks"[28] of all creatures that ever existed, or will ever exist. These atoms flow backward and forward in such useful but artificial constructs as time and space, in the same universal rhythms, universal breath as the tides and stars, joining both the living and the dead in that energy which animates the universe. What is changeless and immortal is not individual body-mind but, rather, that Mind which is shared with all of existence, that stillness, that incipience which never ceases because it never becomes but simply IS. This teaching, still manifest in the Hindu and Buddhist religions, goes back at least as far as the doctrine of Maya that emerges in the Vedic civilizations and may well derive from much more ancient cultures; Maya is Time, the illusion of the ego, the stuff of individual existence, the dream that separates us from a true perception of the whole. It is often likened to a sealed glass vessel that separates the air within from the clear and unconfined air all around, or water from the all-encompassing sea. Yet the vessel itself is not different from the sea, and to shatter or dissolve it brings about the reunion with all universal life that mystics seek, the homegoing, the return to the lost paradise of our "true nature."

Today science is telling us what the Vedas have taught mankind for three thousand years, that we do not see the universe as it is. What we see is Maya, or Illusion, the "magic show" of Nature, a collective hallucination of that part of our consciousness which is shared with all of our own kind, and which gives a common ground, a continuity, to the life experience. According to Buddhists (but not Hindus), this world perceived by the senses, this relative but not absolute reality, this dream, also exists, also has meaning; but it is only one aspect of the truth, like the cosmic vision of this goat by the crooked door, gazing through sheets of rain into the mud.

Tomorrow begins the trek into the north. By the Jang Pass, we cross the Dhaulagiris to the Bheri River; we ascend the Suli Gad and the Phoksumdo River, and by the Kang Pass cross the Kanjiroba Range to Crystal Mountain. In spring or summer, a fortnight might suffice, but there is snow in the high passes, and we shall be lucky to arrive at all.

In early afternoon, the sun appears—the first full sunshine in more than a week. Dhorpatan Valley, which had seemed so grim, is beautiful. I walk down into the valley pastures and circumambulate a great prayer wall of heavy stones, old and new, flat and round, of many colors and from many places—how and when the oldest of them got here, no one seems to know. From four tall poles, blue and white prayer flags—the celestial colors—snap in the crisp wind, sending OM MANI PADME HUM to the ten directions. The skies are shifting, and at dusk a peak of Annapurna rises, far away over the eastern end of the valley. On recent mornings, the low mountains all around this valley have turned white.

northward

O, how incomprehensible everything was, and actually sad, although it was also beautiful. One knew nothing. One lived and ran about the earth and rode through forests, and certain things looked so challenging and promising and nostalgic: a star in the evening, a blue harebell, a reed-green pond, the eye of a person or a cow. And sometimes it seemed that something never seen yet long desired was about to happen, that a veil would drop from it all; but then it passed, nothing happened, the riddle remained unsolved, the secret spell unbroken, and in the end one grew old and looked cunning . . . or wise . . . and still one knew nothing perhaps, was still waiting and listening.

HERMANN HESSE
Narcissus and Goldmund

Monk: What happens when the leaves are falling, and the trees are bare?
Unmon: The golden wind, revealed!

Hegikan Roku (The Blue Cliff Records)

OCTOBER 10

In the glory of sunrise, spiderwebs glitter and greenfinches in October gold bound from pine to shining pine. Pony bells and joyous whistling; young children and animals jump as if come to life. One beautiful child has a silver necklace and red-green strips of rag braided into crow-black hair; the infant she carries papoose-style is her own.

A day so fine for travel is also fine for harvesting potatoes. The new porters refuse to depart, nor will they give up the pay advanced to them to buy food. "Dhorpatan no-good people," says Phu-Tsering. To find nine men, Jang-bu stays behind, and Gyaltsen stays with him, guarding the loads while his friend searches for porters. GS will wait awhile to see what happens. I set out with the rest, and do not see GS again until day's end.

The northward path ascends the Phagune Gorge through resined air of pine forest and cedar. A crimson-horned pheasant, or monal, bursts into the air over the valley, and the small marmot-like pikas are sunning at their holes, ignoring the flights of sweet-voiced alpine birds. Silver lichens, golden moss, the whistle of a falcon: the view south down the Phagune Gorge is full of light.

We climb toward Dhaulagiri, the "White Mountains."

Yesterday's snow retreats uphill as the sun rises, and we do not overtake it until afternoon, at 12,400 feet. The snow is gray, on steep gray slushy scree, and the trail rises into clouds that hide the snow peaks. Cotoneaster of deep green, with its red berries, is the lone piece of color in the grayness.

It is hard going in this mush: the summit never comes. The pass is a V far off and high against a sky that withdraws into swift, fitful weather, and when it is reached, it is only the portal to a higher valley, with yet another V at its far end. In the wet snow, the narrow path traversing the steep slopes is hard to trace, and treacherous. Phu-Tsering and Dawa have mountain boots inherited from past expeditions, but most of the Tamangs go barefoot so that the sneakers provided for them may be sold another day in Kathmandu. Even so, they keep up better than bow-legged old Bimbahadur, who starts off ahead of the others every morning and by evening has fallen far behind.

Due to boot blisters, I am wearing sneakers, and my wet feet are numb. Dawa, clumping steadily along with the basket of camp cooking gear, overtakes me as I near the pass, at 13,400 feet. Here, the clouds have thickened so that we can scarcely see each other; there is strong wind and light snow. From behind and below, in the Phagune Gorge, rumbling rockslides are followed by deep silence. Uneasy, Dawa sets his basket down and works back a little way to whistle to Phu-Tsering and the others.

I wait, facing the north; instinct tells me to stand absolutely still. Cloud mist, snow, and utter silence, utter solitude: extinction. Then, in the great hush, the clouds draw apart, revealing the vast Dhaulagiri snowfields. I breathe, mists swirl, and all has vanished—nothing! I make a small, involuntary bow.

A downward path is forged through the wet snows, striking a tree line of dwarfed cedar six hundred feet below, and emerging at dusk on a saddleback ridge of alpine tundra where it is flat enough to pitch a tent. Here Tukten and GS catch up with us. Just at darkness, the clouds lift: at 12,500 feet, the campsite is surrounded by bright glaciers. The five peaks of Dhaulagiri shine in the black firmament, and over all this whiteness rings a silver moon, the full moon of October, when the lotus blooms.

OCTOBER 11

In the clear night, bright stars descend all the way to the horizon, and before dawn, a band of black appears beyond the peaks, as if one could see past earth's horizon into outer space. The circle of silver peaks turns pink, then a fresh white as the sun ignites Churen Himal, 24,158 feet high, and Putha Hiunchuli, just four hundred feet below. The air is ringing. GS declares that in eastern Nepal, under Mount Everest, he saw nothing to match the prospect from this aerie, all but encircled by great pinnacles of ice.

The mountain sky is bare—wind, wind, and cold. Because of the cold, the Tamangs squashed into the Sherpas' tent, but in the night gusts, the tent collapsed, and at daybreak all are singing from beneath it. Now, half-naked in the brittle air, the Tamangs hunch barefoot at the fire, kneading *tsampa* and humming softly in the smoke; they remind me of young Machiguenga Indians at the Andean river campfires of long ago. Jang-bu and Gyaltsen, with new porters, must have stopped somewhere on the south side of the pass; because of the cold, we break camp quickly and continue down the north side without waiting.

From deep in the earth, the roar of the river rises. The rhododendron leaves along the precipice are burnished silver, but night still fills the steep ravines where southbound migrants descend at day to feed and rest. The golden birds fall from the morning sun like blowing sparks that drop away and are extinguished in the dark.

With the first sun rays we come down into still forest of gnarled birch and dark stiff firs. Through light filtered by the straying lichens, a silver bird flies to a cedar, fanning crimsoned wings on the sunny bark. Then it is gone, leaving behind a vague longing, a sad emptiness.

The path continues down into the oaks. A thousand feet below is a mountain meadow, and here by a herdsman's shed of stone, we wait for Jang-bu. I sit back in straw and dung warmth against the sunny stones. A brilliant black-red beetle comes, and a husky grasshopper, rubbing its fiery legs. A crow flaps to a cedar by the river, and the crow's wings, too, are filled with the hard silver light of the Himalaya. "Wherever you go, the crow shows up, sooner or later," GS remarks, "and of all the crows, I like the raven best. In Alaska, at forty below, no sign of life—and there's the raven!" (GS had a pet raven while attending the University of Alaska, and this bird brought about his first encounter with the girl who became his wife: her attention was drawn to a man shouting at the sky, commanding an unseen raven to come back.)

With its crows and river willows and snow mountains all around, this bowl might be in western North America. D would have loved these mountains. As a girl, my wife had spent much of her time in the Rocky Mountains of Colorado, and later in the Alps in southern France; she always wished to see the Himalaya.

> When I was a child I rode my horse to the top of the mountain where the sun shone down on me, and the valley green in meadow grass lay far below. I looked to the sky and waited, filled with longing. Nothing sounded. In sorrow I lay down on the earth, my arms outstretched to hug it. O Earth, warm and just right, everything just right, the shape of bark, and smell of grass, and sound of leaves brushing the wind, I wanted to be just right too.
>
> But no voice tells me I am and I rise from the mute ground and get on the horse and ride back down the mountain.[1]

Lovely in person and in spirit, a gifted writer and wonderful teacher with a passionate, inquiring mind, exceptionally intelligent and kind—such was the view of all who knew her well.

One friend remarked, "She has no mud on her soul." Yet at times, there was an above-life quality as if she were practicing for the day when the higher state that she aspired to must come. To live with a saint is not difficult, for a saint makes no comparisons, but saintlike aspiration presents problems. I found her goodness maddening, and behaved badly. My days with D were tainted with remorse; I could not abide myself when near her, and therefore took advantage of my work to absent myself on expeditions all around the world—once I went away for seven months. Yet love was there, half-understood, never quite finished; the end of respect that puts relationships to death did not occur.

The sword light on the peaks brings back the snows of Courchevel, in the French Alps, where we went skiing just a year before D died. It was a happy trip, and gave us new hope for the future. From Courchevel we drove to Geneva, from where she would fly to America next day. I was on my way to Italy, to sell a small farmhouse in the mountains of Umbria where she refused to go.

In the dark winter afternoon, in the old quarter of Geneva, we discovered a most beautiful bowl in a shop window, seven elegant thin black fishes in calligraphic design on old white and pale blue; the bowl, fired at Istafahan in the thirteenth century, seemed to float in the hands like an old leaf. But it was too expensive, and I found her something else. Next morning, her plane left an hour before mine, and in this interim, carried away by the drama of our parting, I telephoned the antique shop and arranged to buy the Istafahan bowl, which was eventually sent on to Italy to be carried home. The delicate thing was a symbol of a new beginning, and I meant to surprise D with it on her birthday, but when that day came we quarreled, and the bowl, put away for a better occasion, was forgotten altogether as the marriage came apart. No parting was quite final, each wild reconciliation was followed by new crisis; an exhausted decision to divorce was made on a late summer's morning just five months before her death. That decision was firm, we made it calmly and were both relieved. The very next day, acting on an imperious inner command, I made a commitment to D, this time for good. She understood; sipping coffee in the sun, she merely nodded.

It seems to me now that this mystifying command was related to an earlier intuition. For several years the certainty had deepened that my life was rushing toward a drastic change, and the strength of the premonition made me wonder if I was going to die. I had spoken to a few friends of this foreshadowing, and was working intensely on a book on Africa, knowing that very soon the work must stop; I wanted to finish while all research and impressions were fresh in my head. The book went to the typist on the day before D's first entry into the hospital, in late November, and I did not write again for nearly a year.

In the autumn, D had begun to suffer from obscure pains that the doctors could not identify; she grew thin, wide-eyed, very beautiful. She came home from the hospital in early December, when no clues to her pain were found, but two weeks later metastatic cancer was discovered, and she entered another hospital just before Christmas. She was frightened and depressed, and wished desperately to know that the love I felt for her was not just pity, that it had been there in some measure all along. I remembered the Istafahan bowl.

On Christmas Eve, I had gone home to patch together some sort of Christmas for the children, but I forgot to bring the bowl back to New York. Had I given it to her earlier, she would have understood just what it meant; but by January, D was in such pain and so heavily sedated that any sort of present seemed forlorn. She scarcely knew friends who came to visit: what could she make of a bowl she had seen just once, on another continent, a year before? I had missed a precious chance, and I remember that as I propped her up in bed, coaxing her to concentrate, then opened up the box and placed the bowl in her hands, my heart was pounding. I could scarcely bear to watch how D stared at the bowl, grimacing in the effort to fight off the pain, the drugs, the consuming cancer in her brain. But when I prepared to take it back, she pressed it to her heart, lay back like a child, eyes shining, and in a whisper got one word out: "Swit-zerland!"

———————

Far overhead, the great lammergeier turns and turns.

The porters are cooking their midmorning meal; they will eat the second of two daily meals at the end of the day's trek, in late afternoon. There is still no sign of Jang-bu, and no voice from the mountain; perhaps he is still in Dhorpatan, hunting for porters, or perhaps he has had trouble with them on the way. Phu-Tsering sends Dawa back in search, and the tireless Tukten volunteers to keep Dawa company; they go back up the steep mountain. In less than an hour, the Sherpas return, having seen the others on the upper trails. When Jang-bu and Gyaltsen come, at noon, the new porters set about their morning meal, and so we are delayed an hour longer.

We wait by the stone hut. GS, beside himself, expends his energy by hiking off upriver; returning, he scans the mountains with his spotting scope. Blue sheep could occur here on the bare upper slopes, but they have been hunted heavily in this region by Pahari Hindus working out of Dhorpatan, and none are seen. On a high wooded ridge, however, he locates two Himalayan tahr, an archaic animal that is a transitional form between goat-antelopes and goats. Under the sky, the dark creatures are still, yet they give life to the whole mountain, and the Tamangs, looking through a telescope for the first time in their lives, dance and whistle in excitement.

The new porters are dirt-colored men in dirty rags and small black caps, carrying the curved Gorkha hatchet-knife called the *kukri*. They are not interested in the telescope. Most are "Kami" people of the blacksmith caste, soot-faced familiars of the smelting fire and the iron stolen from the rock, feared and despised as black magicians by primitive people throughout Eurasia and Africa since the beginning of this Dark Age of Iron. With them are two young Tibetans, who carry the heaviest loads, not only because they are smallest and weakest but because, being Buddhist, they are treated as inferior even by low-caste Hindus such as these.

The "Dirty Kamis" are a sharp-eyed lot, so we are watchful, too. And we have hardly set out down the valley when the first malingerers fall by the wayside, pleading sore feet and dysentery; they fade with their loads into the bushes. We rout them out again, and stay behind them, to keep them from making off with our few supplies. During their frequent rests, sly Tukten infiltrates their ranks, smoking and grumbling with them, winking at us, and confusing them altogether.

The trail follows the south bank of the Ghustang, a wild torrent off the Dhaulagiri glaciers that cascades down over rust-colored boulders through a forest of great evergreens, merging farther to the west with the Uttar Ganga and the lower Bheri. Where bamboo appears, four thousand feet below our Dhaulagiri camp, a log bridge crosses the torrent and a trail climbs an open, grassy slope of stolid oaks and lithe wild olives that dance in the silver breeze of afternoon.

At the valley ridge, the trail moves westward, down a hogback spine. There are droppings of fox and the yellow-throated marten, but excepting three startled pheasants, birds are few. Clouds come, and a light steady rain that ends at dusk, when wild rays of late sun bombard the mountains; far behind us and above, near snow line, a sun ray isolates the site of our Dhaulagiri camp.

The trail descends again, down through hill pasture to the hamlet of Yamarkhar, a cluster of stone huts on the steep hillside. We arrive in darkness. Jang-bu is hunting out a place to sleep; since the porters have no tents, they must find shelter. All day we have gone steeply down and steeply up and down again, from 12,400 feet at our Dhaulagiri camp to 8000 feet at Yamarkhar. I have sore feet, a sore knee, and a sore back, and I think about the lammergeier seen this morning; in fifteen minutes, in a single glide, the great vulture could go where we have gone in ten hard hours.

In the canyon, night has come. Though the moon is hidden by the peaks, its light points up the depth of the ravines. On the dark wall opposite us, the wink of a lone fire seems infernal, like a chink of light from fires in the mountain.

OCTOBER 12

The Dirty Kamis, in the great tradition of porters all around the world, will go no farther; no doubt they are daunted—I am, too—by the sight of the precipitous trail up the mountain face across the river. With a last, despairing look at the unlooted loads, they set off for Dhorpatan, taking the two Tibetan boys along. Though glad to be rid of them, we now discover that there are no porters to be had at Yamarkhar, and Jang-bu is bargaining with the hut's owner for the hire of five ponies. What the ponies will do in the snows of the Jang Pass is a problem we shall have to deal with when we get there.

Because of high mountains to the east, this village will be dark until midmorning, but the upper slope of the mountain opposite is already in the sun when GS and I make the long slippery descent through the farm terraces into bamboo at the Pema torrent, which roars through the cold gloom of the ravine. A remarkable wood bridge has boarded sides that are carved in flowers, while the four posts at the bridge ends are sculpted crudely as paired *dhauliyas,* or "guardians," representing local deities of the old religions; such male and female portal figures are also made by coastal Indians of the Pacific Northwest. The females are holding their vulvae wide, as if in welcome to the realms of the mountain gods; sternly we cross the bridge and climb anew.

The path meets the sun at a small hamlet, source of the fire seen last night in the moon shadow, and one of the very primitive communities still to be found in these deep inner canyons of the Himalaya. As the falcon flies, this place is not a mile from Yamarkhar, yet they might be in different lands, in different centuries. The stone houses of Yamarkhar are well separated, as in Tibet, while the dwellings here are all in one stepped pueblo on the hillside, so that the roof of one house is another's terrace, the levels connected by crude ladders hewn in a single log. Yamarkhar people dress like Nepali peasants; here the men wear loincloths and a blanket across the shoulders, and the women wind their hair in gigantic buns, which they comb in the sunlight with stiff broomlike brushes. Several women and one man wear striking necklaces of the white tusks of musk deer, one of the many primitive animals that are found in this evolutionary backwater, cut off from the rest of Eurasia by high mountains; the long recurved canine tusks are replaced in modern deer by antlers. This little deer is killed mostly for its musk, used as a perfume base; because one musk pod (a large gland in the male's belly skin) brings up to five hundred dollars in Kathmandu, the musk deer is disappearing from Nepal.

Observing the inhabitants of this strange place is like watching people from a place of hiding, for they make a point of pretending we are not there. One man, leaning his head far back, smokes a primitive tubular pipe, while a woman grinds maize in a stone mortar, and three girls sit cracking small dark walnuts from the only trees left standing on the mountain. On a covered porch, two children dance; another beats a tom-tom. A very old man, bent double, creeps past a tobacco patch at the base of the buildings, in the hands behind his back an empty bowl.

GS lingers and I keep on climbing, then pause to drink and wash in a mountain brook. Greenfinches come, and a hawk flies down the valley. Asters and everlasting, lavender and white; the soft humming of a bumblebee consoles me. Sitting awhile on a warm rock, I enjoy the view of Yamarkhar as it comes into the sun. At this season, the flat roofs are bright with the fire colors of the harvest, which will sustain the inhabitants through the long winter—yellow squash, red peppers, bronze tobacco, a red millet, maize, and hemp, which is used for twine and cooking oil as well as marijuana.

The path climbs onward to a dark new-broken field under the sky. A ragged man bawls at two humped black cattle as a crude plowshare bucks and lunges at the stony soil; such wood-tipped plows were used three thousand years before the time of Christ. Higher still, in scattered oak forest, a herder leads his string of shaggy ponies, forty or more, down from summer pasture near the summits, and once again that feeling comes that in starting north across the Himalaya, we move unnaturally against the seasons. A boy runs back and forth over the acorns, shying quick stones to keep the beasts in line, and a little girl with a long stick brings up the rear. Startled by my presence in the wood, she darts aside; once safely past, she calls out a shy question, "Who are you?" Or that is what her soft voice seems to say. I cannot understand, and cannot answer. We smile, and she brings her hands up into prayer position—*"Namas-te!"* I do the same: *"Namas-te!"* "I salute you!" And she skips away downhill after her ponies.

I wait in an oak grove for the others. Far below, in a burst of white, snow pigeons plummet from the sun into the darkness of the gorge. In the snap of white wings in the morning light I hear the pigeons that I kept in the barn of New England childhood. I have always been drawn to the wild doves and pigeons, and especially the mourning dove of home.

Three thousand feet above the Pema, the trail runs north, traversing upper valleys. GS has come and, like foraging bears, we strip the bushes of tart barberries and rose hips as we move along. Now the trail penetrates a dank rock gorge without sun, higher and higher, passing big caves and a lonely cairn of stones. We bivouac where the head of this canyon opens out under the sky, in hopes that Jang-bu will turn up at evening with the ponies.

OCTOBER 13

The monsoon rains, supposed to end by the first week in October, still beset us; we are mired down. By the time Jang-bu and the pack ponies appeared, toward eight last evening, a cold rain was falling, and at noon today it is still raining hard. This morning the ponies broke loose in the storm, and their owner is out hunting them over the mountains; perhaps they have run back to Yamarkhar. My bedding is soaked by the mud puddle in the foot of my tent, which is pitched on a slant for want of flat terrain. With luck there will be sun to dry the gear before we climb up higher: I am cold already. All this rain must be snow at Jang La, three days away, but we are committed to this route; it is too late to retreat, to attempt to go around by the Jamoson-Tscharka route, or to fly to Jumla, even if new permits could be obtained. GS calls out through the rain, "We *have* to get across that pass, even if it takes a week—otherwise, we're finished."

Yet morale is high, with Dhorpatan behind us. I am in no hurry to get anywhere, and GS is busily composing haiku. Belatedly, though they were not asked to do so, Dawa and Gyaltsen are digging rain trenches around our tents—in the case of my tent, a more or less useless precaution—and the others have rigged a fly over the fire and are making tea for us in this downpour. Phu-Tsering's sweet infectious laugh rings out at something said by Tukten, who is after all a Sherpa, and drops his porter's load at the day's end to help the others pitch the tents or fetch the firewood and water.

Tukten has been an expedition hand since 1960, when he accompanied a British team to Annapurna; that same year, he was cook-Sherpa to a British botanical expedition into eastern

Nepal. The next year he joined the 6th Gurkha Regiment of the British Army and served in the cook corps for ten years, coming out in time to sign on as cook for the British Annapurna South Face Expedition; later he was a Sherpa on a Japanese expedition to Dhaulargiri One. Last spring he was again cook-Sherpa to a British botanical expedition, this time to the Tscharka region of eastern Dolpo. On his way home, he stopped off at a Sherpa community near Pokhara, where Jang-bu found him.

"Dolpo village many smelly, sah," says Tukten, the only man among us who has been there: one senses that, in one life or another, he has been everywhere on earth. Of his wide experience, Tukten tells tales in that soft voice, and so the other Sherpas listen, but he is not one of them. Ordinarily Tukten would remain among the porters who have taken shelter in a cave down in the canyon, but he is helpful and ingenious, and his mesmerizing voice, coming and going on the wind and rain, seems to fascinate the younger Sherpas, although they are wary of him, and keep their distance. One feels they are afraid of him—not of his violence, though they say he fights when drunk, but of his power. Whatever this man is—wanderer or evil monk, or saint or sorcerer—he seems touched by what Tibetans call the "crazy wisdom": he is free.

The young Tamangs, being inseparable, are exclusive, and so Tukten dines commonly with Bimbahadur, who is dull and gentle, a stumpy old lump-headed bumbler with gnarled legs and worn feet, who clings to his guardsman's mustache and remnant regimental rags. He, too, merely tolerates Tukten, for Bimbahadur has withdrawn from life; he must be with people, to earn his keep, but not among them—in the world but not of it, as the Sufis say. Side by side, hunched low in the light rain, the two outcasts dip up *tsampa,* the roasted maize or barley meal, ground to powder and cooked as porridge or in tea, that is subsistence food in the Himalaya. Weathered faces crusted with white paste, they hunch like specters over the fire stones and blackened pot; perhaps they will rise and, in dead silence, perform the slow dance of the *sennin*—wild mountain sages of the ancient days in China and Japan who give no formal teaching but redeem all beings by the very purity of their enlightenment.

The *sennin* are a favorite subject of the great Zen painters, and sometimes their dance of life is staged against a landscape copied from these paintings, as if to suggest that such free beings perceive a master work in all of nature. Kanzan is studying a scroll while Jittoku leans easily on a broom; when the painting comes to life, the *sennin* begin the steps of a strange dance.

Soon Kanzan pauses, stands apart, gazing away into infinity. Jittoku, much moved, lifts his hands in an attitude of prayer and circles Kanzan with simple ceremony, kneeling beside him and lifting his gaze in reverent expectancy. Becoming aware of him, Kanzan inclines his head in acquiescence and kneels with dignity beside Jittoku. Together they open the scroll and hold it before them; the audience cannot see what is written, can only watch as the *sennin* read silently together. Now the two are struck by a perfect phrase, and they pause in the same instant to regard each other; the power of the revelation lifts them to their feet as they read on, eagerly nodding. Soon they finish, sigh, and turn away into the dance; for a moment, the scroll's face comes into view. It is pure white, void, without the smallest mark. Kanzan rolls it with great attention as Jittoku, smiling to himself, retrieves the broom.

Now Jittoku brings wine, but in his transport, he is holding the flagon upside down; the wine is gone. Not caring he refills it from the stream, and the *sennin* are soon intoxicated on this pure water of high mountains. Kanzan must be supported in the dance, and for a time it seems that the two might sink away in drunken sleep. But they are summoned by the sublime song of a bird, and complete the dance by resuming the attitudes seen in the painting. Kanzan seems to smile, while Jittoku, regarding the audience for the first time, laughs silently, with all his heart. Before the audience can grasp what this might mean, the screen is drawn in a swift rush; there is only silence and the empty curtain.[2]

In early afternoon, when the downpour ends and the sound of the brook is audible under the oaks, the pony man appears, sniffing the weather; he has decided to return to Yamarkhar with his five animals. Sheepishly he says goodbye, and from his tent, GS bursts out, "Goodbye, you sonofabitch: I don't like fair-weather people who back out on an agreement, leaving others stranded!" Jang-bu does not bother to translate this rhetorical address, since the speaker's sentiments are clear.

Tibetans say that obstacles in a hard journey, such as hailstones, wind, and unrelenting rains, are the work of demons, anxious to test the sincerity of the pilgrims and eliminate the fainthearted among them. GS has certainly been tested: still three days short of the Jang La, we are now stranded in heavy rain, with no help to be had from the only settlement between Dhorpatan and Tarakot, which lies on the far side of the Jang. To make things worse, Bimbahadur, who has passed this way before, says that tomorrow this trail climbs above tree line, and that besides the loads, we must carry enough firewood for the next three days. But perhaps because GS is not fainthearted, there falls almost immediately a stroke of luck, as astonishing in its timing as the cutting of the stave that saved me from that mastiff in Dhorpatan. Since leaving Dhorpatan, we have seen not a single traveler going in either direction, yet it turns out that travelers came last night and took shelter in a nearby cave, that they, too, are bound for Tarakot, and that their leader, who is the headman of that village, has agreed to let his men serve us as porters.

This miracle comes slightly tarnished, since the headman is demanding and receiving three times the normal porterage— "They know we are stranded, and they have us against the wall, it's perfectly natural!" GS says, instructing Jang-bu to cut down the number of load baskets by two and spread the extra weight among the Tarakots—but it is great good fortune all the same.

The wind freshens, and blue patches appear among the tree-tops. Surely the monsoon has broken at last, with fair weather certain for tomorrow. Or so GS believes: I feel superstitious in this realm of mountain gods, and knock on one of the wind-warped oak trees in the grove. Fires have been built against the greatest of these trees to kill and bring them down, and all the rest are girdled and cropped for firewood and goat fodder; the deformed shapes twist on the restless skies.

OCTOBER 14

Last night, for the first time in my life, I was conscious of hallucinating in a dream. I was sitting in the shadows of a hut, outside of which the figure of a friend was sitting with a dog beside a rock. Then everything became vibrant, luminous, and plastic, as in psychedelic vision, and the figure outside was seized up by some dreadful force and cast down, broken and dead. Throughout, it seemed to me that I stood apart, watching myself dreaming, watching myself stand free of my body: I could have gone away from it but hesitated, afraid of being unable to return. In this fear, I awoke—or rather, I *decided* to awake, for the waking- and dream-states seemed no different. Then I slept again, and a yellow-throated marten—the large Himalayan weasel whose droppings we have seen along the trail—jumped with cub in mouth into a tree. As it set the cub down in a crotch of branches, a squirrel leaped from a higher limb, and the marten intercepted it in midair. For seconds, gazing at me, the marten remained suspended in the air beside the tree, mouth grotesquely spread by the squirrel's body; then it was on its branch again, gutting the squirrel, and letting fall the head and skin of it. From the ground, the squirrel's eyes in its head gazed up at me, alive and bright. Both dreams seemed more like hallucinations, experienced in the waking state, and left me with a morbid feeling in the morning.

These dreams do not seem to evaporate—can I be dead? It is as if I had entered what Tibetans call the Bardo—literally, between-two-existences—a dreamlike hallucination that precedes reincarnation, not necessarily in human form; typical of the dream-state visions is the skull cup full of blood, symbolizing the futility of carnal existence, with its endless thirsting, drinking, quenching, and thirsting anew.

In case I should need them, instructions for passage through the Bardo are contained in the Tibetan "Book of the Dead" which I carry with me—a guide for the living, actually, since it teaches that a man's last thoughts will determine the quality of his reincarnation. Therefore, every moment of life is to be lived calmly, mindfully, as if it were the last, to insure that the most is made of the precious human state—the only one in which enlightenment is possible. And only the enlightened can recall their former lives; for the rest of us, the memories of past existences are but glints of light, twinges of longing, passing shadows, disturbingly familiar, that are gone before they can be grasped, like the passage of that silver bird on Dhaulagiri.

Thus one must seek to "regard as one this life, the next life, and the life between, in the Bardo." This was a last message to his disciples of Tibet's great poet-saint the Lama Milarepa, born in the tenth century, in the Male Water-Dragon Year, to a woman known as "the White Garland of the Nyang." Milarepa is called Mila Repa because as a great yogin and master of "mystical heat" he wore only a simple white cloth, or *repa*, even in deepest winter: his "songs" or hortatory verses, as transcribed by his disciples, are still beloved in Tibet. Like Sakyamuni, he is said to have attained nirvana in a single lifetime, and his teaching as he prepared for death might have been uttered by the Buddha:

> All worldly pursuits have but the one unavoidable and inevitable end, which is sorrow: acquisitions end in dispersion; buildings, in destruction; meetings, in separation; births, in death. Knowing this, one should from the very first renounce acquisition and heaping-up, and building and meeting, and . . . set about realizing the Truth. . . . Life is short, and the time of death is uncertain; so apply yourselves to meditation. . . .[3]

Meditation has nothing to do with contemplation of eternal questions, or of one's own folly, or even of one's navel, although a clearer view on all of these enigmas may result. It has nothing to do with thought of any kind—with anything at all, in fact, but intuiting the true nature of existence, which is why it has appeared, in one form or another, in almost every culture known to man. The entranced Bushman staring into fire, the Eskimo using a sharp rock to draw an ever-deepening circle into the flat surface of a stone achieves the same obliteration of the ego (and the same power) as the dervish or the Pueblo sacred dancer. Among Hindus and Buddhists, realization is attained through inner stillness, usually achieved through the *samadhi* state of sitting yoga.[4] In Tantric practice, the student may displace the ego by filling his whole being with the real or imagined object of his concentration; in Zen, one seeks to empty out the mind, to return it to the clear, pure stillness of a seashell or a flower petal. When body and mind are one, then the whole being, scoured clean of intellect, emotions, and the senses, may be laid open to the *experience* that individual existence, ego, the "reality" of matter and phenomena are no more than fleeting and illusory arrangements of molecules. The weary self of masks and screens, defenses, preconceptions, and opinions that, propped up by ideas and words, imagines itself to be some sort of entity (in a society of like entities) may suddenly fall away, dissolve into formless flux where concepts such as "death" and "life," "time" and "space," "past" and "future" have no meaning. There is only a pearly radiance of Emptiness, the Uncreated, without beginning, therefore without end.[5]

Like the round-bottomed Bodhidharma doll, returning to its center, meditation represents the foundation of the universe to which all returns, as in the stillness of the dead of night, the stillness between tides and winds, the stillness of the instant before Creation. In this "void," this dynamic state of rest, without impediments, lies ultimate reality, and here one's own true nature is reborn, in a return from what Buddhists speak of as "great death." This is the Truth of which Milarepa speaks.

At daybreak comes a light patter of rain on the tent canvas, although there had been stars all night before, and GS, who is not often profane, is cursing in his tent. As soon as the rain ceases, we break camp. Setting out ahead, I meet almost immediately with a hoopoe, oddly tame. Such tameness must be a good omen, of which we are in need, for the hoopoe walks around before my feet on the wet grass under the oaks as if waiting to conduct us farther.

The path enters a narrowing ravine that climbs to a high cleft between boulders, and the cleft is reached at the strike of the rising sun, which fills this portal with a blinding light. I emerge in a new world and stare about me. A labyrinth of valley mounts toward the snows, for the Himalaya is as convoluted as a brain. Churen Himal looms in high mist, then vanishes. A pheasant hen and then three more sail down off a lichened rock face with sweet chortlings; the crimson cock stays hidden. Far below, over dark gorges where no sun has reached, a griffon circles in the silence. The forest on this ridge is oak and maple, and a mist of yellow leaves softens the ravine sides all around: on a golden wind comes a rich humus smell of autumn.

Now GS comes, and we climb quickly to 12,000 feet. The paths around these mountainsides are narrow, there is no room for a misstep, and at this altitude, one is quickly out of breath. Gradually I have learned to walk more lightly, legs loose, almost gliding, and this helps a lot in times of vertigo. Some of the cliffside trail is less than two feet wide—I measure it—and skirts sheer precipice; nor is the rest very much better, for these mountainsides of shining grass are so precipitous, so devoid of trees or even shrubs, that a stumbler might tumble and roll thousands of feet, then drop into the dark where the sun ends, for want of anything to catch hold of.

My sense of dread is worsened by last night's lingering dreams. "The dream . . . wherein phenomena and mind were seen as one was a teacher: did you not so understand it?" I have not quite apprehended this idea—that man's world, man's dreams are both dream-states—but Milarepa has been of help in other ways. Returning to his village after many years (he was born about fifty miles north of Kathmandu, on the Tibetan side of the present-day frontier), Mila discovers the decayed corpse of his mother, no more than a mound of dirt and rags in her fallen hut; shaken by grief and horror, he remembers the instruction of his guru, the Lama Marpa, to embrace all that he most fears or finds repugnant, the better to realize that everything in the Universe, being inseparably related, is therefore holy. And so he makes a headrest of the sad remains of the erstwhile White Garland of the Nyang and lies upon them for seven days, in a deep, clear state of *samadhi*. This Tantric discipline to overcome ideas of "horror," often performed while sitting on a corpse or in the graveyard in the dark of night, is known as *chöd*. Since trusting to life must finally mean making peace with death, I perform some mild *chöd* of my own, forcing myself to look over the precipice whenever I can manage it. The going in the weeks ahead is bound to worsen, and hardening myself might make less scary some evil stretch of ledge in the higher mountains. It helps to pay minute attention to details— a shard of rose quartz, a cinnamon fern with spores, a companionable mound of pony dung. When one pays attention to the present, there is great pleasure in awareness of small things; I think of the comfort I took yesterday in the thin bouillon and stale biscuits that shy Dawa brought to my leaking tent.

The trees die out in a rock garden of dwarf rhododendron, birch, and fire-colored ash, set about with strap fern, edelweiss, and unknown alpine florets, fresh mineral blue. Then a woodpecker of vivid green appears, and though I *know* that I am awake, that I actually see such a bird, the blue flowers and green woodpecker have no more reality, or less, than the yellow-throated marten of my dream.

Sun comes and goes. The monsoon is not done with us, there is wind and weather in the east, but to the south, the sky of India is clear. GS says, "Do you realize we haven't heard even a distant motor since September?" And this is true. No airplane crosses such old mountains. We have strayed into another century.

This wayfaring in shifting sun, in snow and cloud worlds, so close to the weather, makes me happy; the morbid feeling of this dawn has passed away. I would like to reach the Crystal Monastery, I would like to see a snow leopard, but if I do not, that is all right, too. In this moment, there are birds—red-billed choughs, those queer small crows of the high places, and a small buteo, black against the heavens, and southbound finches bounding down the wind, in their wake a sprinkling of song. A lark, a swift, a lammergeier, and more griffons: the vultures pass at eye level, on creaking wings.

At a low pass stands a small cairn topped with sticks and rags, and an opening on the eastern side for offerings: the rag strips or wind prayers bring good luck to travelers who are crossing a pass for the first time. Perhaps because we ignore the cairn, the mountain gods greet us with a burst of hail, then sun, then both together. A patter of ice dies away as the clouds turn. We wait. Tukten, an hour behind us, is a good half hour ahead of all the rest and, for his pains, is chastised by GS as representative of the lead-footed porter breed. Slowly, he puts down the load that he has humped two thousand feet uphill, observing GS in the equable way in which he observes everything: giving thanks for his arrival at the pass, he places a small stone upon the cairn.

The Tamangs come, then the Tarakots, and we descend steeply to a brushy gulley, where the porters throw their baskets down and start a fire, in preparation for the first of their two meals. After their hard climb, this is understandable, but after our wait of an hour and a half, it is damned frustrating; in the long delay, we assumed they must have eaten. We curse them as we have each day for not taking this main meal before starting out, when fires are already built, and water boiling; this two-hour stop, more days than not, has meant wasting warm sunny hours on the trail and setting up camp in rain, cold, and near-darkness.

The new delay makes GS desperate: we are sure to miss the blue-sheep rut if we don't move faster. But the porters can see the snow that fills the north end of this canyon; chivvy them as we may, they will go no farther than that snow this afternoon.

Ranging back and forth, GS nags Phu-Tsering about wasting sugar and cooking precious rice instead of using the potatoes, which are heavy and still locally available. The cook's happy-go-lucky ways can be exasperating, although GS learned in eastern Nepal that his merry smile more than compensates for any failings. And the Sherpas accept his reprimands in good spirit, since GS is faithfully considerate of their feelings and concerned about their welfare, and rarely permits their child-like natures to provoke him.

Since no brush occurs between this point and the far side of Jang La, we scavenge shrubby birch and rhododendron and gather old stalks of bamboo, which flowers every twelve or thirteen years, then dies over vast areas. In a semicave I find some faggots left half-burnt by other travelers, and bind them across my rucksack with the rest.

The trail ascends the torrent called Seng Khola, under looming cliffs, and in this gloom, in the roar of the gray water, I half expect the visage of a mountain god to peer over the knife edge of the rim. Clouds creep after us, up the canyon, and for once skies look more promising ahead: a shaft of sun that lights the snow at the head of the Seng Khola is a beacon. Then come the first gray drops of rain, this cold rain with a cold wind behind it that overtakes us every afternoon. The river is somber, with broken waterfalls and foaming rock, in a wasteland of sere stubble and spent stone, and I wonder why, in this oppressive place, I feel so full of well-being, striding on through the rain, and grateful in some unnameable way—to what? On the path, the shadow of my close-cropped head is monkish, and the thump of my stave resounds in the still mountains: I feel inspired by Milarepa as described by one of his disciples, walking "free as an unbridled lion in the snowy ranges."

At a canyon bend stands the headman of Tarakot, who wears Hindu puttees and carries no pack of any kind. He is pointing at the bouldered slopes across the stream. "Na!" he cries. "Na!" Then he goes on. A pale form jumps across a gully, followed quickly by six more; the animals move up a steep slope to a haze of green between the rocks and snow. I watch them climb until, at snow line, they are swept up and consumed by clouds that have rushed up the valley from the south: this wonderful silver-blue-gray creature is the bharal, the blue sheep of the Himalaya—in Tibetan, *na*—that we have come so far to see.

We camp on a flat ledge by the river, just beneath the snows. A dipper plunges into the cold torrent, and a pair of redstarts pursue some tardy insect over the black boulders. The altitude is nearly 13,000 feet, says GS as he comes up: it is dark and cold. GS, too, has seen blue sheep, and later, after tents are pitched, he goes out and finds more. He returns at dusk, delighted— "The first data in a month and a half!" he cries. And I tell him of a small find of my own. Back down the trail there was a solitary print, as if a dog had cross the path and gone its way, leaving no trace on the stony ground to either side. There were no signs of human travelers on the wet earth, and the print was fresh. Therefore a dog seemed most unlikely, and having assumed it was a wolf, which still occurs in the wilder regions of Tibet, I had not checked for foretoes on the print. "This is perfect country for the snow leopard," says GS. The headman of Tarakot declares that snow leopards occur here in the Jang region, but the all-knowing Tukten shakes his head. "Only on Dolpo side," says Tukten, "not in Nepal." Dolpo lies on the Tibetan Plateau, and it interests me that he regards it as a foreign land.

In his abrupt way, more in exuberance than rudeness, my friend hurls goggles through my tent flap, to protect my eyes from tomorrow's sun and snow. Excited, I lie awake much of the night, my head out of the tent. The night is clear, clear, clear and very cold. Before dawn, black turns black-blue over the mountains, and there is fire-glow high in the heavens.

OCTOBER 15

We set out before daybreak, crossing a treacherous ice glaze on stream boulders, following the Seng Khola northward. In the solitudes of snow far up the canyon, we come on barefoot human prints. "Yeti," GS says, sardonic, but even for him, the sight is startling, unsettling: something is imminent in this frozen shadow world below the sun. Then the world stirs. In the half-light, a bent figure moves under overhanging rocks across the torrent, cowled, ragged, brown, with a long stave— a mountain lunatic, a *sennin*. Though howling, he cannot be heard over the roaring water; he brandishes his stick.

Astonished, we see that this cowled figure is Bimbahadur; he tries to indicate the direction of the trail. Later we learn that he had walked three miles upriver in the rain, the night before, to sleep alone in a cave of his own ken, and was now on his way down again to fetch his load. To attain solitude, the oldest and slowest of the porters has given himself an additional six miles of stony walking.

Leaving the river, we climb toward the northwest.

Higher, where the snow has melted, a hill fox jumps from tussock grass and runs to a group of rocks, then turns to watch. Its black points and rich red coat are set off by a frosty face and chest and an extraordinary long thick tail, dark brown and black with a white fluffy tip; the tip remains visible long after the creature's glowing colors sink among the stones.

The light on the upper slopes slowly descends the mountain: where we have climbed is still in deep night shadow. Meeting the sun, I rest on the dry lichens that crown a granite islet in the whiteness. Three snow pigeons pass overhead, white wings cracking in the frozen air. To the east, a peak of Dhaulagiri shimmers in a halo of sun rays, and now the sun itself bursts forth, incandescent in a sky without a cloud, an ultimate blue that south over India is pale and warm, and cold deep dark in the north over Tibet—a blue bluer than blue, transparent, ringing. (Yet that "blue" went unperceived until quite recent times: in the many hundred allusions to the sky in the Rig Veda, the Greek epics, even the Bible, there is no mention of this color.[6]

GS, who is a mountaineer, tells me to hold my stave short, on the uphill side, the better to punch it through the crust should my boots slip, for the slope is very steep and the snow is glazed. But he interrupts himself, dropping to one knee and pointing upward, even as he digs into his rucksack for binoculars. Four bharal rams pick and jump on the white outcrops, climbing the ridge, the big horned heads outlined on the blue. We are delighted by this sight, all the more so because this fellowship of rams is sign that the autumn rut has not begun, that after all we may reach Shey in time.

I find the going hard. The footing is treacherous, the air thin, the brightness dazzling, and I am breaking through the crust up to the crotch. In the next hour, GS moves steadily ahead, until his blue parka turns to black against the snow. The emblematic figure rounds a pyramid of white; then there is nothing.

Out of nothingness comes a faint whispering. Fine crystals dance upon the light as snow falls from high monuments of rock. A bird has flown north toward Tibet, a small white falcon. In vertigo caused by exhaustion and the glare, staring straight up at this heraldic bird, I gasp for breath; there is no white falcon in the Himalaya. (Later this day I saw a merlin-sized falcon with black mantle, white beneath; passing overhead, it would have seemed to be a pure-white bird.)

Snowfields climb in sparkling curves into the blue. As the sun rises, I plunge over and over through the weakening crust, and stop every few steps to grab for breath. In late morning, after a four-hour climb, I reach the ridge, and crouch to escape the icy wind cutting across it. "I made it," I blurt out, head spinning. GS is scanning with binoculars. "There's no pass here," he says. "No way to go on." Over the rim lies an awesome drop to the floor of a broad canyon, and the line of porters is just visible, ascending this canyon into the northwest. The four-hour climb to 15,000 feet has been in vain; we misread Bimbahadur's signal, and will have to backtrack down this mountain, and then climb anew.

The splendor of Churen Himal and Putha Hiunchuli, east of us now instead of north, does not console me. In silence, we eat a bit of sausage and a handful of peanuts, then start back along the ridge, in search of a short and safe route down. (GS's idea of a safe route is not the same as mine. After so many years in the high mountains in pursuit of animals, his step and balance are marvelously sure: one of my first impressions of this man, in East Africa, in 1969, was the sight of him standing casually on the very edge of a towering granite outcrop, in hard wind, scanning the Serengeti Plain through these same binoculars.)

A band of thirteen bharal, caught dozing in the snow, jumps up as one animal just yards away. Wild sheep are unwary when approached from above, being conditioned to expect danger from below, and in this wonderful light, the blue-silver creatures observe us calmly before moving off, while GS classifies them as to sex and age, photographs them thoroughly, and scribbles data in his notebook. Then a Himalayan snow cock, white and gray, goes sailing past, gliding down around the mountains—why had it come so high, to this deep snow?

An hour later, having stumbled and slid down the canyon side, we start a new ascent to the northwest. Out of the wind, in the clarion air, the sun burns very hot, and in this flux of white and blue, I feel dizzy and half-blind. My legs are gone, and the valley snow has turned to mush that engulfs the knees at every other step. The one consolation is a grim relief that the pony man quit us when he did, for his animals could not have made it, and we would have been stuck in deep, wet snow with seven extra loads.

At 14,000 feet, the ascent eases, and there is a fine cross-country trek over the snowfields. In midafternoon, the sun sinks behind a ridge, but an hour later it bursts forth once more in a startling way, filling the mouth of a ravine far down among the mountains. Moments later, it is gone again. In twilight, we cross the Saure Khola and bivouac on a bluff.

For most of this afternoon we trailed the porters, one of whom left a blood spoor in the snow; as it turns out, this was Pirim, who failed to wear the sneakers issued him and cut his leather feet on the icy crusts. The blood spots made us wonder if any of the porters had taken precautions against snow blindness; by the time we overtook them, any warnings would have been too late. But this evening, although three complain a little of sore eyes, they seem cheerful enough, taking turns at the telescope and shouting at some *na* high on the ridge. The Tamangs make wind shelters in the ruins of some herdsmen's fallen huts, and the Sherpas take the headman into their tent, but the Tarakots are satisfied to hunch like growths among the snow patches, wrapped in old blankets, doing nothing at all to better their condition, despite the prospect of a long night of bitter cold. They have carried no firewood, and must scavenge rice from us, and most are barefoot.

OCTOBER 16

Last night I dined in GS's tent—two people cannot fit into mine—and though elated by the day in the snow mountains, I was reeling with the altitude, with a bad headache, and a face baked stiff by sun. This morning I am fine again, but not so the poor porters. All are moaning with snow blindness, a very disagreeable burning of the corneas which comes on with little warning and has no cure other than time; the sensation is that of sand thrown in the eyes. The Tarakots are still huddled in their pile outside our tents, blowing pathetically through cloths into each other's eyes. Refusing to carry, they stagger off eventually toward home.

Our own porters are suffering, too, and so are the Sherpa camp assistants, who should have known better. Only Phu-Tsering looks happy as ever; he is actually amused. "*Solu!*" he says of Dawa and Gyaltsen, referring to a valley clan; they are not true mountaineers such as himself. Phu-Tsering comes from Khumbu, southwest of Everest, where most high-altitude Sherpas are born; he has accompanied expeditions that climbed Makalu (French, 1971: 27,790') and Manaslu (German, 1973: 26,658') and has all sorts of certificates. The cook has his own snow goggles; Jang-bu, though improvident, had borrowed a spare pair from GS; and Tukten and two of the Tamangs had sense enough to tie slitted rags around their heads, to squint through—but why didn't all have sense enough? GS, disgusted, says he is continually astonished by the poor adaptation of Himalayan peoples to their environment.

And so we are stuck in the snows for another day, and perhaps more. Unlike the Tarakots, our own brave invalids consent to carry lightened loads, although they stagger and moan each time we glance at them. They bind on eye rags without slits, and the ever-cool, resilient Jang-bu leads them off into the snows like a chain of blind, hoping to return from Tarakot tomorrow with new porters. Phu-Tsering will stay to cook for us and guard the camp, and Bimbahadur will also stay, being too far gone to walk. His eyes are swollen tight and his legs are rickety; as if some spell had been cast upon him, he has turned overnight into a dotard. Yesterday, as we caught up with him, he stumbled and fell on the ice and toppled his basket, and Phu-Tsering and Jang-bu had to retrieve his load from the bottom of a steep incline of ice and snow. Now GS fixes him a tea-leaf poultice, which seems to ease his pain a little, and later I daub some cream on his broken lips, and this poor old man, who only came with us from Dhorpatan because he wanted to be helpful, groans with the ordeal of life on his crude bed of straw in the ruined hut.

GS frets about time lost and additional expense, but there are blue sheep here, and he'll make the most of them. Having pitched our tents again, we set off up the steep mountain, which has open grass on these lower slopes due to south exposure. Soon a hill fox appears, intent upon its hunting, ignoring us, it makes six pounces in eight minutes, four of them successful, though its game is small. One victim is a mouse—mouse holes and snow tunnels, exposed by thaw, are everywhere around our feet—and two more, seen through the spotting scope, look like big grasshoppers, and the fourth is a long thin gleam of life that is perplexing. Later, when the sun is high, I find some shiny striped gray skinks that solve the mystery. Despite the unseasonal blizzards of the late monsoon, this midautumn mountainside is still alive, and the seeds and myriad insects stuck to the snow patches attract the migrant redstarts as well as large mixed flocks of pipits, larks, rose finches, and the like. Dwarf rhododendron, edelweiss, blue gentian occur sparsely, and above 15,000 feet, wherever stone protrudes, bright lichens of all colors deck the snow. The white is patterned by the pretty tracks of snow cock, blue sheep, fox, and smaller creatures: we look in vain for the pug marks of snow leopard. And soon we drift apart like grazing animals, in silence, as we do almost every day along the trail. GS pursues three blue sheep that move diagonally up the slope, while I climb to the base of a huge rock pile on the sky.

In a niche of lichens, out of the cold wind, I contemplate the still white mountains to the south. The effect of sun and light here is so marked that south slopes with north exposure are locked in snow right down to the river, while on this north side, facing south, the slopes are open. Thus, one bank of the Saure is a sheet of white, while across the torrent, a few yards away, the warm grass swarms with grasshoppers and skinks.

Overhead, pale griffons turn on the deep blue. How silent vultures are! From this aerie, no sound can be heard but the rush of the Saure torrent far below.

Traversing the slope to its north ridge, I scan the valley that leads north to the Jang, then return slowly down the mountain. Phu-Tsering gives me warm chapatis, and hot water for a wash in the cold sun. He is wearing his amulets outside his shirt, but tucks them away, embarrassed, when I ask about them; they were given him by his lama, he murmurs, feeling much better when I show him that I, too, wear an "amulet," a talisman given to me by the Zen master Soen Roshi, "my lama in Japan." He admires this smooth plum pit on which a whole ten-phrase sutra is inscribed in minute characters, and is awed when I tell him that the sutra honors the most revered of all those mythical embodiments of Buddhahood called Bodhisattvas, the one known to Phu-Tsering as "Chen-resigs" (literally, *sPyan ras gzigs*), who is the Divine Protector of Tibet and is invoked by OM MANI PADME HUM. In the Japanese sutra inscribed upon this plum pit, this Bodhisattva is Kanzeon, or Kannon (in China, Kuan Yin; in southeast Asia, Quon Am). To Hindus He is Padmapani, and in Sanskrit, He is Avalokita Ishvara, the Lord Who Looks Down (in compassion). Like all Bodhisattvas, Avalokita represents "the divine within" sought by mystics of all faiths, and has been called the Lord Who Is Seen Within.[7]

Like most good Buddhists, Phu-Tsering chants OM MANI PADME HUM each day, and in time of stress; he also clings to

fear of demons, and is frightened by the dark. Walking behind
GS one night in eastern Nepal, he chanted this mantra so inces-
santly that GS longed to throw him off the cliff. But the faithful believe that the invocation of any deity by his mantra will
draw benevolent attention, and since OM MANI PADME HUM is
dedicated to the Great Compassionate Chen-resigs, it is found
inscribed on prayer stones, prayer wheels, prayer flags, and
wild rocks throughout the Buddhist Himalaya.

ཨོཾ་མ་ཎི་པ་དྨེ་ཧཱུྃ

Pronounced in Tibet *Aum—Ma-ni—Pay-may—Hung,* this
mantra may be translated: *Om!* The Jewel in the Heart of the
Lotus! *Hum!* The deep, resonant *Om* is all sound and silence
throughout time, the roar of eternity and also the great stillness
of pure being; when intoned with the prescribed vibrations, it
invokes the All that is otherwise inexpressible. The *mani* is the
"adamantine diamond" of the Void—the primordial, pure, and
indestructible essence of existence beyond all matter or even
antimatter, all phenomena, all change, and all becoming.
Padme—in the lotus—is the world of phenomena, samsara,
unfolding with spiritual progress to reveal beneath the leaves of
delusion the *mani*-jewel of nirvana, that lies not apart from daily
life but at its heart. *Hum* has no literal meaning, and is variously
interpreted (as is all of this great mantra, about which whole vol-
umes have been written). Perhaps it is simply a rhythmic exhor-
tation, completing the mantra and inspiring the chanter, a
declaration of being, of Is-ness, symbolized by the Buddha's gesture of touching the earth at the moment of Enlightenment. *It*
is! *It* exists! All that is or was or will ever be is right here in this
moment! *Now!*

I go down along the canyon rim and sit still against a rock.
Northward, a snow cone rises on the sky, and snowfields roll
over the high horizon into the deepening blue. Where the Saure
plunges into its ravine, a sheer and awesome wall writhes with
weird patterns of snow and shadow. The emptiness and silence

of snow mountains quickly bring about those states of consciousness that occur in the mind-emptying of meditation, and
no doubt high altitude has an effect, for my eye perceives the
world as fixed or fluid, as it wishes. The earth twitches, and the
mountains shimmer, as if all molecules had been set free: the blue
sky rings. Perhaps what I hear is the "music of the spheres,"
what Hindus call the breathing of the Creator and astrophysi-
cists the "sighing" of the sun.

Before me on a simple stone I place this plum pit, minutely
inscribed to the Lord Who is Seen Within:

> Kanzeon! Devotion to Buddha!
> We are one with Buddha
> In cause-and-effect related to all Buddhas
> And to Buddha, Dharma, Sangha.
> Our true Bodhisattva Nature is Eternal, Joyful, Selfless, Pure.
> So let us chant each morning Kanzeon, with Nen!
> Every evening Kanzeon, with Nen!
> Nen, Nen arises from Mind.
> Nen, Nen is not separate from Mind.[8]

Kanzeon is Kannon or Avalokita. Cause-and-effect is karma.
Dharma is the great wheel of Universal Law set in motion by
Sakyamuni Buddha; and Sangha is the community of Buddha's
followers, past and present. "Eternal, Joyful, Selfless, Pure" are
the qualities of nirvana in which the Dream-state, "the Many,"
of samsara, is transmuted into Awakening, "the one."[9] Nen is
mindfulness, attention to the present with a quality of vibrant
awareness, as if this present moment were one's last. Mind is
Universal Mind of which individual minds are part, in the way
of waves; the waves do not derive from water, they *are* water,
in fleeting forms that are not the same and yet not different
from the whole.

In November 1971, I attended a weekend retreat at the New
York Zendo. All-day meditation in the lotus postures can be arduous, and D, who had been suffering for two months with
mysterious pains, decided to limit herself to the Sunday sittings.

On Saturday evening, when I returned to where we were staying, she opened the door for me; she was smiling, and looked extremely pretty in a new brown dress. But perhaps because I had been in meditation since before daybreak and my mind was clear, I saw at once that she was dying, and the certainty of this clairvoyance was so shocking that I had to feign emergency and push rudely into the bathroom, to get hold of myself so that I could speak.

Before dawn on Sunday, during morning service, D chanced to sit directly opposite my own place in the two long facing lines of Buddha figures—an unlikely event that I now see as no coincidence. Upset by what I had perceived the night before, by pity and concern that this day might be too much for her, I chanted the Kannon Sutra with such fury that I "lost" myself, forgot the self—a purpose of the sutra, which is chanted in Japanese, over and over, with mounting intensity. At the end, the Sangha gives a mighty shout that corresponds to OM!—this followed instantly by sudden silence, as if the universe had stopped to listen. And on that morning, in the near darkness—the altar candle was the only light in the long room—in the dead hush, like the hush in these snow mountains, the silence swelled with the intake of my breath into a Presence of vast benevolence of which *I was a part:* in my journal for that day, seeking in vain to find words for what had happened, I called it the "Smile." The Smile seemed to grow out of me, filling all space above and behind like a huge shadow of my own Buddha form, which was minuscule now and without weight, borne up on the upraised palm of this Buddha-Being, this eternal amplification of myself. For it was *I* who smiled; the Smile was Me. I did not breathe, I did not need to look; for it was Everywhere. Nor was there terror in my awe: I felt "good," like a "good child," entirely safe. Wounds, ragged edges, hollow places were all gone, all had been healed; my heart lay at the heart of all Creation. Then I let my breath go, and gave myself up to delighted immersion in this Presence, to a peaceful *belonging* so overwhelming that tears of relief poured from my eyes, so overwhelming that even now, struggling to find a better term than

"Smile" or "Presence," the memory affects me as I write. For the first time since unremembered childhood, I was not alone; there was no separate "I."

Already the Buddha-Being was dissolving, and I tried to convey gratitude, to inform It about D, but gave this up after a moment in the happy realization that *nothing was needed*, nothing missing, all was already, always, and forever known, that D's dying, even that, was as it should be. Two weeks later, describing to Eido Roshi what had happened, I astonished myself (though not the Roshi, who merely nodded, making a small bow) by a spontaneous burst of tears and laughter, the tears falling light and free as rain in sunlight.

One *intuits* truth in the Zen teachings, even those that are scarcely understood; and now intuition had become knowing, not through merit but—it seemed—through grace. The state of grace that began that early morning in the Zendo prevailed throughout the winter of D's dying, an inner calm in which I knew just how and where to act, wasting no energy in indecision or regrets: and seemingly, this certainty gave no offense, perhaps because no ego was involved, the one who acted in this manner was not "I." When I told the Roshi that I felt this readiness and strength, even a kind of crazy exaltation, he said quietly, "You have transcended." I think he meant "transcended your ego," and with it grief, horror, and remorse. As if awakened from a bad dream of the past, I found myself forgiven, not just by D but by myself, and this forgiveness strikes me still as the greatest blessing of my life.

In those last months, it seemed that love had always been there, shining through the turbulence of waves, like the reflection of the moon in the Zen teachings; and love transformed the cruel and horrid face that cancer gives to death. One day, knowing she was dying, D remarked, "Isn't it queer? This is one of the happiest times in all my life." And another day, she asked me shyly what would happen if she should have a miraculous recovery—would we love each other still, and stay together, or would the old problems rise again to spoil things as before? I didn't know, and that is what I said. We had tried to be honest, and anyway, D would not have been fooled. I shrugged unhappily, she winced, then we both laughed. In that moment, at least, we really understood that it didn't matter, not because she was going to die but because all truth that mattered was here and now.

After D's death, I wondered if the specter of remorse might overtake me. It never did. In the grayest part of the empty months that followed, my heart was calm and clear, as if all that bad karma of the past had been dissolved on that early morning in November.

Toward the Presence who prepared me for D's death I was filled with gratitude, quite different from the thankfulness I felt toward Eido Roshi and toward D, toward kind family and friends and children. It was not that I felt grateful to myself, yet the question seemed inescapable: where could that vast Smile reside if not in my own being? In chanting the Kannon Sutra in such desperation, I had invoked Avalokita, but I had been paying no attention to the words, only to D, who sat in the line of Buddha forms across the way. And so it was hard to identify Avalokita with that Presence unless He was also D, also myself—in short, what Meister Eckhardt meant: "The Eye with which I see God is the Eye with which God sees me." Or Jesus Christ: "I and my Father are One."[10] Surely those Christian mystics spoke of the Lord-Who-Is-Seen-Within.

That year I was a new student of Zen, expecting nothing, and almost another year had passed before something said by an older student made me realize what had happened. I went to Eido Roshi, who confirmed it. But a *kensho,* or *satori,* is no measure of enlightenment, since an insight into "one's True Nature" may vary widely in its depth and permanence: some may overturn existence, while others are mere tantalizing glimpses that "like a mist will surely disappear."[11] To poke a finger through the wall is not enough—the whole wall must be brought down with a crash! My own experience had been premature, and a power seeped away, month after month. This saddened me, although I understood that I had scarcely started on the path; that but for D's crisis, which had cut through forty years of encrustations, I might never have had such an experience at all; that great enlightenment was only born out of deep *samadhi*. In this period the invitation came to go on a journey to the Himalaya.

Wind brings swift, soft clouds from the south that cast shadows on the snow. Close at hand, a redstart comes to forage in the lichens, followed soon by a flock of fat rose finches. I do not stir, yet suddenly all whir away in a gray gust, and minutely I turn to see what might have scared them. On a rock not thirty feet away, an accipitrine hawk sits in silhouette against the mountains, and here it hunches while the sun goes down, nape feathers lifting in the wind, before diving after unseen prey over the rim of the ravine. Then the great lammergeier comes, gold-headed and black-collared, a nine-foot blade sweeping down out of the north it passes into the shadows between cliffs. Where the river turns, in a corner of the walls, the late sun shines on a green meadow, as if a lost world lay in that impenetrable ravine, so far below. The great bird arcs round the wall, light glancing from its mantle. Then it is gone, and the sun goes, the meadow vanishes, and the cold falls with the night shadow.

Still I sit a little while, watching the light rise to the peaks. In the boulder at my back, there is a shudder, so slight that at another time it might have gone unnoticed. The tremor comes again; the earth is nudging me. And still I do not see.

OCTOBER 17

Jang-bu hoped to be back today by noon, but perhaps he is having trouble finding porters. Rather than wait another day, GS and I will take two loads over the Jang Pass while Phu-Tsering and Bimbahadur guard the rest. This high valley between snows would be a bad place to be caught by storm, with no firewood and sick, ill-equipped porters, but blizzard now seems most unlikely: last night was so clear that the Milky Way rose in a mist out of the snows, and for the third day in a row, the dawn was cloudless. The end of the monsoon, a fortnight late, is here at last.

I start early, climbing toward the sun. Until now we have carried rucksacks only, leaving to others our books and heavy gear. Today we will carry our full backpacks, together with bedding, tents, and food, and GS will also take his telescope and camera.

From the crest of the first ridge, getting my breath, I turn for a last look down the Saure ravine; absurdly, I feel homesick for that green meadow under the dark walls where in this lifetime I shall never go. I move on quickly, to gain altitude before the sun softens the snow, crossing a stream of icy boulders, climbing on. The trail made by the Tarakots and Jang-bu is easy to follow in the snow, and the high pack protects my brains from the rising sun, and my boots crunch reassuringly upon the crust. Soon the track enters the long white valley that rises to Jang La. How strange it seems that the blue sky is so much darker than the mountains! This morning the moon is centered in a crescent between the white peaks, off to the south. A neat fox foot trails snow-cock prints to three pools like black mirrors. The ice-free pools are springs of a stream that flows away under the snow and falls over a cliff into the Saure.

Behind and below, among swirls made by snow gleam and the ice-broken black brook, a surreal figure very like my own pursues me across the vast floor of the mountains. It crosses the shining boulders, coming on with slow, portentous step. The sight of this figure brings a small foreboding, as if it were the self of dreams who seeks me out with the coming of the day at the black labyrinthine river, in dead whiteness.

At this altitude the white is thick and silent, only a soft murmur of snow-shrouded streams. The moon rests on the white crescent. All is still, I walk in sun-filled dream, as wind blows sparkling snow from the rock faces.

From a summit where torn choughs are flying, a small cairn rises like a man. If this is Jang La, its fearsomeness has been exaggerated. "Jang" means "green," which seems to suggest that it is rarely snow-bound; and "La" signifies a pass—more properly, the deity or keeper of the pass who may or may not let the traveler cross over. The cairn marking this place is no more than a heap of stones with sticks and rags upon which, in propitiation of the mountain gods, some traveler has set two skulls of *na*. The north face of the cairn is under snow, and down the north side of the pass the snow descends unbroken to the tree line. GS, who overtakes me at the summit, reads 14,880 on his altimeter, which is accurate within one hundred feet; in Kathmandu, we were informed that this pass lies at 17,000 feet. Similarly, the headman of Tarakot had assured us that from the Saure Camp up over Jang La and down to tree line was a journey of seven hours; carrying full loads, we shall make it without difficulty in four. True, we left early enough to make good time on the hard snow. whereas the local people will slog extra hours through wet mush rather than break camp before sun strikes it.

GS is discoursing happily on the freedom of carrying one's own pack, of being "independent of childish people who've lived all their lives in the mountains and won't wear rag strips on their eyes in snow—do you realize we could travel for a week this way, and make good time, with just what we have here on our backs?" I do realize this, and am happy, too, watching him tramp off down the mountain; the sense of having one's life needs at hand, of traveling light, brings with it intense energy and exhilaration. Simplicity is the whole secret of well-being. ("I could not simplify myself"—the explanation of the suicide Nezhdanov.)[12] Jang La is behind us, my lungs are holding up in this thin air, my dour boots show some signs of relenting. And starting a relaxed descent, I enjoy the view of distant shadows that mark the deep gorge of the Bheri River. Beyond the Bheri the steep mountains rise toward the snow peaks of the Kanjiroba Himal; on the far side of those distant peaks lies Crystal Mountain.

Liberation, freedom—unaccountably I think about a girl I talked to once in a marine-supplies store where she was buying rope, just a few years ago. The next day, with her young husband and a British companion, she rose in a balloon from the Long Island farmland, waving goodbye to a cheering crowd, and headed eastward, bound for England over the Atlantic Ocean. None of the three was ever seen again. At this moment I feel moved, not by the disappearance of that girl (which was no tragedy, only a brave essay that was lost) but by the name of their great adventure—the Free Life Balloon. Perhaps the voyagers on the Free Life Balloon meant "free life" as described by a mountaineer: "The mountains had been a natural field of activity where, playing on the frontiers of life and death, we had found the freedom for which we were blindly groping and which was as necessary to us as breath." But the same mountaineer, after nearly losing his life, wrote of "freedom" in a quite different way: "I saw that it was better to be true than to be strong. . . . I was saved and I had won my freedom. This freedom, which I shall never lose . . . has given me the rare joy of loving that which I used to despise. A new and splendid life has opened out before me."[13] This is closer to my own idea of freedom, the possibility and prospect of "free life," traveling light, without clinging or despising, in calm acceptance of everything that comes; free because without defenses, free not in an adolescent way, with no restraints, but in the sense of the Tibetan Buddhist's "crazy wisdom," of Camus's "leap into

the absurd" that occurs within a life of limitations. The absurd-
ity of a life that may well end before one understands it does
not relieve one of the duty (to that self which is inseparable
from others) to live it through as bravely and as generously as
possible.

I feel great gratitude for being here, for *being*, rather, for
there is no need to hide oneself to the snow mountains in order
to feel free. I am not here to seek the "crazy wisdom"; if I am,
I shall never find it. I am here to be here, like these rocks and
sky and snow, like this hail that is falling down out of the sun.

Cruck! My stave makes a blue hole in the snow.

Down the glazed surface of the slope blows a cold wind, the
wind of Jang. A dry moth is transfixed upon the glaze, and a
caterpillar that followed some dim impulse to crawl up from
below, but in this icy place there are no birds to eat them. A
black tumulus, snow-sheathed and treacherous, twists the boots.
Then the track rounds the mountain and comes down from
winter into an autumn kingdom where brown swifts flicker in
pursuit of the warm insects, over golden woods. Like a bharal,
I jump down through patchy snow and red wildflowers.

By the path, GS is glaring toward high glaciers on the
Dhaulagiris, which we are skirting on our journey to the north.
"We made a mistake, leaving today," he says. "This isn't blue-
sheep habitat at all." He is also upset that we have not met
Jang-bu, and we eat in silence. But we have scarcely set off
again when Jang-bu turns up on the trail below. It is fortunate
that we have carried our full loads, for he has no new porters,
only Tukten, Gyaltsen, and the singing young Tamang called
Karsung—the only men well enough to return today. Tired from
the trek the day before, they had left Tarakot late, carrying firewood, thick green discs of buckwheat bread, and a flask of
arak. We celebrate for a few minutes on the sunny mountainside before these cheerful fellows climb onward to Jang La. Already it is afternoon, and it will be dark, in snow and stars,
before they reach the Saure.

In high spirits, we continue down through alpine pastures to
dry slopes of oak and pine. Below, the Bheri Valley can be seen,
winding down out of dark canyons to the north and east.

Camp is made on a sunny ledge, near a shadowed stream; here spruce and fir and pine all live together.

At the fire, we cook rice before dusk falls; and afterward, I climb the hill and sit under a pine and watch the stars appear over Tibet. Then the planet Mars, bright orange-gold, rises swiftly over night snows in the northeast. How clear it is! How imminent!

An owl hoots, deep in the black needles.

Whooo—ooo.

OCTOBER 18

I am up before the sun, and make a fire. The water boils as the sun ignites the peaks, and we breakfast in sunshine on hot tea and porridge. A nutcracker is rasping in the pines, and soon the crows come, down the morning valley; cawing, they hide among long shimmering needles, then glide in, bold, to walk about in the warming scent of resin, dry feet scratching on the bark of fallen trees.

Since Jang-bu cannot reach Tarakot before the evening, we have time. I walk barefoot in the grass, spreading my gear with ceremony: today, for the first time in weeks, everything will be dry, a great event in expedition life. Then with my stave I prop my pack upright and sit back against the mountainside, my face in cold shade and hot sun on my arms and belly.

Pine needles dance in a light breeze against the three white sister peaks to the northwest. I sit in silence, lost in the burning hum of mountain bees. An emerald butterfly comes to my knee to dry its wings, gold wings with black specks above, white polka dots beneath. Through the frozen atmospheres, the sun is burning.

In the clearness of this Himalayan air, mountains draw near, and in such splendor, tears come quietly to my eyes and cool on my sunburned cheeks. This is not mere soft-mindedness, nor am I all that silly with the altitude. My head has cleared in these weeks free of intrusions—mail, telephones, people and their needs—and I respond to things spontaneously, without defensive or self-conscious screens. Still, all this *feeling* is astonishing: not so long ago I could say truthfully that I had not shed a tear in twenty years.

In the early afternoon, we go down through the hill pastures to Tarakot, a group of villages set on terraces high above the upper Bheri, near the confluence of the Tarap River with smaller streams that come down off Dhaulagiri. In the days before the Gorkhas made a nation of Nepal, this medieval place was the capital of the old kingdom of Tichu-Rong (from the Tibetan: Valley of Fragrant Waters), and it is still known to its inhabitants as Dzong (the Fortress). Seen from above, in the distilled air, Tarakot seems not quite real; the sunlight is too soft, too gilded, and the shade too black, as in an illuminated painting from some ancient book.

On the hillside above Tarakot is a pageant of tall poles crowned by symbols of sun, moon, and fire; brown, white, and gray Tibetan ponies graze among white prayer flags, which snap OM MANI PADME HUM on the autumn wind. (Is it the flag that moves? Is it the wind? Neither, said Hui-Neng, the sixth Ch'an Buddhist Patriarch of China: It is your mind. The Sixth Patriarch's comment is treasured to this day by Zen roshis and Tibetan lamas alike.)

The path winds among potato patches and terraces of red buckwheat. Under the eaves of a lone hut, a bright-colored fresco in blue, gold, green, and red portrays seven Buddha figures in symbolic postures that represent idealized aspects of Sakyamuni's life. These Buddha aspects, "celestial Buddhas," Bodhisattvas, and other embodiments of Buddha-hood are all given separate names and attributes; and in these Himalayan lands, the chaotic nature of Buddhist iconography is compounded by the fact that everywhere, and almost from the start, Buddhists have adapted and adopted local deities rather than eradicate the old religions, so that even the most pernicious demon might be sanctified as a "Protector of the Dharma." Then, in the first centuries after Sakyamuni's death, certain yoga teachings of Vedic origin became systematized in esoteric treatises, called Tantras (it is sometimes claimed that they are the Fifth Veda) and the Tantric influences of these yoga cults brought about the creation of female wisdom principles, or *prajnas,* for each of the already numerous demons and divinities.

Avalokita, for example, was given a female counterpart called Tara; as a merciful savior, Tara became so popular that, in certain lands, She tended to displace Him. Kuan Yin, as Avalokita is known in China, is distinctly a female presence, while the Japanese Kannon is given neither sex, or both. By the sixth century A.D., Tantric worship of female energies was dominant in both Hinduism and Mahayana Buddhism, and it was this Tantric form of Buddhism that was carried north into Tibet.

The histories relate that an extraordinary *naljorpa* named Padma Sambhava, or Lotus-Born, established Buddhism in Tibet in the eighth century. Yogins from northwest India—Kashmir, Gilgit, and Ladakh—had carried certain teachings to western Tibet before this time, but Padma Sambhava, by discrediting the old B'on religion, established Buddhism on a firm basis and introduced the occult yogic Tantras (corresponding to kundalini yoga), some of which, tradition says, originated in the lost realm of Shambala, "in the north." (Padma Sambhava himself is supposed to have come originally from the "north country" of Urgyan, or Udyana, which is identified sometimes with Shambala but more often with a region north and west of the Indus River in what is now Afghanistan.) He is also credited with compiling the *Bardo Thodol*, or "Book of the Dead," as well as with founding Nyingma, the "Old Sect" of Tibetan Buddhism, which later developed the forms of Tantric practice that in Western eyes seemed decadent and orgiastic. Despite his persecution of B'on sorcerers, Padma Sambhava, in the Buddhist tradition of absorbing the local religions, seems to have tolerated the inclusion of much B'on magic in Nyingma, including the grim *chöd* rites from the pre-Buddhist Tibetan manuscripts known as "Heart-Drops from the Great Space."[14] The *chöd* rites may well be much older than B'on itself, deriving from archaic practices of sacrifice and exorcism. And the supreme Buddha figure of Nyingma, known as Samantabhadra, derives from an ancient deity who is probably close kin to such eminent sky gods as Zeus, Jupiter, and the Dyans-Pita of the Aryans, all of whom, it is supposed, had a common ancestor in the cultures of Central Asia.

In Chinese and Japanese Buddhism, only a few Bodhisattvas

and the historical Buddha, Sakyamuni, are commonly por-
trayed, and the Ch'an or Zen sect in particular has cut away
most iconography, in keeping with its spare, clear, simple style;
in its efforts to avoid religiosity, to encourage free-thinking and
doubt, Zen makes bold use of contradictions, humor, and ir-
reverence, applauding the monk who burned up the wood altar
Buddha to keep warm. Tibetan Buddhism, on the other hand,
having incorporated the Hindu pantheon as well as B'on, must
pay homage to a multitude of Buddha aspects and manifestations, with varying orders of precedence and emphasis according to the sect. In such remote corners of the Himalaya as
Tichu-Rong, the people still favor the Nyingma with its ves-
tiges of B'on; here the B'on sky divinity who became king on
earth lends his celestial colors of sky-blue and snow-white to
Buddhist prayer flags. In the Tarakot stupa, Samantabhadra
and Padma Sambhava, the traditional founder of Nyingma, are
given precedence over the Buddha Sakyamuni.

The stupa is a monument, shrine, and reliquary that traditionally derives from the Buddha's tomb, but has come to symbolize existence. On a square red base (signifying earth) sits a
large white dome (water) with a sort of spire (fire) crowned
with a lunar crescent (air) and a solar disc (space); such structures guard the approaches to towns and villages throughout
the Buddhist Himalaya. Larger stupas may enclose a room decorated with mandalas and iconographic paintings: the inner
west wall of the Tarakot stupa, for example, portrays three
Bodhisattvas, while on the east wall are three Buddhas. One is
a Buddha of past ages (the light-giver, Dipankara), another the
historical Buddha (Sakyamuni), the third the Buddha-to-come
(Maitreya, who exists at present as a Bodhisattva but will be
reborn as the Buddha in a future age).

Tarakot's Tibetan-speaking people are not Bhotes but Magars
who made their way up the river valleys long ago and later
adopted Buddhism; or perhaps they were refugees from the Muslim holy wars that eradicated Buddhism from India in the twelfth
century. The town itself is flat-roofed, built of stone, each
building a several-storied fortress topped by prayer flags. The

women wear the brass earrings of the valley peoples as well as the striped blankets of the hills, and the men, too, lack a definitive costume, though the poorest tend to dress like Tibetan herdsmen while the headman, he whom we met in the mountains north of Yamarkhar, attires himself like a Hindu of the towns.

Dawa and the sick Tamangs await us at the headman's house, which except in size is typical of Tarakot. The ground floor is a stable for goats, cattle, and sheep, and the only access to the floors above is by a narrow steep log ladder from the stable yard, the top of which is guarded by a grim dog on a chain. The stable roof is the clay floor of the next story, which is occupied by most of the human inhabitants as well as goat kids, lambs, and chickens. The chicks run free, peeping among brass canisters and water urns and stacks of firewood; at night they are kept beneath overturned wicker baskets, used by day for carrying dry cargo on the human back. The house entrances are holes in the wall well above floor level (much like those in the old Anasazi dwellings at Mesa Verde and other locations in the American Southwest), and the wall itself is decorated by big round white spots; irregular wood windows let a small amount of light into the outer room, but the inner chambers are entirely dark. Animal heads are carved at the ends of the eave poles, from which hang sheepskins, calabashes, drying meat.

From the terrace on the stable roof, another ladder mounts to the second story, where hens and hen dung are discouraged; here, warm piles of buckwheat, barley, maize, peas, hemp, and millet are spread out to dry on straw mats or homespun blankets, and one man, scattering the tree sparrows, piles big yellow pumpkin squashes in a corner. In the fall days before the snows, on all the roofs of Tarakot, people are turning winter provender toward the sun, baling up hay for their animals, and stacking brushwood for the winter's fuel. Once the buckwheat is winnowed, the chaff is stacked up with the hay for winter fodder. To one side is a great wood pot of fermented barley, used in the brewing of the local beer, called *chang;* the dregs will be given to the cattle, for nothing in this old economy is wasted.

A sheepish Dawa, eyes still swollen, gives us tea when we arrive, and the Tamangs jump up from the mats where they were sleeping. Pirim (Pirimbahadur Lama; "Lama" is their own word for "Tamang") runs to my pack unasked and spreads out to dry the sleeping bag that was dried thoroughly this morning on the mountain: I thank him warmly. He is happy to see us, and delighted that I call him "Lama" with mock reverence, as if he were my guru. The rest of the Tamangs hover about, half-blind, in eagerness to be of service. In late afternoon, the Sherpas turn up with Bimbahadur, who salutes the sahibs in old regimental style and goes immediately to his rest.

Tarakot is in twilight shadow by midafternoon, while the mountainside across the Bheri, facing south, lies in full sunshine. In a strong dusk, the women gather up the grain in homespun sacks to store inside. Now the snow peaks take on color, and whistling boys bring kine and sheep and goats from the high pastures. A rooster and a barking dog, the sting of sticks on the hard flanks of the cattle, the cry of the village termagant, unceasing, is the voice of autumn twilight in every peasant village across time. But Tarakot is the capital of Tichu-Rong, and from the police house comes flat tin music from a small radio with weak batteries, the first such noise we have heard since late September. "A note of the twentieth century in the seventeenth," GS sighs, as sorry as myself that we have heard it.

Toward seven, the radio goes dead and the din of the village ceases. We lie down in the open, on the roof. On this long trek, to limit weight, precious kerosene and flashlight batteries must be conserved, and so the nights are long: like the local people, we go to bed at dark and rise at dawn.

For a time I watch the coming of the night. A bat chitters and stars loom, and somewhere on the far side of this earth, the sun is burning. Soon Mars appears over the dark split in the northern mountains where the Tarap River comes down from the Land of Dolpo, and in the snug warmth of my sleeping bag, I float under the round bowl of the heavens. Above is the glistening galaxy of childhood, now hidden in the Western world by air pollution and the glare of artificial light; for my children's children, the power, peace, and healing of the night will be obliterated.

Every little while I wake and watch the spiral of the heavens.

Orion rises, and the Pleiades. Shooting stars are in the shimmering void of the black universe, and toward four the sky is parted by a satellite, mercifully silent, like a probe from another world, a distant century.

A horse screams.

The moon is up over Tibet, and in the southern mountains, over Jang, the planet Mars is disappearing. How much dignity the moon has lost, now that man has left his disrespectful litter, his cute golf balls! But the moon retains its mystery for the dogs of Tichu-Rong, which howl in awe at its first appearance, and set one another off the whole night through; while its fellows rest, the dog next door harangues the cosmos for an hour. The mastiffs sleep much of the day and are let loose at night to deal with wolves and robbers; in the absence of such, they will make do with strangers. Not caring to venture out into the streets when such brutes are abroad, I follow the custom of the town, standing on the roof edge and urinating into the mud street, in daybreak light.

OCTOBER 19

At sunrise, in our sleeping bags, we are served oatmeal by the gold-toothed Phu-Tsering, and from one of the friends that Tukten makes everywhere he goes, I buy a blanket of striped homespun, multicolored, strong. Meanwhile Jang-bu has conscripted seven porters and so, this morning, we depart the fabled Dzong.

Bimbahadur will not go with us. Standing at attention, tears in his eyes, the old Gurkha salutes us, crying, "Sahib!" New white sneakers and white ski socks, presented to him by GS, and pulled up high on his short rootlike legs, give Bimbahadur a peculiar air of misplaced ceremony, but above the knees, he wears his usual arrangement of brown rags and gritty blankets. Now he turns away and sets off up the mountainside, leaning heavily upon his stave, bound south over the blue heights of Jang La and across the snows to his cave on the Seng River, thence to Yamarkhar and Dhorpatan, and east to the Kali Gandaki.

The police official at Tarakot, having given us bored, pompous audience, has referred us to his superior at Dunahi, not having the authority, it seems, to make things hot for us himself. We leave before he thinks of something, taking the path that drops straight down through garden terraces to the Bheri. In the terraces are four kinds of millet-like grains, not quite familiar, such as might have been grown millennia ago by the people of the Middle East who are thought to have first domesticated the wild cereals. Squash and beans are plentiful, and in my need to supplement our dead white diet, I pick and eat raw purple kidney beans all the way downhill.

Near the river, a troupe of Himalayan langurs has invaded a garden of red millet. The monkeys are forty-one in all, including six infants that are carried, and they are knocking down in play the plants they are not eating. Gleeful, Tukten yells, "*Ho, Diddi!*" ("Hey, Sister!") and a woman comes running from the garden, slinging stones. Curltailed, the langurs move into the rocks, in no great hurry, and there turn to observe man at their leisure. They are big handsome silver-brown creatures, one of the most beautiful of primates, with frosted faces and an expression so entirely detached as to seem disdainful—a very suitable expression, at least in the lead male, which upon taking control of a band customarily sets about the systematic killing of its infants, thereby bringing the females quickly into estrus, and preparing them for the perpetuation of his genes.

The langur is sacred to all Hindus as the manifestation of the monkey god Hanuman, and is also the beast most commonly brought forth to account for footprints of the "abominable snowman," although bears, snow leopards, great-footed birds, and melting snow have their supporters. In the half century since big, upright creatures, leaving hundreds of tracks, were seen in the high snowfield on the north side of Mount Everest by a band of British mountaineers, the *ye-teh*, or yeti, has met with a storm of disapproval from upset scientists around the world. But as with the sasquatch of the vast rain forests of the Pacific Northwest, the case *against* the existence of the yeti—entirely speculative, and necessarily based on assumptions of foolishness or mendacity in many observers of good reputation—is even less "scientific" than the evidence that it exists. Photographs and casts of the yeti footprint are consistent—a very odd, broad primate foot—and so are the sight records, most of which come from the populous Sherpa country of eastern Nepal.

The yeti is described most often as a hairy, reddish-brown creature with a ridged crown that gives it a pointed-head appearance; in size, despite the outsized foot (entirely unlike the long foot of a bear, in which the toes are more or less symmetrical), it has been likened to an adolescent boy, though much larger individuals have been reported. There are no brown bears (*Ursus arctos*) on the south side of the Himalaya, where both black bear and langur are well known and unmistakable. Bears hibernate in winter, when yetis are most often seen (in lean times, they appear to scavenge near monasteries and villages), and most yeti tracks are much too large to be made by monkeys, even in melting snow. Langurs are rarely seen in snow, or yetis either, if it comes to that: while the yeti may cross the snows on foraging excursions to higher elevations or into the next valley, its primary habitat must be the cloud forest of the myriad deep Himalayan canyons, which are exceptionally inhospitable to man. From a biologist's point of view, in fact, most of the Himalayan region is still *terra incognita*. As GS says, almost nothing is known of the natural history of the snow leopard, and we are walking a long way indeed to find out some basic information about the relatively accessible Himalayan bharal.

One evening last month in Kathmandu, a young biologist in charge of a field project in the Arun Valley of eastern Nepal set down on our dinner table a big primate footprint in white plaster; this cast had been made in the snow outside his tent six months before.[15] The tracks had led down across steep snowfields into valley forest; he and his colleagues were not able to follow. Plainly the creature being spoken of was the "abominable snowman," and I waited for GS to express skepticism. But he merely nodded, picking up the cast with care, turning it over, and setting it down again, his face frowning and intent; what interested him most, he said at last, was the similarity of this yeti print to that of the mountain gorilla. And later he told me that he was not being polite, that there was no doubt in his mind that a creature not yet scientifically described had made this print. Despite the scoffing of his peers, GS has believed in the existence of this creature ever since the mountaineer Eric Shipton took the first clear photographs of yeti prints on Everest in 1951. "At least ninety-five percent of the yeti material is nonsense," GS said, "but I'm convinced, on the basis of the Shipton photographs and some other evidence, that an animal unknown to science occurs here." (He still has doubts about the sasquatch, the existence of which has been accepted by no less an authority on primates than Dr. John Napier of the University of London; Napier, on the other hand, has no faith in the yeti, although he is disturbed by Shipton's photographs.)[16] A theory that the yeti is a relict species of early man, driven long ago into dense forests by the surge of *Homo sapiens* that presumably eliminated more primitive hominids, is not helped by its strange, bestial foot, which would seem to place it closer to a subhominid such as *Gigantopithecus* or even to the apes; yet the hundreds of photographs and casts of sasquatch tracks show a very large, crude humanoid footprint with the big toe close to all the rest, not separate as in all other known primates—a footprint such as might have been made by a large Australopithecine species of early man. (This raises the interesting possibility that the sasquatch is not "unknown to science" but, like the coelacanth, was prematurely classified "extinct.")

A strong argument against the existence of both sasquatch and yeti (and the whole world-wide phenomenon called "Bigfoot") is that man's expeditions in pursuit of these elusive creatures have all failed. However, this may only prove that Bigfoot habitat is virtually impenetrable, and that after long centuries of hiding, these rare creatures are exceptionally wary. Perhaps the best way to find Bigfoot is to set up camp in a likely region and live there quietly until this creature, in its primate curiosity, makes a few investigations of its own.

The Nepal government takes yeti seriously, and there is a strict law against killing them. But one of the Arun Valley scientists has a permit that would allow him to collect one of these creatures, and I asked him what he would do if, one fine morning, a yeti presented itself within fair range; it seemed to me that this decision should not wait for an event. The biologist was unsettled by the question; he had not made this hard decision, or if he had, was not at peace with it.

After a moment, looking up, he asked me a hard question of his own. He could understand why GS, as a biologist, would walk hundreds of miles over high mountains to collect wildlife data on the Tibetan Plateau. By why was *I* going? What did I hope to find?

I shrugged, uncomfortable. To say I was interested in blue sheep or snow leopards, or even in remote lamaseries, was no answer to his question, though all of that was true; to say I was making a pilgrimage seemed fatuous and vague, though in some sense that was true as well. And so I admitted that I did not know. How could I say that I wished to penetrate the secrets of the mountains in search of something still unknown that, like the yeti, might well be missed for the very fact of searching?

We cross the river on an old wood bridge and descend the Bheri Canyon. Today I feel a little sad and a little sick. GS thinks this is the sudden loss of altitude—we have dropped seven thousand feet from the Jang La—and I regret all those raw purple beans; whatever it is, my gut feels as heavy as my spirits, which had been so exhilarated in the snows.

Though these journals remind me of the date, I have long since lost track of the day of the week, and the great events that must be taking place in the world we left behind are as illusory as events from a future century. It is not so much that we are going back in time as that time seems circular, and past and future have lost meaning. I understand much better now Einstein's remark that the only real time is that of the observer, who carries with him his own time and space. In these mountains, we have fallen behind history.

I long to let go, drift free of things, to accumulate less, depend on less, to move more simply. Therefore I felt out of sorts after having bought that blanket—another *thing,* another burden to the spirit. The weaver wished a most reasonable price for a heavy blanket of fine colors. But with Tukten's encouragement, I bargained him down, and though this was expected, it depressed me, all the more so because, for Tukten and Pirim, who were present as cheerful translators in the transaction, the cost of this blanket—eighteen dollars—was twelve times their porter's wage of fifteen rupees a day. The Sherpas fare scarcely any better, even those who risk their lives on climbing expeditions; until recently, at least, the daily wage on even the most perilous peaks was about four dollars, whereas Sherpas on treks such as our own receive but two.

Across the canyon, on the steepest slope, a slash-and-burn agriculture has been attempted, for along the Bheri, as in most of Nepal, the good land has run out. The great pines still clinging to the inaccessible corners of this canyon are monuments to a ruined wilderness: very soon, the last of the trees that hold these mountainsides together will be gone. The flood carries eroded stone down from the glaciers, and the deep canyon it has carved across the ages, with its extraordinary layers of folded rock, is remarkably hot and dry, almost xerotic, by comparison to river canyons at this altitude on the far side of the Jang. We notice, too, that the clouds that come up every afternoon south of the Jang are missing here as we draw closer to the mountain deserts of the Tibetan Plateau, which is cut off from the monsoon rains by the rising of the Himalaya. Yet despite the heat, a cool breeze is flowing up the canyon, and the river path is pleasant. On rock tumulus I spy a goral, a neat small brown goat-antelope related to the chamois and the North American mountain goat; otherwise, a hoopoe and white butterflies are the only signs of life.

A sparkling tributary, the Jairi Khola, falls in cascades from a snow peak called Dwari Lekh. We make camp on the riverbank not far beyond, and Phu-Tsering obtains maize on the cob and small tomatoes for our supper. The hamlet here is just east of Dunahi, which is the frontier administration post for Dolpo.

The Bheri continues west as far as Tibrikot, on the main trade route between Tarakot and Jumla, in far western Nepal; our own route turns north across the river bridge, a few miles down, and climbs the Suli River. From the administrative point of view, we enter Dolpo once we cross the Bheri, but the "Land of Dolpo" of my own imagination lies off there on the farther side of the Kanjirobas.

At Dhorpatan we had been warned that the police checkposts at Tarakot, and perhaps at Dunahi, might ignore our trekking permits and forbid us to continue into Dolpo; worry on this point, with debates on strategy, has occupied us for some days. A chronic problem all along the way has been the language barrier, which fills the regional officials (already suspicious of our avowed interest in wildlife) with insecurity and often leads them to face-saving stubbornness. The Sherpas, being Buddhist, are not acceptable as witnesses on our behalf, and thus there is considerable risk that after walking for three weeks, we shall be stopped for no good reason, just one week—as we suppose—from our destination.

OCTOBER 20

The police official at Dunahi is absent on a journey, and instead we are dealt with by the local member of the Nepal Panchayat, or Parliament; police underlings make no effort to contest this sophisticated man who speaks good English, understands our aims, and offers tea. Greatly relieved, we get under way as quickly as we can, before something can go wrong. The Kang Pass in the Kanjirobas is now the last serious obstacle on our journey to the Crystal Mountain.

At Dunahi, the bridge crosses the Bheri, and the path climbs steeply up dry mountainside of sage and spear grass and the silver-leaved wild olive. Far below, the river curves in a broad bend of burnished gravel bars toward its confluence with the Suli Gad, which rushes down from Phoksumdo Lake and the snows of the Kanjirobas, holding its turquoise blue for a short reach along the north bank of the Bheri before subsiding into the gray glacial flood. The Suli Gorge is so precipitous that the path must climb high above the Bheri before rounding the steep mountainside above the confluence and entering this canyon, and even here, one thousand feet or more above the water, the incline is such that the path is scarcely two feet wide in places, sometimes less; where the path has slid away or been blotted out by slides, we scrabble across loose rocks as best we can.

GS seems casual on ledges, although the telescope strapped across his rucksack, caught upon a rock, could nudge him off the edge; I can scarcely look. However, I am getting hardened: I walk lighter, stumble less, with more spring in leg and lung, keeping my center of gravity deep in the belly, and letting that center "see." At these times, I am free of vertigo, even in dangerous places; my feet move naturally to firm footholds, and I flow. But sometimes for a day or more, I lose this feel of things, my breath is high up in my chest, and then I cling to the cliff edge as to life itself. And of course it is this clinging, the tightness of panic, that gets people killed: "to clutch," in ancient Egyptian, "to clutch the mountain," in Assyrian, were euphemisms that signified "to die."[17]

Before departing, I had taken leave of Eido Roshi, and spoke to him of odd death whispers that had come for several months. He nodded; perhaps what such whispers anticipated was a spiritual "great death" and a rebirth. "The snow," he murmured, "may signify extinction, and renewal." After a pause, he warned me, "Expect nothing." The Roshi was pleased that there would be but two of us—this seemed to him a condition of true pilgrimage. He instructed me to recite the Kannon Sutra as I walked among the mountains, and gave me a *koan* (a Zen paradox, not to be solved by intellect, that may bring about a sudden dissolution of logical thought and clear the way for direct *seeing* into the heart of existence):

All the peaks are covered with snow—why is this one bare?

The Roshi rose from his black cushion and, taking me by the shoulders, touched my forehead three times with his own, then smote my back, and sent me on my way with a great shout.

"Expect nothing." Walking along, I remind myself of that advice; I must go lightly on my way, with no thought of attainment. Instead of the Kannon Sutra, I intone OM MANI PADME HUM, which is addressed to the same great Bodhisattva and, when recited one word for each step, has a resonant and mighty sound much better suited to this slow tread up the mountain.

Aum . . . Ma-ni . . . Pay-may . . . Hung!

Disputing the path is a great copper-colored grasshopper, gleaming like amber in the sun; so large is it, and so magical its shimmer, that I wonder if this grasshopper is not some old *naljorpa,* advanced in the art of taking other forms. But before such a "perfected one" can reveal himself, the grasshopper springs carelessly over the precipice, to start a new life hundreds of feet below. I choose to take this as a sign that I must entrust myself to life, and thanking the grasshopper, I step out smartly on my way.

An empty village on the path above the Suli Gad is used in winter by the yakherders of Inner Dolpo, whose animals find forage on these lower slopes. But in the autumn, in the morning shadow and clear light, the doorways and windows are black as eyeholes in a skull, and the emptiness is deepened by a prayer flag's tatter on the wind, and a child's call from higher up the valley. Under the village, a stream comes down the mountain, and while GS goes up the gully a short way, trying to photograph a troupe of langurs, I wash myself in the warm sunlight where the water sparkles cold and clear over flat stones. Eventually GS returns, the Sherpas come, and we all eat together in the willow and aspen shade at streamside, flavoring the chapatis with seeds of the small wild *Cannabis,* for which we compete with the Himalayan goldfinch.

From this place there is a very steep ascent of an hour or more. The Tarakot porters grumble, and even the Tamangs struggle for breath, all but Karsung, who is singing. A Bhotia family without animals descends the trail, nods shyly, and is gone. At 9400 feet, the path reaches the cliff top, leveling off as it winds around the mountain. The Bheri is far behind us and below, and a snow peak of the Kanjirobas is rising, quiet as a cloud, on the northern blue. A claterynge of choughs, lifting along upon the air currents, delights me, and for want of a fresh way to let well-being overflow, I talk to GS rapturously about my boots, which are broken in at last and give me no end of honest pleasure. Mildly alarmed by my euphoria, he goes on rapidly. Left to myself, I listen contentedly to the leather creak of my back harness and beloved boots, the steady thump of my faithful stave upon the mountain, feeling as indomitable as Padma Sambhava, who carried the Dharma from India into Tibet.

Upon the path, in the glint of mica and odd shining stones, lies the yellow and gray-blue feather of an unknown bird. And there comes a piercing intuition, by no means understood, that in this feather on the silver path, this rhythm of wood and leather sounds, breath, sun and wind, and rush of river, in a landscape without past or future time—in this instant, in all instants, transience and eternity, death and life are one.

Higher still, a crude cave has been dug out of the mountainside. Awed by wind, the precipice, the roar of the wild river far below, travelers have thought it prudent to construct a group of cairns. On the east face of each edifice is a rough niche for offerings, and one cairn is decorated with fresh marigolds, no doubt placed there by the folk met earlier along the trail. According to Tukten, who lifts his palms together in mock supplication and wild nervous glee, these cairns are dedicated to an ancient mountain god called Masta.

To the north, high on the mountain's face, has come in view the village called Rohagaon. The track passes along beneath wild walnut trees. The last leaves are yellowed and stiff on the gaunt branches, and the nuts are fallen; the dry scratch and whisper of sere leaves bring on the vague melancholy of some other autumn, half-remembered. Cracked nutshells litter big flat stones along the path, and among the shells lie fresh feathers of a hoopoe, perhaps killed in the act of gleaning by the accipiter that darts out of the bush ahead and down over the void of the Suli Gorge. In a copse below Rohagaon, maple, sumac, locust, and wild grape evoke the woods of home, but the trees differ just enough from the familiar ones to make the wood seem dreamlike, a wildwood of children's tales, found again in a soft autumn haze. The wildwood brings on mild nostalgia, not for home or place, but for lost innocence—the paradise lost that, as Proust said, is the only paradise. Childhood is full of mystery and promise, and perhaps the life fear comes when all the mysteries are laid open, when what we thought we wanted is attained. It is just at the moment of seeming fulfillment that we sense irrevocable betrayal, like a great wave rising silently behind us, and know most poignantly what Milarepa meant: "All worldly pursuits have but one unavoidable and inevitable end, which is sorrow: acquisitions end in dispersion; buildings, in destruction; meetings, in separation; births, in death. . . ." Confronted by the uncouth specter of old age, disease, and death, we are thrown back upon the present, on this moment, here, right now, for that is all there is. And surely this is the paradise of children, that they are at rest in the present, like frogs or rabbits.

From somewhere comes the murmur of a hidden brook, and the chill air of autumn afternoon carries a mineral smell of humus. GS and I put down our packs and gather wild walnuts in the wood; soon the Sherpas and porters come, and we run about in happy adolescence, and crack small grudging nuts in the twilight haze beyond the trees before climbing up the last steep path into Rohagaon.

If Tarakot had a medieval air, one enters the Dark Ages in Rohagaon. The approaches to the place are guarded by *dhauliyas,* "protectors," crudely inscribed on big flat stones, and on the primitive entrance stupa (like a huge cairn) has been laid a god's supply of marijuana. Neither Buddhism nor Hinduism has displaced the old religions of this Thakuri folk, who heap up offerings of goat heads in their primitive temple to Masta. Brutal human effigies in wood protect the low stone huts, and half-wild curs rage at strangers from the rooftops; the dead crows hung from high poles in the turnip gardens, feathers lifting in October evening wind, are the primordial scarecrows of mankind.

As we enter the village, the men stare stupidly as if transfixed, but the dour women soon resume their labors; one pounds millet with an outlandish wooden pestle, another bends beneath a crude wood cask, which even in Tarakot had been replaced by the brass water urn. The women wear black cloth, the men soot-colored clothes of other cultures, the children rags; every face is masked in black, black even by the standards of this region, where ceaseless exposure to manure dust, pine smoke, and soot makes filth endemic. But for all their grime, the children lack the cloddish grimness of their parents: rushing about as we set up tents, playing loud games for our benefit, they celebrate this moment of their life.

Rohagaon on the mountainside has a majestic prospect down the valley of the Suli Gad to the low snow peaks in the western reach of Dhaulagiri. Soon stars fill this southern sky, and at the sight of the moon rising, the mongrels go berserk. The October moon reminds me that at home it will soon be Halloween, and I wonder if my son will carve a pumpkin. He has a skeleton costume, white bones painted on black cloth, but this year his colt legs in their high sneakers will certainly stick out too far beneath—what will he wear? What mask will cover my child's face on All Hallow's Eve, as he celebrates the festival of fire and death? I lie sleepless, shouting hopelessly, as the exalted dog in the house above, crazed by the pale tents in the moonlight, barks unceasingly from midnight until dawn, without the smallest loss of tone or volume.

OCTOBER 21

We leave Rohagaon as the first light tints the snow peaks to the south.

Outside the village, two little girls in wool boots and bead necklaces, carrying water, tarry on a corner of the trail to watch us go; minutes later, I look back, and still they stand there, little ragged stumps on the daybreak sky.

All around, the sun fires the summits, yet these steep valleys are so shut away from light that on this trail above the Suli Gad we walk for two hours in dim daybreak shadow. Here and there wild roses gather in clear pale-yellow bloom, and a flight of snow pigeons wheels up and down over the canyon far below; we look in vain for tahr or other creatures on the slopes across the valley. Wildlife has been scarce all along the way, with no sign at all of exotic animals such as the moon bear and red panda.

The trail meets the Suli Gad high up the valley, in grottoes of bronze-lichened boulders and a shady riverside of pine and walnut and warm banks of fern. Where morning sun lights the red leaves and dark still conifers, the river sparkles in the forest shadow; turquoise and white, it thunders past spray-shined boulders, foaming pools, in a long rocky chute of broken rapids. In the cold breath of the torrent, the dry air is softened by mist; under last night's stars this water trickled through the snows. At the head of the waterfall, downstream, its sparkle leaps into the air, leaps at the sun, and sun rays are tumbled in the waves that dance against the snows of distant mountains.

Upstream, in the inner canyon, dark silences are deepened by the roar of stones. Something is listening, and I listen, too: who is it that intrudes here? Who is breathing? I pick a fern to see its spores, cast it away, and am filled in that instant with misgiving: the great sins, so the Sherpas say, are to pick wild flowers and to threaten children. My voice murmurs its regret, a strange sound that deepens the intrusion. I look about me— who is it that spoke? And who is listening? Who is this everpresent "I" that is not me?

The voice of a solitary bird asks the same question.

Here in the secrets of the mountains, in the river roar, I touch my skin to see if I am real; I say my name aloud and do not answer.

By a dark wall of rock, over a rivulet, a black-and-gold dragonfly zips and glistens; a walnut falls on a mat of yellow leaves. I wonder if anywhere on earth there is a river more beautiful than the upper Suli Gad in early fall. Seen through the mist, a water spirit in monumental pale gray stone is molded smooth by its mantle of white water, and higher, a ribbon waterfall, descending a cliff face from the east, strikes the wind sweeping upriver and turns to mist before striking the earth; the mist drifts upward to the rim, forming a halo into the guarding pines.

Leaving the stream, the trail climbs steeply through the trees, then down again under the rock of a dripping grotto, a huge cave of winds. Beyond rises a grassy hill set about with red cotoneaster berries and the yellows, blues, and whites of alpine flowers, and above the hill, like an ice castle set atop a nearer peak, soars Kanjiroba. In twilight, the path descends again to the upper Suli, where camp is made beside the roaring water. We shout to one another and cannot be heard; we move about like shades in the dark canyon.

OCTOBER 22

At dawn on this east side of the canyon, the ground is frozen, making a ringing sound under the stave, and ice slivers glimmer in the brooks that flow into the torrent. Moving upriver in near darkness, we find a bear's nest in a hackberry—our first sign of the Asiatic black bear, called the "moon bear." The bear sits in the branches and bends them toward him as he feeds on the cherry-like fruits; the broken branches make a platform which the bear may then use as a bed. In a corner of this nest, a blue rock dove—the wild ancestor of the street pigeon—has late-October young, as yet unfledged. We make a bear's breakfast of wild berries touched by frost.

A forest of dead pines, dank river caves, and hearths of travelers; two caves are fitted with wood shelves, as if these places had been hermit habitations. The shelves are marked with the swastika, that archaic symbol of creation that occurs everywhere around the world except south of the Sahara and in Australia. It was taken to North America by the ancestors of the American aborigines; in the Teutonic cultures, it was the emblem of Thor; it appeared at Troy and in ancient India, where it was adopted by Hindus, then Buddhists. The reversed swastika 卐 is also here, in sign of the B'on religion, still prevalent in old corners of these mountains; since it reverses time, it is thought to be destructive to the universe, and is often associated with black magic.

Faint musical cries ring through the trees above the water noise. In the dim light, I cannot find the caller, and walk on. He calls again, and now I see him, in a small woodland grove across the river; he is a settler, cutting the wild grass for winter hay. I am glad to see him, yet sad that he is here; even this wild region of the Suli Gad will disappear. Because we cannot speak over the river, we merely smile, and he puts his sickle down and lifts his hands, placing his palms together in simple greeting. I do the same; we bow, and turn away.

Near a fork where a tributary stream flows down from the B'on village at Pung-mo, the deep forest across the torrent has been parted by avalanche, and on this brushy slope, a dark shape jumps behind a boulder. The slope is in bright morning sun, but I glimpse the creature only for an instant. It is much too big for a red panda, too covert for a musk deer, too dark for wolf or leopard, and much quicker than bear. With binoculars, I stare for a long time at the mute boulder, feeling the presence of the unknown life behind it, but all is still, there is only the sun and morning mountainside, the pouring water.

All day I wonder about that quick dark shape that hid behind the rock, so wary of a slight movement on the far side of a rushing torrent; for I was alone, and could not have been heard, and was all but invisible in the forest shades. In the list of Himalayan mammals, black bear and leopard seem the best choices, but no bear that I ever saw moved like this animal, and no leopard is a uniform dark red or brown. Could it have been a melanistic leopard—a "black panther"? But I have seen leopards many times in Africa, where the species is the same; in rough terrain of brush and boulders, the leopard is much less apt to spring for cover than to crouch, flatten, and withdraw.

And so—though I shall assume it was a musk deer—it is hard to put away the thought of yeti. This forested ravine of the upper Suli Gad is comparable in altitude to the cloud forests of eastern Nepal that are thought to shelter "the man-thing of the snows"; so far as I know, no yeti have been reported from west of the Kali Gandaki, but in reference to a creature as rare and wary as the yeti is presumed to be, this may only mean that these northwestern mountains are far less populous, far less explored.

At 10,800 feet, the canyon opens out into high valleys. A herd of the black shaggy oxen known as yak are moving down across a hillside of cut barley, preceded by a cold thin tink of bells; in these mountains, a faint bell is often a first sign of human presence. The lead animals, carrying packs, are decked out in red collars and bright tassels, and soon a man and wife come down the path in full Tibetan dress, the man in blanket, belted cloak, and baggy pants tucked into red wool boots tied around the calf, the woman in striped apron and black cloths.

On a long slope, in buckwheat fields, is the settlement called Murwa, which takes its name from a kind of mountain millet. The Murwa folk are very clean by comparison to the people of Rohagaon, and their stone houses, yards, and fields are well ordered and well kept; they have red dogs and well-fed stock, and sell a few eggs and potatoes to Phu-Tsering. The sunny hillside is protected all around by snow peaks, and down the high wall to the west roars the great waterfall from Phoksumdo Lake, joining the Murwa stream to form the Suli. I am sorry we must march straight through this restful place in order to reach Phoksumdo Lake before the evening.

In a cold wind at the Murwa stream, we take off boots and pants and wade the current, which is strong and swift, over slick rocks. I hurry in the icy water, for my numb feet find no footing; suddenly I am plunging like a horse, on the brink of a frigid bath, or worse. Moving diagonally upstream, I make it safely after some bad moments and dry myself on a sunny rock, out of the wind.

From Murwa there is a steep climb through scrub juniper and deodar cedar to a ridge at 12,500 feet—the natural dam that holds Phoksumdo Lake among the snow peaks. I am some distance ahead of GS when a man on horseback, crossing the ridge, demands to know my destination. "Shey Gompa," I declare—the Crystal Monastery. "Shey!" he repeats doubtfully, looking behind him at the peaks to the northwest. He points toward the south and then at me. "Tarakot," I say, "Dhorpatan." Nodding, he repeats "Dhorpatan." Probably he is going there, and is glad to learn that we have got across Jang La; I neglect to warn him that his pony will not make it.

A boy and girl appear among the cedars. In her basket is a cask of goat cheese, and cheese wrapped in birch bark; she presents me with a bit, and I buy more, and out of the wind, on warm needles in the shelter of the evergreens, I eat it up, with half of a big raw radish from Rohagaon.

From the forest comes the sound of bells, and horse hooves dancing on the granite: a man in clean cloak and new wool boots canters up on a pony with silver trappings. This horseman, too, demands to know my destination, and he, too, frowns to learn that it is Shey. With a slashing movement of his hand across his throat, he indicates a depth of snow, then rides off in a jangle of bright bells.

Clouds loom on the mountains to the south; the cold wind nags me. Soon GS comes, having had the same report: he fears we may have trouble getting in. I nod, though what concerns me more is getting out. The snow already fallen at Kang La will not melt this late in the year, it can only deepen. To be trapped by blizzard on the far side of the Kang would be quite serious, since the food that remains cannot last more than two months.

Northward, the ridge opens out in a pine pasture at 12,000 feet where a herd of yaks, like so many black rocks, lies grouped in the cold sun. The yak has been domesticated from wild herds that still occur in remote parts of Tibet. The female yak is called the bri, and her bushy-tailed, short-faced calf looks like a huge toy. Among these yaks are some yak-cattle hybrids, known as *dzo*. On the shaggy coats, the long hairs shine, stirred by the wind; one chews slow cud. Manure smell and finch twitterings, blue sky and snow: facing the cold wind from the south, the great animals gaze down across the cliff to where the Bauli Gad, descending from Phoksumdo, explodes from its narrow chute into two, then three broad waterfalls that gather again at the Murwa stream below.

In the granite and evergreen beyond the yaks, a lake of turquoise glitters beneath the snow peaks of the Kanjirobas. I walk down slowly through the silent pines.

A geologist would say that Phoksumdo Tal, three miles long, a half-mile wide, and reputed to be near a half-mile in depth, was formed when an earthquake collapsed the mountain on this side of the high valley, blocking the river that comes down from the Kanjirobas at what is now the north end of the lake. But local tradition has a different explanation:

When B'on was the great religion of the Land of B'od, of which this region was once part, there was a village where this lake now lies. In the eighth century, the great Buddhist saint Padma Sambhava, the "Lotus-Born," came to Phoksumdo with the intent of vanquishing the mountain demons. To this end, he persecuted a B'on demoness who, fleeing his wrath, gave these villagers a priceless turquoise, making them promise not to reveal that she had passed this way. But Padma Sambhava caused the turquoise to be turned to dung, upon which the villagers, concluding that the demoness had tricked them, betrayed her whereabouts. In revenge, she wreaked upon them a disastrous flood that drowned the village beneath turquoise waters.[18]

Be that as it may, B'on has persisted in this region, and there is a B'on monastery near Ringo-mo, a village at the eastern end of the lake that cannot differ much from the eighth-century village that vanished in the deluge. From a distance, Ring-mo looks like a fortress in a tale, for the walls are built up like battlements by winter brushwood stacked on the flat roofs. Sky-blue and cloud-white prayer flags fly like banners in the windy light, and a falling sun, pierced by the peaks, casts heraldic rays.

From the pine forest comes a woodcutter in boots and homespun, uttering barbaric cries that go unanswered in the autumn air. I follow this moonstruck figure down the path toward two white entrance-stupas. The stupas, ringed and decorated in warm red, are fat and lopsided, like immense gingerbread houses, and it seems fitting that, nearby, a cave beneath a giant boulder is walled up with stones in which a small crooked wooden door has been inset. All about are red-gold shrubs—barberry, gooseberry, and rose—and a glistening of the last silver wisps of summer's caper blossoms. Beyond the stupas, protecting the walled town like a moat, is the Bauli torrent that falls down from Phoksumdo. A bridge with flags crosses the torrent where it narrows to enter its mile-long chute down around the west end of the ridge to the great falls, and just above this bridge, in the roaring waters, is a boulder that was somehow reached by a believer. OM MANI PADME HUM has been carved there in mid-torrent, as if to hurl this mantra down out of the Himalaya to the benighted millions on the Ganges Plain.

Across the bridge, a third entrance-stupa is built in an arch over the path up to the town. There are snowdrifts under the north walls, and three immense black yaks stand there immobile. Beyond are small patches of barley and buckwheat, and potato, which came to these mountains in the nineteenth century. A small boy leads a team of *dzo* through the potatoes, hauling a crude harrow with wood blade; other children ride the harrow handles to keep the blade sunk in the flinty soil. In their wake, an old man, kneeling, scavenges stray potatoes with a hand hoe, though barely fit to manage his own body. Seeing a stranger, he offers a broken yellow smile by way of apology for his old age.

On the village street stands a tall figure in a red cloak flung over a sheepskin vest that is black with grime; a lavender turban with tassels and once-colorful wool boots deck the extremities of this bandit, who hails me in a wolfish, leering way. Now pretty children run out, smiling, and a silent mastiff runs out, too, only to suffer a rude yank from its chain; its lean jowls curl in a canine smile of pain. Everyone in Ring-mo smiles, and keeping a sharp eye out, I smile, too.

The rough brown buildings have wood doors and arches, and filthy Mongol faces, snot-nosed, wild, laugh at the strangers from the crooked windows. Strange, heavy thumpings come from an immense stone mortar: two girls strike the grain in turn with wood pestles four feet long, keeping time with rhythmic soft sweet grunts, and two carpenters hew rude pine planks with crude adzes. Among the raffish folk of Ring-mo, dirt is worn like skin, and the children's faces are round crusts of sores and grime. Both sexes braid their long hair into pigtails and wear necklaces of beads and dark bits of turquoise, silver, and bone, as well as small amulet packets of old string around their necks. The dress here is essentially Tibetan—cloaks, aprons, belts, and red-striped woolen boots with yak-twine soles.

Through Jang-bu, we question everyone about Kang La and Shey Gompa, as the crowd gives off that heartening smell of uncultivated peoples the world over, an earthy but not sour smell of sweat and fire smoke and the oil of human leather. Goats, a few sheep, come and go. Both men and women roll sheep wool on hand spindles, saying that blizzards have closed Kang La for the winter. On the roofs, culled buckwheat stacked for winter fodder has a bronze shine in the dying sun, and against a sunset wall, out of the wind, an old woman with clean hair turns her old prayer wheel, humming, humming.

OCTOBER 23

The Tamangs will turn back at Ring-mo, for they are not equipped for the Kang Pass. A goat has been found, and some wood flagons of *chang,* to celebrate our weeks together, and they butcher this billy goat with glee. The Sherpas don't participate in the taking of its life, but they will be happy to help eat it.

In early afternoon, bearing away the goat's head and forequarters and five bellyfuls of *chang,* Pirim and his companions cross the torrent and go chattering uphill, past the cake-colored stupas, to vanish among the sunny pines; freed of their loads, they fairly dance. And though I smile to see the way they go, I feel a sinking of the spirit.

Tukten is our sole remaining porter, and he will be paid henceforth as a Sherpa, as he is much too valuable to lose. The decision to keep Tukten on was mine, as despite his ambiguous reputation I find him the most intelligent and helpful of our men; also, I feel that in some way he brings me luck. He will go with me in case I depart from Shey before GS, for Dawa and Gyaltsen speak no English whatsoever, and GS will need both Jang-bu and Phu-Tsering.

A wind out of the north is cold, but behind the high stone walls of the stock compound where the tents are pitched, the sun is warm. Despite all the reports of heavy snow, we have decided against using yaks, which can plow through new snow up to their bellies but are soon immobilized by ice and crusts. And so Jang-bu is organizing a new lot of porters, who are demanding twenty-five rupees a day. Already these noisy fellows lay the groundwork for malingering at the Kang Pass—"What will you pay us if we must turn back?" They say two days are needed to prepare food and patch their clothes, and one man has been all day in our compound, sewing hard gray wool from a spindle whorl (much like the one used by the Hopi) into his calf-high woolen boots, and meditating on our gear the while.

All but the porters have lost interest in us quickly, now that it's clear just how and where the money will be made. In costumes, attitudes, and degree of filth, these Ring-mos cannot have changed much from the eighth-century inhabitants who betrayed the demoness when her turquoise turned to dung. At this season, they live mostly on potatoes, ignoring the autumn bounty of wild fruit that is everywhere around the village. Down by the stream, I persuade two girls to try the gooseberries that grow there. The children are suspicious, tantalized, astonished; in their delight, they stare at each other, then begin to laugh.

While GS climbs the mountainside in search of bharal, I explore the stupas and the town. Even to my untutored eye, the ancient frescoes on the stupa walls, and the ceiling mandalas especially, seem intricate and well designed, for the culture of this region was formerly more vital than it is today. The dominant colors are red ochers, blues, and whites, but yellow and green are also used for certain Buddha aspects and manifestations. The confusion of Buddha figures is compounded here because B'on still prevails, despite the eighth-century inundation of the B'on villagers beneath Phoksumdo. At Ring-mo, Sakyamuni is called Shen-rap, and the faithful swing their prayer wheels left about and circumambulate prayer walls and stupas with left shoulder to the monument instead of right. The swastikas here in the main stupa are reversed, and the prayer stones bear such B'on inscriptions as OM MATRI MUYE SA LE DU ("In clarity unite"),[19] said to derive from the language of Sh'ang Sh'ung, the mysterious kingdom of western Tibet where, according to B'on-pos, the great B'on teachings usurped by the Buddhists first appeared.

"There is no word for Buddhism in Tibet. Tibetans are either *chos-pa* (followers of *chos*—the Dharma or Universal Law as revealed by Buddha) or *bon'pos* (followers of *bon*)."[20] Yet in practice, B'on has adapted itself so thoroughly to Buddhism, and vice versa, that in their superficial forms they are much the same.

At Ring-mo, OM MANI PADME HUM is carved on the river rock, and a blue Buddha manifestation on the frescoes represents the great scourge of B'on, Padma Sambhava; incidental decorations inside and outside the stupas are common symbols of Tibetan Buddhism, such as the conch-shell trumpet of victory, the intertwined snakes, the four-way yin-yang, and the four- and eight-petaled lotuses. B'on has degenerated into a regressive sect of Buddhism and is so regarded, here at least, by its own practitioners. As one of the townsmen says, a little sheepishly, "I am a Buddhist, but I walk around the prayer stones the wrong way."

The path to the B'on monastery crosses the torrent, traversing potato field and pasture to the evergreen forest by Phoksumdo Lake. Ring-mo is a quarter mile or more south of the lake, yet the inhabitants use its Tibetan name, Tsho-wa, or "Lakeside"—could this have been the name of the drowned village? Except for the monastery, there is no habitation near the water, and no boat has ever sailed its surface; its translucent blue-green color must reflect a white sand on the lake floor far below. There are no aquatic animals, and even algae find no place in this brilliant water rimmed around by stone. Truly it is a lake without impurities, like the dust-free mirror of Buddhist symbolism which, "although it offers an endless procession of pictures, is uniform and colorless, unchanging, yet not apart from the pictures it reveals."[21]

The sacred eyes on small stupas by the water's edge follow me along a path of lakeside birch. On the far side of this wood stand the monastery buildings, backed up against the cliffs on the lake's east wall. Seventeen years ago, there were two B'on lamas and twelve monks at Ring-mo, but now it is locked shut, all but abandoned. An ancient caretaker, plagued by goiter, makes wood water casks and prayer stones of poor quality; his old wife squats in a potato patch so small that she can hoe all corners of it from the center. There is a B'on lama up at Pung-mo—they point toward the west peak—but they have no idea when he will come. I go away disappointed. Two days north of Shey is the monastery of Samling, which is said to be the seat of B'on in these far mountains. But if we are to believe these people, our chance of reaching Shey is very small.

OCTOBER 24

A cold wind out of the north. I wash my head. To reduce the drain on our food supplies, Tukten and Gyaltsen leave today for Jumla, where they will obtain some rice and sugar and perhaps mail; if all goes well, they will join us at Shey about November 10.

Yesterday I wrote letters to send off with Tukten, and the writing depressed me, stirring up longings, and worries about the children, and bringing me down from the mountain high. The effort to find ordinary words for what I have seen in this extraordinary time seems to have dissipated a kind of power, and the loss of intensity is accompanied by loss of confidence and inner balance; my legs feel stiff and heavy, and I dread the narrow ledge around the west walls of Phoksumdo that we must follow for two miles or more tomorrow. This ledge is visible from Ring-mo, and even GS was taken aback by the first sight of it. "*That's* not something you'd want to do every day," he said. I also dread the snow in the high passes that might trap us in the treeless waste beyond. These fears just worsen matters, but there's no sense pretending they are not there. It is one thing to climb remote mountains if one has done it all one's life; it is quite another to begin in middle age. Not that forty-six is too old to start, but I doubt that I shall ever welcome ice faces and narrow ledges, treacherous log bridges across torrents, the threat of wind and blizzard; in high mountains, there is small room for mistake.

Why is death so much on my mind when I do not feel I am afraid of it?—the dying, yes, especially in cold (hence the oppression brought by this north wind down off the glaciers, and by the cold chop on the cold lake), but not the state itself. And yet I cling—to what? What am I to make of these waves of timidity, this hope of continuity, when at other moments I feel free as the bharal on those heights, ready for wolf and snow leopard alike? I must be careful, that is true, for I have young children with no mother, and much work to finish; but these aren't honest reasons, past a point. Between clinging and letting go, I feel a terrific struggle. This is a fine chance to let go, to "win my life by losing it," which means not recklessness but acceptance, not passivity but nonattachment.

If given the chance to turn back, I would not take it. Therefore the decision to go ahead is my own responsibility, to be accepted with a whole heart. Or so I write here, in faint hope that the words may give me courage.

I walk down around the ridge to where the torrent falls into the Suli. Beneath evergreens and silver birch, ripples flow along the pale gray rocks, and a wren and a brown dipper come and go where water is pouring into water. The dipper is kin to the North American water ouzel, and the tiny wren is the winter wren of home—the only species of that New World family that has made its way across into Eurasia.

Drowned boulders knock beneath the torrent, and a rock thuds at my back. Transfixed by the bright gaze of a lizard, I become calm. This stone on which the lizard lies was under the sea when lizards first came into being, and now the flood is wearing it away, to return it once again into the oceans.

OCTOBER 25

We must leave Ring-mo before word comes from Dunahi that we must not. But still these B'on-pos yell and shout about their loads until Jang-bu takes cord thongs from their boots, mixes them up, and lays one on every basket, giving each man the load on which his cord is laid. The B'on-pos accept this way of dispensing justice with much grumbling

Gloomy and restless, I set out ahead, and am some little way along the lake ledge when the rest catch up. Parts of the ledge have fallen away, and the gaps are bridged by flimsy scaffoldings of saplings. Certain sections are so narrow and precarious that more than once my legs refuse to move, and my heart beats so that I feel sick. One horrid stretch, lacking the smallest handhold in the wall, rounds a windy point of cliff that is one hundred feet or more above the rocks at lake edge, and this I navigate on hands and knees, arriving a lifetime later—but still in my old life, alas—at one of the few points in that whole first mile where one can lean far enough into the cliff to let another man squeeze by. Gasping for breath, I let the expedition pass.

For some time now, the chattering, laughing voices of the B'on-pos have been coming up behind. At that dangerous point of cliff, an extraordinary thing happens. Not yet in view, the nine fall silent in the sudden way that birds are stilled by the shadow of a hawk, or tree frogs cease their shrilling, leaving a ringing silence in the silence. Then, one by one, the nine figures round the point of rock in silhouette, unreal beneath big bulky loads that threaten each second to bump the cliff and nudge them over the precipice. On they come, staring straight ahead, as steadily and certainly as ants, yet seeming to glide with an easy, ethereal lightness, as if some sort of inner concentration was lifting them just off the surface of the ground. Bent far forward against the tump lines around their foreheads, fingers wide spread by way of balance, they touch the cliff face lightly to the left side, strike the north wind to the right. Light fingertips touch my upper leg, one, two, three, four, five, six, seven, eight, nine hands, but the intensity is such that they seem not to distinguish between cold rock face and warm blue jeans. Mute, unknowing, dull eyes glazed, the figures brush past one by one in their wool boots and sashed tunics, leaving behind in the clear air the smell of grease and fires. When the bad stretch is past, the hooting instantly resumes, perhaps at the point where they left off, as if all had awakened from a trance.

The Sherpas come, and Phu-Tsering smiles gold-toothed encouragement from under his red cap. GS appears, moving as steadily as the rest; I am glad that the cliff corner hid my ignominious advance on hands and knees. Squeezing by, GS remarks, "This is the first *really* interesting stretch of trail we've had so far." How easy it would be to push him over.

The second mile of the ledge path is pleasant, and I am able to enjoy the mythic view. Below lies the turquoise lake that has never known paddle or sail, and above, all around the sky, rise the snow mountains. A ravine that falls from a small glacier splits the rock face, opening out on a small beach of smooth pebbles. From here the trail climbs once again toward the ramparts at the northwest corner of Phoksumdo.

High above the lake, GS turns to wait; he points at something on the trail. Coming up, I stare at the droppings and mute prints for a long time. All around are rocky ledges, a thin cover of stunted juniper and rose. "It might be close by, watching us," murmurs GS, "and we'd never see it." He collects the leopard scat, and we go on. On the mountain corner, in hard gusts of wind, GS's altimeter reads 13,300 feet.

The path descends through snow and ice to silver birch woods by the shore. At its north end Phoksumdo has two arms, not visible from Ring-mo, each leading to a hidden river valley. The eastern arm, across the lake, is very beautiful and strange, rising steeply into the shadows of the mountains. This northwestern arm is the valley of the Phoksumdo River, and its delta of boggy tundra streams, of gravel bars and willow, is so like Alaska that both of us exclaim at the resemblance. A cold wind drives waves onto the dead gray beach, and when the sun sinks behind the Kanjiroba Massif at the head of the valley, it is still very early in the afternoon. Shey is two thousand feet higher than our present camp, and therefore considerably colder; with precious little fuel for lamps and no way to heat the tents, we can only hope that the western mountains there are low, and sunset later.

At dusk, the northern sky is lavender. The cold lake nags at the gray pebbles, and there is no sign of a bird.

From down the lake shore, where the Ring-mos have made camp, comes sound of singing. All day I have thought about the eerie trance state of these people as they passed me on the ledge, and wonder if this might be a primitive form of the Tantric discipline called *lung-gom*,[22] which permits the adept to glide along with uncanny swiftness and certainty, even at night. "The walker must neither speak, nor look from side to side. He must keep his eyes fixed on a single distant object and never allow his attention to be attracted by anything else. When the trance has been reached, though normal consciousness is for the greater part suppressed, it remains sufficiently alive to keep the man aware of the obstacles in his way, and mindful of his direction and goal."[23] *Lung-gom* is, literally, wind-concentration, with "wind" or "air" equivalent to the Sanskrit *prana,* the vital energy or breath that animates all matter: if matter is energy, then *lung-gom* may be simplistically regarded as a manifestation of mind over matter, of matter returning to energy (with a corresponding reduction of weight and gravity) so that it flows. The same yogic command of the physical body might account for the "invisibility" achieved by advanced yogins, who are said to still their being and its vibrations so completely that their corporeal aspect makes no impression on the mind or memory of others; and also for the recrystallizing of energy into other forms, as when Milarepa, to confound his enemies, resorted to his black Nyingma-pa

Tantra and transformed himself into a snow leopard at Lachi-Kang (Mount Everest). That holy men and sorcerers of Asia are capable of such feats has been attested to by astonished travelers since the time of Marco Polo; and very similar trance practice has been reported among native Americans and other traditional people.

In other days, plain levitation was described in Christian and Muslim faiths alike: thus, Saint Joseph of Cupertino, in times of ecstasy, was observed to fly into low trees, and on one occasion, according to a seventeenth-century witness, rose "from the middle of the church and flew like a bird onto the high altar, where he embraced the tabernacle."[24] Such unusual gifts, whether cultivated or not, may deflect the aspirant from his path to true mystical experience of God, and have never been highly regarded by great teachers;[25] one of the four cardinal sins in the monastic order of the Buddha—after unchastity, theft, and killing—was laying claim to miraculous powers. It is related that Sakyamuni once dismissed as of small consequence a feat of levitation on the part of a disciple, and cried out in pity for a yogin by the river who had wasted twenty years of his human existence in learning how to walk on water, when the ferryman might have taken him across for a small coin.

By firelight, we talk about the snow leopard. Not only is it rare, so says GS, but it is wary and elusive to a magical degree, and so well camouflaged in the places it chooses to lie that one can stare straight at it from yards away and fail to see it. Even those who know the mountains rarely take it by surprise: most sightings have been made by hunters lying still near a wild herd when a snow leopard happened to be stalking. (One explorer of Central Asia and Tibet encountered wolves, wild asses, argali or "Marco Polo sheep," orongo antelopes, wild camels, bears, and even the Turkestan tiger, but makes not a single mention of a snow leopard.)[26] In years of searching, GS has seen but two adults and one cub. He got his first look at *Panthera uncia* in the Chitral Gol of Pakistan, in 1970; this past spring, in the same region, after an entire month of baiting with live goats, he made the first films ever taken of this creature in the wild.

The snow leopard is usually found above 5000 feet and occurs as high as 18,000 feet. Though nowhere common, it has a wide range in the mountains of Central Asia, from the Hindu Kush in Afghanistan eastward along the Himalaya and across Tibet into southern China, and also northward in the mountains of the U.S.S.R. and of west China to the Sayan Range, on the Siberian border of Mongolia: the few captive specimens caught in the wild come mostly from the Tien Shan Mountains of the U.S.S.R., where trapping is limited and the animal is otherwise protected.

The typical snow leopard has pale frosty eyes and a coat of pale misty gray, with black rosettes that are clouded by the depth of the rich fur. An adult rarely weighs more than a hundred pounds or exceeds six feet in length, including the remarkable long tail, thick to the tip, used presumably for balance and for warmth, but it kills creatures three times its own size without much difficulty. It has enormous paws and a short-faced heraldic head, like a leopard of myth; it is bold and agile in the hunt, and capable of terrific leaps; and although its usual prey is the blue sheep, it occasionally takes livestock, including young yak of several hundred pounds. This means that man would be fair game as well, although no attack on a human being has ever been reported.

The snow leopard is the most mysterious of the great cats; of its social system, there is nothing known. Almost always it is seen alone; it may meet over a kill, as tigers do, or it may be unsociable and solitary, like the true leopard.

OCTOBER 26

Last night a bonfire was made from deadwood at the mouth of the Phoksumdo River, and for a long time I sat beside it, watching the stars rise from the mountains. The Ring-mos came, singing and laughing, from their own camp in the cave by the lake shore, and mimicked everything that was said by sahib or Sherpa. "Thak you!" "Ferry good!" "Ho! Dawa!" They are jolly and colorful, but there is aggressiveness in their good nature, and we cannot trust them. Yesterday morning, having stalled for two hours before departure to insure themselves three short days rather than two long ones on the trail, they stopped constantly to rest, and now this morning one man is complaining, and stirring up the others to protest their loads. Because Jang-bu seems indecisive with these people, GS shouts to the man to shut up or go home. Today this works, for we are only a few hours out of Ring-mo, but in the snows it may be a different matter altogether. These Red-faced Devils have us at their mercy, and all know it. Perhaps we should adopt the imperial methods of dealing with unruly Tibetans, as described at the turn of the century: "Throwing myself on him, I grabbed him by his pigtail and landed his face a number of blows straight from the shoulder. When I let him go he threw himself down crying and implored my pardon. Once and for all to disillusion the Tibetan on one or two points, I made him lick my shoes clean with his tongue . . . He tried to scamper away, but I caught him once more by his pigtail and kicked him down the front steps which he had dared to come up unasked."[27]

(This forthright Briton was constantly harassed by bandits in western Tibet—one reason, perhaps, why he called his book *In the Forbidden Land.* But Tibet was not always a "Forbidden Land"; it welcomed its rare visitors before the Gorkha invasions of the late seventeenth century and the several Chinese invasions since, including those of 1910 and 1950. Still, it has always been remote and inaccessible, more so than any land on earth; before the last Chinese invasion, the journey from Peking to Lhasa took eight months.)[28]

We left Kathmandu a month ago today: theoretically, we shall arrive at Shey tomorrow, almost two weeks later than expected. GS has been worried by the setbacks, but among the blue sheep on the mountains above Ring-mo there is still no sign of rut. The main effect of the repeated delays has been extra expense: over and over, the porters have been paid to sit and sleep. GS figured his budget rather closely—he is rigorous in his responsibility to the societies that sponsor him—and at Pokhara, the expedition was already so short of money, even with my own thrown in, that we could not afford an extra porter to carry more kerosene for the lamps, or more canned food to vary our diet, or even a single bottle of strong drink. The sausage, crackers, and coffee are all gone, and sugar, chocolate, tinned cheese, peanut butter, and sardines are nearly finished; we shall soon be down to a pallid regimen of bitter rice, coarse flour, lentils, onions, and a few potatoes, without butter. With short days, no heat, dwindling lamp fuel, and white food, life promises to be stringent at Shey Gompa, where much time will be spent in sleeping bags, in order to keep warm; writing notes in this wretched tent, I cannot even sit upright, but must hunch forward with a bent and aching neck.

Red leaves drift on the still lake; a B'on-po coughs. High above this campsite in the silver birches, on a meadow near the sky, blue sheep are grazing. The time of the sun in the high mountains depends upon the placement of the peaks, and this day the sun appears eighty minutes earlier than yesterday, at the head of the wild valley across the lake. Shortly we are under way, headed west up the Phoksumdo Khola to where the Kang stream comes down out of the north.

Small avalanches that resound on Kanjiroba must be falling with the snow melt on the south slopes of the mountain, for there is no snow dust, only that glittering white point on the blue sky. The sound of avalanche evokes the sound of the great waterfall below Phoksumdo, or hurricane, or surf in storm, a cavernous deep thunder like an echo of the roaring of creation.

This valley of warped birches and gaunt willows is gloomy even in bright sun, and the only birds are the numerous dead redstarts on the gravel bars—a whole migratory flight—that must have perished in the early October blizzards. To judge from the glum faces of our people, the dead songbirds and the ominous grumbles from the peaks might be warnings from the mountain demons who plague pilgrims in Tibetan myth. Perhaps tomorrow we shall reach our destination, but as GS says, it is sure to be the hardest day of all, even if our porters prove dependable. He intends to carry his own sleeping bag, and warns me to do the same. In fine weather," he says, "seventeen thousand feet isn't all that high, but weather can change quickly at that altitude, and it isn't a height to fool around with: winds can come up very suddenly that will drop your chilling point by fifteen or twenty degrees. So I like to keep my bag along, in case of emergency or injury." GS, too, appears subdued. Though we don't talk about it, we are both aware that injury or sickness would be serious, and more so every day. When the round trip is considered, Pokhara is now two months away, and the nearest wireless at Dunahi, even if it worked, might or might not locate a doctor who might or might not be able and willing to abandon his practice and make a long trek in over high mountains on behalf of strangers. In short, there is no reason to expect that help would ever come to us over these trails. "One can live with a compound fracture," GS says, "it can always be broken and reset. But a ruptured appendix—" He does not bother to finish.

There is no trail up this gray valley, only dim paths that lose themselves in bogs and willow flats and gravel streams. Several hours pass before we come to the rock outwash of a chasm in the northern walls where the torrent comes down from the ice fields of Kang La. Even at midday the ravine is dark, and so steep and narrow that on the ascent under hanging rocks the torrent must be crossed over and over. Each time we strip off boots and pants, the Ring-mos cheer in simple-hearted hope that the strangers will crack their skulls on the slick rocks or fall into the frigid water. We climb on, numb-legged, without incident. Higher, where the ravine widens, a snow slide comes down from the east, and just above, in a wood of stunted birch, near tree line, the porters dump their loads and quit; farther up, they say, it will be too cold to camp. GS is nowhere to be seen (he told me later that he sat near the trail and watched us pass—he just needed to get away from human company) and since Jang-bu seems so leery of these people, I step in angrily, shouting that for two days now they have got away with a half-day's work, that there is no hope of crossing the high pass to Shey unless we gain more altitude today and get started earlier tomorrow. I am astonished when they heft their loads and go on for another hour.

At a bend in the high canyon where the last shrubs disappear, and the snow deepens, three birch saplings with rocks laid on to steady them served the last traveler as a bridge, for the torrent here is deep and swift, too swift to ford. Spray has built thick crusts of ice on the flimsy saplings, and I cross over without shame on hands and knees. Then our men come, traversing the ice bridge upright with the help of extended arms. But Dawa in his clumpy boots disdains all aid, swaying about on the treacherous sticks as he hacks ice off with the hoe that must serve us as an ice ax at the pass. I am cold and wet, and the foolish fellow is carrying my dry clothes and sleeping bag; at last, he is across.

Above the bridge, we make rough camp at a cave beneath an overhang, near 14,000 feet. To be alone, I walk a little way up-river and, in near-darkness, watch gray finches forage in gray snow. This evening I feel much better—why? I disliked the gray Phoksumdo Khola and hate this black ravine; thick clouds are moving north, with threat of snow, and already the porters are pointing toward the pass, shaking their heads. Yet I feel calm, and ready to accept whatever comes, and therefore happy. The turn in my mood occurred this morning, when the brave Dawa, attempting to catch Jang-bu's pack, hurled across a stream, dropped it ineptly into the water. Wonderfully, Jang-bu laughed aloud, as did Dawa and Phu-Tsering, although it meant wet clothes and a wet sleeping bag for the head Sherpa. That happy-go-lucky spirit, that acceptance which is not fatalism but a deep trust in life, made me ashamed.

OCTOBER 27

In the stone fall of this canyon, my tent is pitched at a sharp angle, with bedroll pinched among sharp rocks. Still, I sleep well and awake happy, and enjoy a breakfast of hot tea and *tsampa*. Then we set off from the Cave Camp in the first light, before the B'on-pos can come up bitching from the birch wood where they spent the night; as long as they remain unpaid, they are bound to follow. GS and I are in high spirits, feeling confident that today we will reach Shey at last.

GS says that yesterday he, too, had felt irritable and morose. "These damned Ring-mo porters are even worse than the Dirty Kamis. And the Sherpas were getting to me, too, wasting and breaking everything: you lend them something, and in one day it looks like they'd used it for a month. Yesterday I was just sick of *people,* that's all." He gazes about him at the still, clear morning, at the canyon side that lies under heavy snow. "This is what it's all about," he says, shouldering his rucksack. "To be able to go up into a valley, and not come on a pile of human dung."

Soon he is gone around a corner of the canyon. In the ringing emptiness I pause to hear the hiss of the swift torrent under ice, then turn in a slow circle, absorbing all this mighty weight of rock and snow and sky. A monumental glacier fills the southern blue like a frozen waterfall, but the sun flowing down that wall of ice has not yet touched the canyon rim over my head. I climb on through gray daybreak worlds toward the light.

Rockfalls half-covered with snow, interspersed with ice and scree, make the ascent arduous. Moving quickly to keep away

the cold, I meet the sun where the canyon opens out, eighteen
hundred feet above the cave. GS's map seems to indicate the
steep climb from this approximate point straight up the valley-
side to the north, but maps of the region are more imaginative
than precise. Seeking Shey Gompa in May of 1956, a scholar of
Tibetan Buddhism (whose fine book[29] enables me to speak
about the iconography of this region with an authority that is
not mine) made camp farther up, at the head of this long
canyon, and he makes no mention of returning to a point
downstream before climbing toward Kang La. Since scholars
are less apt to be mistaken in small matters than in large ones,
it seemed to me that the ascent to the pass would begin at the
head of the valley, a mile farther.

But GS, certain he is right, cuts off toward the north. I wait
here in the sun awhile, to see which way the Ring-mos go, for
two of them have been to Shey in milder seasons. Soon they
appear—the cold in the dark canyon must account for their
brisk pace—and stop at the first sunlight; when they start
again, they move on up toward the head of the canyon. GS has
vanished over a ridge, and there is no answer to my calls in the
empty valley: either he will proceed along the ridge and join the
trail higher up, or he will descend again into this valley and follow our fresh tracks in the snow. There is sheep sign here, and
perhaps he has come upon a band of *na*.

At the canyon's head, a faint path becomes visible, following
a steep series of frozen waterfalls to a point where stream and
path are buried under drifts. The porters have been resting
every little while since emerging from the cold of the lower
canyon, and now they quit again on a narrow ridge, kept clear
of snow by wind. Breaking trail for them, I keep on climbing,
but continually plunge through the crust, over my knees; finally, I cut across to the frozen falls, continuing upward to the
snowfields by way of the half-exposed stream boulders, which
finally vanish underneath the snow.

These snowfields lie high up under the peaks, and in this im-
mensity of silence, they are awesome. No one has followed me,
nor is there sign of GS on the ridges all around. In hopes that
the Sherpas can get the porters going, I try to find a stretch of

snow that will hold my weight, but after ten yards in any direction, in the thick snow and thin air, I am exhausted. The one chance is a straight climb to the western ridge, where the snow appears to be thinned away by wind.

Eventually two B'on-pos without loads come up to have a look; for some reason, the Sherpas stay behind. Having no interpreter, I tease them in pantomime, and get them laughing, and they agree to bring the loads to this plateau. By that time, GS may have turned up, and Jang-bu, and some sort of decision can be made.

But it is early afternoon when the porters' heads appear above the icefalls, and it is plain that the expedition is in trouble; the loads are cast down in a sullen way, and even the three Sherpas look unhappy. I point out the high ridge to the west that looks less locked in snow: Kang La is no more than a two-hour climb, we have only to take turns breaking trail. . . . The Ring-mos shake their heads. These snowfields are impassable, and anyway, it is too late in the day and in the year to go to Shey, and much too high, too cold, to make camp here. Nor are the Sherpas any help. When I persist in my arguments, wondering where in hell GS could be, Jang-bu and Phu-Tsering take me aside and express discouragement about proceeding farther. The Ring-mos have persuaded them that even if Kang La is reached, the north face of the pass is perilously steep and icy: why, last year a man lost his life there! Jang-bu is also worried about his friend Gyaltsen—how would he and Tukten ever find us, since the wind is sure to cover any tracks? It is best that we return to Ring-mo.

Having tried the snow with my minimal load, I cannot blame the porters for wishing to give up. And we have seen blue sheep and sign of snow leopard near Phoksumdo Lake, which is not only strange and beautiful but accessible to the outside world in event of trouble; to cross Kang La only to have the winter snows close the pass behind us is what I fear most. On the other hand, we have come too far to quit—no more than a mile from the Kang Pass, perhaps one day away from Shey—and GS would not consider a retreat even if I abandon him, which I won't do.

To the east and south, dark clouds are drifting on the mountains, and wisps of snow begin to fall. I am worried about GS,
and the Sherpas, though I try to reassure them, are more worried still. Even if the Ring-mos were willing, we cannot go farther, in case GS has had an accident. Perhaps he is waiting for
help in the pit of some crevasse, with bitter night coming on: I
remember with relief that he has his sleeping bag.

The Ring-mos mutter: they wish to leave these cold white
wastes and take shelter in the canyon while there is still light.
With binoculars, I scan the ridges a last time, then give the order to stack the loads against a drift, where a bare place has
been spun by wind on the black scree; the whole lot is covered
with tarpaulin. We shall start from this place early tomorrow, I
announce, getting no response whatever. Dawa and Phu-Tsering
are sent down with a minimum of gear and food to the Cave
Camp, where there is firewood: Jang-bu and I will backtrack,
in the hope of finding our companion before dark.

To comfort Jang-bu, I say that in all likelihood we shall meet
GS on the way down, and we have scarcely started out when he
comes in view across the icy falls. Even from afar it's plain that
he is not happy to see us here on this side of the pass, and upon
his arrival, he insists that his map must be right and these local
people wrong, even though he has not found Kang La. "It
looks like this day has really been bollixed up," says he accus-
ingly, annoyed by the suggestion that his own disappearance, if
nothing else, has prevented us from going farther—though not,
I think, quite so annoyed as he might have been had he been
left lying broken-legged in the ice as darkness fell, while his expedition proceeded on to Shey. I do not point out that both yesterday and today he was elsewhere when the porters quit; that
but for me, we wouldn't have reached the point we did on either day. Instead, I say shortly that the porters won't go farther,
that even our Sherpas advise us to be content with the blue
sheep and snow leopard above Ring-mo. . . . No, he says. The
animals at Ring-mo are wild and scattered due to harassment
by the likes of these scrofulous porters—we will go to Shey.

I grin at Jang-bu, who smiles sadly. Knowing that I am worn
out from my trail-breaking, he has given his own pack to an

unloaded porter and kindly offers to take mine. To mollify GS a little, I say, "No, better take George's." And GS accepts this offer without thanks to either Jang-bu or myself and stalks off down the mountain without a word. Jang-bu hangs back long enough to say, "If this snow keeps up, we shall never reach Shey Gompa." (He actually says something like "More snow, never go Shey," for Sherpa English is more fluent than grammatical.) And I answer that, as the head Sherpa, he must feel free to express his opinion to GS. Whether he ever did or not, I do not know.

I go slowly down the mountain, falling well behind the rest, in no hurry to get back to that dark camp. Despite the hard day that has ended in defeat, despite the loss of three thousand feet of altitude that will have to be so painfully regained, despite the gloomy canyon and uncertain weather and ill humor of my friend, and the very doubtful prospects for tomorrow, I feel at peace among these looming rocks, the cloud swirl and wind-whirled snow, as if the earth had opened up to take me in.

OCTOBER 28

A light snow fell throughout the evening, but this morning it is clear. The Ring-mos demanded a raise in pay before they would try again, and not receiving it, have quit. I agree with GS that they are robbers, but since the total increased expense, on the Asian wage scale, comes to about twenty-five dollars, our decision seems to me a false economy. However, he feels—and very likely he is right—that the Ring-mos are sure to quit short of the pass in any case, leaving us that much poorer and no wiser.

GS left Cave Camp in the early hours, in the hope that the snow crust will support men's weight before it is softened by the sun; he has with him two Ring-mos who agreed to guide but not to carry, and he is also taking Jang-bu, our best interpreter, and Phu-Tsering, our most experienced mountaineer. Traveling light, they will try to reach Shey, where, hopefully, new porters can be recruited. Meanwhile, Dawa will carry a load of firewood up to the snowfields depot, in case GS's party cannot cross Kang La and gets caught by snow or darkness on its return. I shall remain to guard the camp against light-fingered porters, one of whom has already made off with my trusty stave.

Now it is noon, and Dawa has trudged away up the dark canyon. I will enjoy a day here by myself, although Cave Camp is the most inhospitable of any of the camps made since Pokhara. This deep bend in the ravine is stony and narrow and very cold; except for a half hour in the first part of the morning, when the sun crossed like an omen between peaks, the camp has remained in profound shadow. At these altitudes, in the Himalayan autumn, the difference between sun and shade is striking: the stream by my tent is clogged by ice, whereas lizards lie sunning on the rock slope above camp where I climb up to get warm and write these notes.

In early afternoon the sun touches my tent and is quickly gone; a cold wind off Kanjiroba scours the canyon. It is too chilly to sit still in one place, and I go down the ravine a little distance to a point where the high glacier and great icefalls can be seen. The wind blows snow from pristine points that glisten in the light, and there are magic colors in the clouds that sail across the peaks on high blue journeys.

Once again, I am struck by the yin-yang of these rivers—the one slope white, right down to the water, and the other dark, yet with a snow patch on the dark side and a dark rock on the white, each side containing the seed of its own opposite. The balance of cosmic principles, positive (yang) and negative (yin), as taught in the ancient "Book of Changes" (the I Ching), seems to foretell the electron theory of energy as matter, and is also a wonderful emblem of the flow, the interpenetration of all existence, for which the usual Tantric symbol is the *yab-yum* of sexual union. In Tantra, the pessimistic fear of desire and pleasure that characterized early Buddhism was seen as but another form of bondage, and emphasis was placed on being-in-life without suppression of life forces but also without clinging or craving. Tantra concerned itself with the totality of existence, the apprehension of the whole universe within man's being. All thoughts and acts, including the sex energies, were channeled into spiritual growth, with the transcendence of all opposites the goal; in the communion of sex, wine, and feasting, the illusion of separate identity might be lost, so long as a detached perspective was retained. All things and acts were equal, interwoven, from the "lowliest" physical functions to the "highest" spiritual yearning, and even consumption of dead human flesh and filth was recommended as an ultimate embrace of all existence. Thus, Tantra might be interpreted[30] as the practice of mankind's earliest religious intuition: that body, mind, and nature are all one. But decadence weakened all the Tantric sects, especially the Old Sect, or Nyingma, and in the sixteenth century a reformation was begun by the new Gelug-pa sect led by the Dalai Lamas. In this same period, in India (where Buddhism had long since been eradicated by the Muslims), the Mogul Akbar had the Hindu Tantrists tied to elephants and torn asunder.

On my return, Dawa, Phu-Tsering, and the two Ring-mos are squatting on their heels at the cave fire. Phu-Tsering says that we are to strike camp tomorrow. The brown faces stare at me through firesmoke as I cheer and clap my hands like a small boy. But a note from GS, who has gone on to Shey with Jang-bu, dampens my outburst.

1200 hrs Top of Pass

Peter:

The route yesterday was obvious—sorry I was not there. Straight up the ridge you talked about and in two hours you're at the pass.

Move all gear to Camp 2. Establish Camp 3 on pass. Two trips a day can easily be made.

With your trusty knife cut some thin 2-3' long willow wands and mark the trail every few hundred feet, in case it drifts over.

Pay porters 80R's each.

GBS

I go out among the river rocks with Dawa's inlaid bronze-and-silver *kukri* and slash crossly at the stunted springs of willow. Why does GS want to establish a "Camp 3" on a windy snow pass near 18,000 feet when we must keep returning anyway to "Camp 2" (I presume he means the snowfields depot), a much more sheltered site a thousand feet below? For twenty-five dollars' worth of porterage, I fume, we could have been across this pass with its wind, cold, and deep snow. True, my attitude is not improved by the note's peremptory tone, nor by its seeming suggestion that if GS had been there, the porters would have gone on to Shey yesterday afternoon.

Then I relax; surely he does not mean this note the way I take it. What seems abrasive in GS's behavior is often merely abrupt, as when he flings something that he wishes me to look at through my tent flap; once I flung something right back out again, as a hint that I didn't care much for these manners. But as I learn more about this man, I see that such acts are not bad manners but the intense respect of a private soul for the privacy of others; for all he knew, I was taking notes, or meditating, and might not welcome an exchange of any kind. On a hard journey, with no respite from each other, such consideration (extended also to the Sherpas) is far more valuable than mere "good manners," which sometimes hide a mean spirit beneath, and may evaporate when things get rough.

In the lowlands, GS was a formal man who could not quite communicate his feeling; in the freedom of the snow mountain he is opening out in true, warm colors. On two occasions, he has managed to say how glad he is of my company on this trip, and he astonished me the other day in Ring-mo when he spoke of an impulse to "cuddle" a child (the child being snot-nosed and filthy, the impulse was stifled). And so, for all his thorns, a gentleness shines through. The Sherpas see it; they are fond of him and respect him very much. Phu-Tsering, hunkered on his heels, is often to be seen humming contentedly at "Chorch's" knee.

I wax my boots, I wash my socks, I listen to Phu-Tsering hum as he rolls out his chapatis on a small round piece of wood. With the Sherpas, I have supper in the cave, huddled close to the small fire, which bends low in the night winds of the ravine. Phu-Tsering tells me that this past September, while he and four or five other villagers were digging potatoes at Khumbu, in eastern Nepal, a small yeti appeared, the size of a "big sheep," moving along a hillside more or less on all fours, as if foraging; when it fled, Phu-Tsering says, it rose on its hind legs and moved much faster. It has a distinct pointed head, and was "between black and red" in color. I thought of the unknown creature I had seen in the upper Suli Gad, which had looked darker than the reddish color usually attributed to the yeti: "Between black and red" was about right, and well describes many primate creatures, which often have black hair in early life and tend toward reddish as they age. Perhaps Phu-Tsering is untruthful or deluded, or is concocting something that the sahib might wish to hear. It is also possible that what he says is true.

Phu-Tsering's awestruck face, so like a child's, reminds me of GS's story of the time in eastern Nepal when our cook received a letter saying that his wife had left him for another man. Weeping, Phu-Tsering had got to his feet and read the letter aloud to all the Sherpa villagers where they were camped, and the people had all stood there and wept with him. As GS commented, "A Westerner would have slunk off and kicked stones; you have to admire the Sherpas for being so open about everything"—so open, so without defense, therefore so free, true Bodhisattvas, accepting like the variable airs the large and small events of every day.

OCTOBER 29

With a full pack, I leave at dawn, and make good time up to the sun, at 15,500 feet. The trek is fun, for knowing the way I can enjoy details. On bare places in the ice-fretted snow, rubbery red succulents grow among the stones, and many stones hold fossils from the epochs when these earth summits lay beneath the sea.

In the snow mountains—is it altitude?—I feel open, clear, and childlike once again. I am bathed by feelings, and unexpectedly I find myself near tears, brought on this time by the memory of an early-morning phone call from the hospital, in the last week of D's life. For days, D had been in what the doctors thought was her last coma, yet a nurse's voice said that my wife wished to speak with me: she had to assure me that there was no mistake. Then I heard this very weak clear voice out of D's childhood, calling as if I were far away across a meadow, "Peter? Peter? Come right away! I'm very very sick!" She must have sensed that she was close to death, and the bewilderment in her voice broke my heart. I ran there through the winter streets, past pinched city faces glaring in suspicion, steam rising from beneath the street in frozen wisps, blowing away.

Now, halfway around the world, as tears freeze at the corners of my eyes, I hear strange sounds, a yelping like a lonely mountain fox, and a moment later burst out laughing, thinking how D herself would laugh at an idea so delicious as wailing with lost love in the snow mountains. The tears and laughter come and go, and afterward I feel soft, strung out, and relieved magically of the altitude headache with which the day had started.

At the snowfields depot there is nothing but snow and silence, wind and blue. I rest in the warm sun, enveloped in the soft shroud of white emptiness; my presence in such emptiness seems *noticed,* although no one is here.

When Phu-Tsering comes, we pitch two tents in the gravel gully between drifts; the loads lie in a mist of wind-blown snow. My missing stave is here, stuck in a snowbank by the B'on-po who made off with it when he passed my tent at the start of yesterday's climb. Now Dawa arrives, it is just past noon, and when we finish these chapatis, we shall carry three loads to the pass, descending again to this camp for the night. Despite his bitter experience in the Dhaulagiris, Dawa wears a rag over his eyes only because I forbade him to leave camp without it. Earlier this year, he worked at the base camp of an American expedition to Annapurna Four: he has had no experience as a mountaineer, and not much, it appears, as a grown man.

It is windless and hot, and the knee-deep snow has softened in the sun, and our boots break through the steps made by GS's party while the snow was hard yesterday morning. I am toting a burlap sack of lentils in a broken basket, and can testify that the porters would have quit within the first one hundred yards in the unlikely event that GS had charmed them into going on. The thin straps bite at my shoulders, the broken wicker stabs holes in my parka, and the basket itself on its crude harness rolls heavily from side to side, throwing me off-balance: I pant so in the thin air that I feel sick. I keep my gaze fixed on the misted footprints that weave back and forth up the steep slope, so as not to be disheartened by the distance still to go; the sun is shimmering in waves off the bright snow.

With no landmarks, only this hallucinating whiteness blurred by the salt sweat in my vision, the way to the pass mounts in crazy spirals to a white crescent on the blue. From somewhere comes the rumble of an avalanche. Here I am at 17,000 feet, in desperate need of air; instead, I am floundering through soft snow beneath sixty pounds of lentils. Every few feet, I come to a gasping halt, lungs bursting. The stress brings an upsurge of yesterday's rage; I curse the thrift that has brought us, so to speak, to this pretty pass. Today we shall have carried loads from Cave Camp to the Kang, four thousand feet up through ice and heavy snow; two more loads apiece must come up from the Snowfields Camp tomorrow. Why aren't GS and Jang-bu back today to help? Why are we setting our willow sticks for Tukten and Gyaltsen, when it is plain that the absent Sherpas will never get this far without a guide? If GS had packed a sack of lentils more than a thousand feet up a steep slope, knee-deep in this blazing slush, he would send no more damned messages about two easy trips a day.

Then I come to my senses, as if hearing a distant bell: all this raging is absurd. I know this man, and if he has stayed in Shey (the alternative explanation for his absence—accident—is unthinkable) he has good reason. My anger is wasting energy I badly need, and realizing this, it is easy to put it aside.

As the slopes steepen, I am almost on all fours, knuckles brushing the snow, and this simian stance shifts the weight forward, saving my lacerated shoulders. Three thoughts carry me ahead; the prospect of the northward view over Dolpo to Tibet; the prospect of a free descent across these brilliant snowfields to hot tea and biscuits; and the perception—at this altitude, extremely moving—that these two hands I see before me in the sun, bracing the basket straps, hands square and brown and wrinkled with the scars of life, are no different from the old hands of my father. Simultaneously, I am myself, the child I was, the old man I will be.

Three hours of brute labor are required to reach the pass, where a very cold wind from the north makes us lie flat out on our bellies. What the Kang turns out to be is the only point on a narrow spine between two crags where a descent might be attempted into the great snow bowl beyond. Even here, the drop in the first hundred feet is too precipitous for creatures without hands; a slip would mean a roll and tumble of a good half-mile.

At 17,800 feet, Kang La is much higher than any peak in the United States outside Alaska, yet in three directions rise mountains of greater altitude, for excepting Tibet, Nepal is the highest country in the world. The horizon north across the mountains, in deep purple shadow, is the Land of B'od. These ravines on the north side of the Kang are deep in twilight; one of them must lead down to Shey Gompa.

Confronted with this emptiness, it is not hard to imagine that somewhere down among those peaks—like that green place under the Jang Pass in the Saure ravine—the center of the world, Shambala, might exist. Tradition says that the venerable Lao-tzu, having propounded the Tao to the Keeper of the Pass, vanished with his ox into such emptiness; so did Bodhidharma, the First Patriarch, who carried the Dharma from India to China. But what I see in this first impression is a chaos of bright spires, utterly lifeless, without smoke or track or hut or passing bird.

To the south, under the Kanjirobas, the point of brown color that is camp lies in full sun. I retreat down the snow slopes, starting to run, as the oppression of that northern prospect lifts away. The glaciers glow in sunset light, as the ice face of Kanjiroba comes in view. In the last of a flying, swift descent I leap and bound.

At sundown, a black eagle crosses between peaks; then bitter cold descends from the swift fierce stars. With no fuel to spare, we turn in quickly, to wait out the night.

OCTOBER 30

At daybreak, when I peek out at the still universe, ice fills my nostrils; I crouch back in my sleeping bag, cover my head. If GS and Jang-bu do not come today, there are hard decisions to be made. Since our path of retreat is a descent down icy boulders, this is no place to be caught in a storm, and, anyway, we cannot stay, as fuel is almost gone. The spell of silence on this place is warning that no man belongs here.

At dawn, the camp is visited by ravens. Then a cold sun rises to the rim of the white world, bringing light wind.

This morning we shall carry three more loads up to Kang La, and then three more. That will make nine; there are fourteen altogether. To avoid the bitter cold, we wait until the sun touches the slopes, then climb hard to take advantage of the snow crust, reaching the pass in an hour and a half. In the snowbound valleys to the north, still in night shadow, there is no sign of our companions, no sign of any life at all.

The Sherpas start down immediately; they, too, seem oppressed by so much emptiness. Left alone, I am overtaken by that northern void—no wind, no cloud, no track, no bird, only the crystal crescents between peaks, the ringing monuments of rock that, freed from the talons of ice and snow, thrust an implacable *being* into the blue. In the early light, the rock shadows on the snow are sharp; in the tension between light and dark is the power of the universe. This stillness to which all returns, this is reality, and soul and sanity have no more meaning here than a gust of snow; such transience and insignificance are exalting, terrifying, all at once, like the sudden discovery, in meditation, of one's own transparence. Snow mountains, more than sea or sky, serve as a mirror to one's own true being, utterly still, utterly clear, a void, an Emptiness without life or sound that carries in Itself all life, all sound. Yet as long as I remain an "I" who is conscious of the void and stands apart from it, there will remain a snow mist on the mirror.

A silhouette crosses the white wastes below, a black coil dangling from its hand. It is Dawa Sherpa carrying tump line and headband, yet in this light, a something moves that is much more than Dawa. The sun is roaring, it fills to bursting each crystal of snow. I flush with feeling, moved beyond my comprehension, and once again, the warm tears freeze upon my face. These rocks and mountains, all this matter, the snow itself, the air—the earth is ringing. All is moving, full of power, full of light.

Eager to make my second climb while the snow is firm, I travel quickly. This time I have a sack of onions in my basket—how *onion* is this onion reek in the stiff snowbound air!—and the onions seem much heavier than, in their onion nature, they have any right to be. Later I find that the sly Phu-Tsering has cached two gallons of cooking oil beneath the onions; he giggles gleefully behind me.

Already the snow has lost its edge, and I break through here and there on the ascent: this trip takes a good half hour longer than the first, although an hour less than yesterday. The pass is reached a short time after noon, and Phu-Tsering, first to gaze down into the snow bowl, turns back toward me, his grin of pleasure turning to a frown. "There is Chorch." He signs. "No porters." Wearily, Dawa and I sit back against bare scree to shed our harness. Far below, Chorch in his bright-blue parka is plodding upward; lower still, Jang-bu rests on a white rock. In full sun, the mountains to the north look less forbidding, but it is clear from the way GS is moving that the route to Shey lies under heavy snow. We gaze down, stupefied, as the hot sweat on our backs turns cold.

Today the thin air and heavy load bother me less than the shining snow, which after two days had cooked my head, eyes, brains, and all—in my addlement, I reel around on the high rim of the world. Phu-Tsering and Dawa are also burned and dizzy—Dawa, despite repeated warnings, is still careless about his eye rag—and as we are hungry after our two climbs, we descend to the Snowfields Camp again without waiting for GS and Jang-bu. Though none of us say so, we are all disheartened; this job of moving fourteen loads from Snowfields Camp up over Kang La and down to Shey will have to be finished by just five of us.

In early afternoon, our friends reach camp with their bad tidings: at Shey, there are no porters and no food. The early October storms that held us up in Dhorpatan have been blizzards in these peaks, just as we feared, and the unseasonal snow had caused the people to lock up the Crystal Monastery, abandon Shey, and cross the eastern mountains to Saldang, leaving two women to guard the remnant stores.

GS brings up of his own accord what he refers to as his "curt note" of two days before, explaining that it was so cold and windy at the Kang Pass that he could not write more than bare essentials; he had ordered me to pay off the two Ring-mos because his frozen fingers could not count out money, which might have blown away into Tibet. I admit to him that I didn't care much for the note and offer to say why, but he anticipates my objections, saying that the note meant no criticism of my actions but only recognition that my instincts about the route had been correct, whereas he had held us up by "waiting too long on the wrong mountain." That he wrote it as he did, and that I took it so amiss, he ascribes to the pressure of the days preceding and also the high-altitude irritability that has ruined so many mountain expeditions. Everything he says rings true to me, and I feel foolish: I recall my first visit to high altitudes, in the Andes, when I was so volatile that any sudden noise inspired fury. Quickly and happily we drop the entire business. We are glad to see each other—and a good thing, too, since in this camp we shall have to share this one small tent—and full of excitement about Shey, for there is good news, too: the blue sheep there are plentiful and tame, and the rut we have come so far to see has scarcely started.

Early tomorrow, if fair weather holds, we shall pack the last five loads up to Kang La, then slide all fourteen down the northern face to a strange black tarn in the bottom of the snow bowl. From there the loads will be moved in relays, three hours downriver to Shey. At Snowfields Camp we shall leave a cairn with food for Tukten and Gyaltsen, and instructions to ignore advice from the denizens of Ring-mo and to push on to Shey; being lightly loaded, they might reach Shey from Snowfields Camp in a half day. If the pass is closed by blizzard, they should try to reach us by a long alternate route, from Murwa by way of Saldang; there are three high passes on that route, say the Shey women, but none of them is so formidable as this one. All else failing, they are to await us at Dunahi.

In a dream I am walking joyfully up the mountain. Something breaks and falls away, and all is light. Nothing has changed, yet all is amazing, luminescent, free. Released at last, I rise into the sky. . . . This dream comes often. Sometimes I run, then lift up like a kite, high above earth, and always I sail transcendent for a time before awaking. I *choose* to awake, for fear of falling, yet such dreams tell me that I am a part of things, if only I would let go, and keep on going. "Do not be heavy," Soen Roshi says. "Be light, light, light—full of light!"

In recent dreams, I have twice seen light so brilliant, so intense, that it "woke me up," but the light did not continue into wakefulness. Which was more real, the waking or the dream? The last Japanese character written in this life by Soen Roshi's venerable teacher, and the last word spoken, was the word for "dream."

OCTOBER 31

Today is the last day of October.

I am tired, and the early climb takes a half hour longer than the climb at the same hour yesterday. At the rim we rest briefly before starting the descent into the blue shadows of the bowl. I plant my stave, then kick a foothold into the snow wall, then move the stick down, kick another step—"Never move more than one thing at a time!" GS calls—until, reaching a point just above a chute of sharp jutting shale, I level a platform for both feet and prepare to receive the loads. Out of the sun, the air is very cold. GS lowers my backpack, then a sack of lentils, then our supply of flour in a big neoprene bag. I work the lentils and the flour over to my right, to a point where they will clear the stretch of shale, then let them fall. The lentils in their squashy sack soon come to rest where the wall becomes steep slope, a hundred yards below, but the slick neoprene bag sails so far down into the bowl, and at such speed, that the Sherpas, whose heads have now appeared over the rim, give it a cheer.

With my backpack, punching with my stick, I descend carefully to the lentils, then keep on going, sliding the rough sack alongside. Even here, the bowl side is so steep that facing the slope on all fours, I am almost upright, and I must kick the steps into the hard crust as I go down, to avoid a long and lacerating fall.

The figures above, bringing more loads to the rim, look very small; I see Phu-Tsering make his way down to the platform. Then, from the sky, as the imminent sun shoots cold rays over the ice rim of the Kang, comes a cry of warning.

A load is falling.

Black figures on the sky, a doomsday sun, the blaring ice, and this dark bounding thing, quite small at first, looming larger with each carom as it comes: a load is falling. Clumsy with my pack, I clutch the crust, afraid that any move may be the wrong one, since the trajectories of the dark thing are so erratic; I kick desperately at the ice, making a purchase for a leap aside at the last second. Someone yells as the lunging shape strikes the slope above me and takes off again, filling the sky: that it will strike precisely where I lie seems astonishing even in this last hallucinatory second. I leap leftward, and GS's big case—books, spare boots, camera equipment—splits the glazed snow where I had been and whistles downward. I have lost my hold on the slope, and start to fall, but my stave, punched through the crust, comes to my rescue, and I lie spread-eagled, forehead to the snow, gasping for breath. Far above, GS's voice is high, berating Phu-Tsering for his carelessness. Later, when I tease Phu-Tsering ("I thought you were my friend!"), he laughs wildly out of nervousness, saying, "I sorry!"

We hoped to have the loads down to the snow lake by midday, but the warmth and windlessness now work against us. In the steep stretch, the loads slide well upon the crust, even with one man for three loads, but later, when the sun is overhead, they bog down and must be dragged through softening snow. Frequently we sink up to the crotch, and it is midafternoon before the first loads reach the snow lake; the rest lie scattered on the slopes above. GS, on snowshoes, has fared better than the rest of us, but we are all soaked and exhausted.

The sunset behind the steep walls of the bowl will bring instant cold. The Sherpas, unladen, set off rapidly for Shey, although they cannot reach there before dark. Much as I wish to go to Shey this evening, it is folly to set out wet and tired down a tortuous three-hour course of drifts and ice-stream boulders and floes: I say I shall camp here. GS agrees. Although we did not eat at noon, we are too tired to be hungry. And so we bivouac by the strange pond—a depression of black clay where, at this season, snow and ice melt at midday—and share the last tin of sardines, and are huddled in our sleeping bags when darkness comes in the late afternoon.

A sundown wind has died away to utter stillness, and a good thing, too, since the snowbanks all around are deep and dry, all set to drift. GS is a remorseless sleeper, but for me the night will be a long one. I think about the great black eagle that crossed the sky at twilight: this can only be the golden eagle, which I last saw in western mountain lands of North America. Perhaps this eagle is the one that passed over Snowfields Camp at just this time of day. What can it be hunting, this heroic bird, in bitter white waste, at the edge of darkness?

at crystal
mountain

As the hand held before the eye conceals the greatest mountain, so the little earthly life hides from the glance the enormous lights and mysteries of which the world is full, and he who can draw it away from before his eyes, as one draws away a hand, beholds the great shining of the inner worlds.

RABBI NACHMANN OF BRATZLAV

Days and months are the travelers of eternity. So are the years that pass by. . . . I myself have been tempted for a long time by the cloud-moving wind—filled with a strong desire to wander. . . . I walked through mists and clouds, breathing the thin air of high altitudes and stepping on slippery ice and snow, till at last through a gateway of clouds, as it seemed, to the very paths of the sun and moon, I reached the summit, completely out of breath and nearly frozen to death. Presently the sun went down and the moon rose glistening in the sky.

BASHO
The Narrow Road to the Deep North

NOVEMBER 1

This Black Pond Camp, though well below the Kang Pass, lies at an altitude of 17,000 feet, and an hour after the sun sinks behind the peaks, my wet boots have turned to blocks of ice. GS's thermometer registers −20° Centigrade (4° below zero Fahrenheit) and though I wear everything I have, I quake with cold all night. Dawn comes at last, but making hot water from a pot of ice is difficult at this altitude, and it is past nine before boots are thawed and we are under way.

The snow bowl is the head of an ice river that descends a deep canyon to Shey. In the canyon we meet Jang-bu and Phu-Tsering, on their way up to fetch some food and pots: Dawa, they say, is down again with acute snow blindness.

Sherpa tracks in the frozen shadows follow the glassy boulders of the stream edge, and somewhere along the way I slip, losing the hoopoe feather that adorned my cap. The river falls steeply, for Shey lies three thousand feet below Kang La, and in the deep snow, the going is so treacherous that the Sherpas have made no path; each man flounders through the drifts as best he can. Eventually, from a high corner of the canyon, rough red-brown lumps of human habitation come in view. The monastery stands like a small fort on a bluff where another river flows in from the east; a mile below, the rivers vanish into a deep and dark ravine. Excepting the lower slopes of the mountainside behind the monastery, which is open to the south, most of this treeless waste lies under snow, broken here and there by calligraphic patterns of bare rock, in an atmosphere so wild and desolate as to overwhelm the small huddle of dwellings.

High to the west, a white pyramid sails on the sky—the Crystal Mountain. In summer, this monument of rock is a shrine for pilgrims from all over Dolpo and beyond, who come here to make a prescribed circle around the Crystal Mountain and attend a holy festival at Shey.[1] What is stirring about this peak, in snow time, is its powerful shape, which even today, with no clouds passing, makes it appear to be forging through the blue. "The power of such a mountain is so great and yet so subtle that, without compulsion, people are drawn to it from near and far, as if by the force of some invisible magnet; and they will undergo untold hardships and privations in their inexplicable urge to approach and to worship the centre of this sacred power. . . . This worshipful or religious attitude is not impressed by scientific facts, like figures of altitude, which are foremost in the mind of modern man. Nor is it motivated by the urge to 'conquer' the mountain. . . ."[2]

A gravel island under Shey is reached by crossing ice and stones of a shallow channel. At the island's lower end are prayer walls and a stone stockade for animals; farther on, small conduits divert a flow of river water to a group of prayer mills in the form of waterwheels, each one housed separately in its own stone shrine. The conduits are frozen and the wheels are still. On top of the small stupas are offerings of white quartz crystals, presumably taken from the Crystal Mountain in the summer, when the five wheels spin five ancient prayer drums, sending OM MANI PADME HUM down the cold canyon.

On the far side of a plank bridge, a path climbs the bank to two big red-and-white entrance stupas on the bluff: I go up slowly. Prayer flags snap thinly on the wind, and a wind-bell has a wooden wing in the shape of a half-moon that moves the clapper; over the glacial rumble on the river stones, the wistful ring on the light wind is the first sound that is heard here at Shey Gompa.

The cluster of a half-dozen stone houses is stained red, in sign that Shey is a monastery, not a village. Another group of five small houses sits higher up the mountain; above this hamlet, a band of blue sheep may be seen with the naked eye. Across the river to the north, stuck on a cliff face at the portals of the canyon, is a red hermitage. Otherwise, except for prayer walls and the stone corrals, there are only the mighty rock formations and dry treeless mountainside where snow has melted, and the snow and sky.

I move on slowly, dull in mind and body. Gazing back up the Black River toward the rampart of icy cornices, I understand that we have come over the Kanjirobas to the mountain deserts of the Tibetan Plateau: we have crossed the Himalaya from south to north. But not until I had to climb this short steep path from the wintry river to the bluffs did I realize how tired I was after thirty-five days of hard trekking. And here I am, on this first day of November, standing before the Crystal Monastery, with its strange stones and flags and bells under the snows.

The monastery temple with its attached houses forms a sort of open court facing the south. Two women and two infants, sitting in the sun, make no sign of welcome. Fearing Kham-pa brigands, the women had locked themselves into their houses a few days ago, when Jang-bu and GS first appeared, and plainly they are still suspicious of our seemingly inexplicable mission. The younger woman is weaving a rough cloth on an ancient loom. When I say, "*Namas-te!*" she repeats it, as if trying the word out. Three scraggy *dzos* and an old black nanny goat excepted, these are the only sentient beings left at Shey, which its inhabitants call Somdo, or "Confluence," because of the meeting of rivers beneath its bluff—the Kangju, "Snow Waters" (the one I think of as Black River, because of the black pond at its head, and the black eagle, and the black patterns of its stones and ice in the dark canyon), and the Yeju, "Low Waters" (which I shall call White River, because it comes down from the eastern snows).

For cooking hut and storeroom, Jang-bu has appropriated the only unlocked dwelling. Like all the rest, it has a flat roof of clay and saplings piled on top with brushwood, a small wooden door into the single room, and a tiny window in the western wall to catch afternoon light. The solitary ray of light, as in a medieval painting, illumines the smoke-blackened posts

that support the roof, which is so low that GS and I must bend
half-over. The earth floor is bare, except for a clay oven built
up in three points to hold a pot, with a hole near the floor to
blow life into the smoky fire of dung or brushwood. Jang-bu
and Phu-Tsering's tent is just outside the door, while Dawa will
sleep inside with the supplies. GS pitches his blue tent just uphill from the hut, while I place mine some distance away, facing
east up the White River toward the sunrise.

The cooking hut is the sometime dwelling of the brother of
the younger woman, Tasi Chanjun, whom the Sherpas call
Namu, meaning hostess. (Among Tibetans as among native
Americans, it is often rude to address people by their formal
name.) Her little boy, aged about four, is Karma Chambel, and
her daughter, perhaps two, is Nyima Poti. Nyima means "sun"
or "sunny"—Sunny Poti! The old woman's name is Sonam: her
husband, Chang Rapke, and her daughter Karima Poti have
gone away to winter in Saldang, and Sonam lives alone in the
abandoned hamlet up the mountain. Namu says that before the
snows there were forty people here, including twenty-odd
monks and two lamas: all are gone across the mountains to Saldang, from where—is this a warning to outlandish men who
come here without women?—her husband will return in a few
days. Namu's husband has the key to the Crystal Monastery, or
so she says, and will doubtless bring it with him when he comes
to visit, in four or five days, or in twenty. Namu is perhaps
thirty years old, and pretty in a sturdy way, and self-dependent.
She speaks familiarly of B'od but not Nepal; even Ring-mo is a
foreign land, far away across Kang La.

That the Lama is gone is very disappointing. Nevertheless,
we are extremely happy to be here, all the more so since it often seemed that we would never arrive at all. Now we can
wake up in the morning without having to put on wet boots,
break camp, get people moving; and there is home to return to
in the evening. There are no porters harassing our days, and we
are sheltered, more or less, from evil weather. The high pass between Shey and the outside world lies in the snow peaks,
ghostly now in the light of the cold stars. "God, I'm glad I'm
not up there tonight," GS exclaims, as we emerge from the

smoky hut, our bellies warm with lentil soup. We know how fortunate it was that the Kang Pass was crossed in this fine, windless weather, and wonder how long fair skies will hold, and if Tukten and Gyaltsen will appear. It is November now, and everything depends upon the snows.

NOVEMBER 2

At almost 15,000 feet, Shey is as high as the Jang Pass. It is located in what has been described as Inner Dolpo,[3] which is walled off from eastern Dolpo by a surrounding crescent of high peaks, and must be one of the highest inhabited areas on earth. Its people are of pure Tibetan stock, with a way of life that cannot differ much from that of Ch'ang Tartars out of Central Asia who are thought to have been the original Tibetans, and their speech echoes the tongue of nomads who may have arrived two thousand years ago. Dolpo was formerly a part of western Tibet, and it is certain that some form of Buddhism came here early. Beyond the Karnali River, to the north and west, the Tibetan Plateau rises to Kailas, the holy "Mount Sumeru" or "Meru" of Hindus and Buddhists, home of Shiva and the Center of the world; from Mount Kailas, four great rivers—the Karnali, the Indus, the Sutlej, and the Brahmaputra—flow down in a great mandala to the Indian seas.

Shey Gompa (in Tibetan, *Shel dgon-pa*) is a monastery of the Kagyu sect, which was established in the eleventh century as a departure from the Kalachakra Tantrism of the Old Sect, or Nyingma. Kalachakra (Circle of Time) came to Tibet in the same century; it traditionally derives from a Tantra or treatise known as *Journey to Shambala,* which teaches the adept how to transcend time (death), and is supposed to be the Book of Wisdom that appears in portraits of the Bodhisattva called Manjusri.[4] In Kalachakra, the already numerous Buddha aspects are split once more into peaceful and wrathful forms of the same deity; thus, Avalokita, the Great Compassionate One, is also perceived as Mahakala, or Great Time, the Lord of Death—the Tantric personification of the disintegrating forces of the Cosmos, often depicted wearing skulls and human skins, brandishing darts, and stamping upon copulating humankind. Mahakala will liberate those who can die to their past in order to be reborn, and terrify those who cling to the worldly existence of samsara, the thirsting and quenching and thirsting anew that is symbolized by the priest's skull cup full of blood. For better or worse, the Kalachakra pantheon of peaceful-and-wrathful deities was retained by the "reformed" sects—the Kagyu-pas, the Sakya-pas, and, much later, the Gelug-pas, led by the Dalai Lamas, who have dominated Tibetan Buddhism since the sixteenth century.

The Kagyu sect was established by the great Lama Marpa, the "Translator," who made three trips to India to study with a famous teacher called Naropa. When Marpa returned to Tibet, he transmitted the Dharma to Milarepa. Subsequently, Milarepa's disciples split off from Kagyu as the Karma-pas, and this new school, in the thirteenth century, was the first Tibetan sect[5] to establish influence with the emperor of China, Kublai Khan. (Subsequently, according to the chronicles of Marco Polo, the Khan's conversion was strengthened by a lama who triumphed over competing divines of Christian, Muslim, and Taoist persuasions by causing a cup to rise to the royal lips of its own accord.)

Gelug-pa reforms since the sixteenth century have not changed the nature of Karma-Kagyu, or not, at least, in such far places as the Crystal Mountain. In its ascetic disciplines and spare teachings, which discourage metaphysical speculation in favor of prolonged and solitary meditation, Karma-pa practice is almost identical to that of Zen, which also emphasizes intuitive experience over priestly ritual and doctrine. Both have been called the "Short Path" to liberation, and although this direct path is difficult and steep, it is also the pure essence of Buddhism, with all religious trappings cut away. It seems to me wonderful karma that the Crystal Monastery belongs to this "Zen" sect, and that the Lama of Shey is a notable *tulku,* or incarnate lama, revered throughout the Land of Dolpo as the present reincarnation of the Lama Marpa. On my way here, I entertained visions of myself in monkish garb attending the Lama in his ancient mysteries, and getting to light the butter lamps into the bargain; I suppose I had hoped he would be my teacher. That the gompa is locked and the Lama gone away might be read as a karmic reprimand to spiritual ambition, a silent teaching to this ego that still insists upon itself, like the poor bleat of a goat on the north wind.

Last night, the temperature sank to $-13°$ Centigrade and a strong east wind rattled my tent: this morning I move the tent into the stockyard of an empty house. On the corral walls lie some excellent stone carvings, one of them portraying Tara (in Tibetan, *Dölma*), born of the compassionate tear of Avalokita (Chen-resigs) and the embodiment of the Bodhisattva spirit. As the feminine aspect of Chen-resigs, Dölma is the great "Protectress" of Tibet, and so I am pleased to find her on my wall.

The temple is distinguished from the buildings that abut it on both sides by the ceremonial raised entrance under a roofed porch and the abundant ornaments upon the roof, which include prayer flags, tritons, the great horns of an argali, and the gigantic antlers of a Sikkim stag, a creature of northern Bhutan and southeastern Tibet. (Since neither animal is supposed to occur here, GS is fascinated by the origins of these horns and antlers, especially since the Sikkim stag is said to be extinct.)[6]

Although the gompa is locked tight, the two large stupas on the bluff over the river bridge give a clue to the iconography within. Perhaps thirty feet high, they have the typical square red base and red-garlanded white dome, with a tapering cone topped by a lunar crown and solar disc. On the four sides of the base are crude clay frescoes of symbolic creatures—elephants on the east face, horses south, peacocks west, and on the north face the garuda, or mythical hawk, here represented as a man with wings bearing what appears to be the sun and moon. The garuda, like the swastikas inside the stupa, is a pre-Buddhist symbol, and so is the yin-yang symbol on the door, which is thought to antedate the early Taoism of three thousand years ago in China.

In the small chamber inside one stupa are two rows of ancient prayer wheels, five to a row, set up in such a way that ten rounds of OM MANI PADME HUM may be turned simultaneously by the visitor; each wheel represents the Wheel of Dharma, first set in motion by the Buddha, and also the rotation of the Universe. On walls and ceilings are bright-painted mandalas and Buddhas, including Samantabhadra and Padma Sambhava, he who scourged the demoness at Phoksumdo Lake, depicted here in his fierce Kalachakra "Tiger-God" aspect, as a protector of the Dharma. A benign presence with four hands, bearing a string of pearls, a lotus, and the blue orb or *mani* that signifies compassion, is Avalokita, or Chen-resigs. Presiding over all is Dorje-Chang, Holder of the *Dorje,* or "thunderbolt," the adamantine diamond, symbol of cosmic energy distilled. Dorje-Chang (Vajradhara) is the primordial Buddha of Tibet, who transmitted the Dharma to the great Indian sage Tilopa, and thus began a celebrated succession of reincarnations— from Tilopa to Naropa to Lama Marpa the Translator to Milarepa, and so forth, to the present day. He also appears outside on a dome fresco with the Pleiades and black sickle moon over his shoulder; his sky-blue color signifies his eternal nature, and he carries a bell that represents the perfect sound of voiceless wisdom. Beside the dome perches a wind-bell, and its very small clear song, in shifts of air, seems to deepen the vast silence of this place.

The second stupa is of like size and character, and between these stupas and the monastery houses, heaped up into a platform five feet high, is a whole field of carved slabs, thousands upon thousands, by far the greatest assemblage of prayer stones that I have ever seen, before or since. OM MANI PADME HUM is the commonest inscription, but there are also wheels of life, carved Buddhas, and quotations from liturgical texts, heap upon heap. The stones vary in weight from ten pounds to several hundred; some are recent, while on others, the inscriptions are worn to shadow by the elements, and all of these conceal the masses more that lie beneath. In addition, a great wall of these stones nearly encircles the monastery and its adjoining houses as well as a group of smaller stupas on the northern side, and there are extensive prayer-stone walls on the river island and along the paths as well. The prayer stones at the bottom of these walls must be many centuries old. Though nobody seems to know who lived here when the first of them were made, the great accumulation of old stones in the Shey region supports the idea that the Crystal Mountain is a very ancient shrine of Tibetan Buddhism, and perhaps B'on before it. Samling Monastery, not far north of this mountain, is an old redoubt of B'on and the repository of B'on's most ancient texts, and I like to imagine that this archaic kingdom might be none other than the Kingdom of Sh'ang-Sh'ung that the B'on-pos claim as the home of their religion. That Sh'an-Sh'ung is deemed "mythical" may be discounted: the Land of Dolpo is not found in the geographies, and it seems mythical even to such people as myself, who like to imagine they have been here.

This morning I bathe inside my sunny tent, and sort out gear. Dawa is still groaning with snow blindness, but Jang-bu and Phu-Tsering have crossed Black River to hunt scraps of low shrub juniper for firewood, and GS is up on this Somdo mountainside viewing his sheep; he returns half-frozen toward midmorning. After a quick meal of chapatis, we set off on a survey of other sheep populations in the region, heading eastward up the Saldang trail, which follows the north bank of the White River. Like the Saure and other east-west rivers in this season, this one is snowbound on the side that faces north, and across the water, we can see snow tracks of marmot, wandering outward in weird patterns from a burrow; perhaps the animals, sent underground too early by those blizzards of the late monsoon, had gone out foraging. But they are hibernated now, there is no fresh marmot sign, the land seems empty.

Snow clouds come up over the mountains, and the shining river turns to black, over black rocks. A lone black *dzo* nuzzles the stony earth. GS has picked up scat of a large carnivore and turns it in his hand, wondering aloud why fox sign, so abundant at Black Pond, is uncommon here at lower altitudes. "Too big for fox, I think. . . ."

As GS speaks, I scan the mountain slopes for bharal: on these rolling hills to the east of Somdo, we have not seen even one. Abruptly, he says, "Hold it! Freeze! Two snow leopard!" I see a pale shape slip behind a low rise patched with snow, as GS, agitated, mutters, "Tail's too short! Must have been foxes—!"

"No!" I say. "Much too big—!"

"Wolves!" he cries out. "Wolves!"

And there they are.

Moving away without haste up an open slope beyond the rise, the wolves bring the barren hills to life. Two on the slope to northward frisk and play, but soon they pause to look us over; their tameness is astonishing. Then they cut across the hill to join three others that are climbing a stone gully. The pack stops each little while to gaze at us, and through the telescope we rejoice in every shining hair: two silver wolves, and two of faded gold, and one that is the no-color of frost: this frost-colored wolf, a big male, seems to be the leader. All have black tail tips and a delicate black fretting on the back. "That's why there's no sign of fox or leopard!" GS says, "and that's why the blue sheep stay near the river cliffs, away from this open country!" I ask if the wolves would hunt and kill the fox and leopard, and he says they would. For some reason, the wolves' appearance here has taken us by surprise; it is in Tibet that such mythic creatures belong. This is an Asian race of *Canis lupus,* the timber wolf, which both of us have seen in Alaska, and it is always an exciting animal: the empty hills where the pack has gone have come to life. In a snow patch are five sets of wolf tracks, and old wolf scats along the path contain brittle gray stuff and soft yellow hair—blue sheep and marmot.

Down the path comes an old woman who has walked alone from Saldang, over the Shey Pass to the east; we are as surprised by her appearance as she is by ours. The old woman has seen the five *jangu,* and two more, but seems less wary of the wolves than of big strangers.

We wonder about that solitary *dzo*, not more than a half mile from the place where we had turned the wolves back toward the east. Later Namu says that wolves kill two or three *dzos* every year, and five or six sheep at a time in the corrals. She sets out upriver to fetch her *dzo*, and is back with the lone beast just before sundown.

NOVEMBER 3

There is so much that enchants me in this spare, silent place that I move softly so as not to break a spell. Because the taking of life has been forbidden by the Lama of Shey, bharal and wolves alike draw near the monastery. On the hills and in the stone beds of the river are fossils from blue ancient days when all this soaring rock lay beneath the sea. And all about are the prayer stones, prayer flags, prayer wheels, and prayer mills in the torrent, calling on all the elements in nature to join in celebration of the One. What I hear from my tent is a delicate wind-bell and the river from the east, in this easterly wind that may bring a change in the weather. At daybreak, two great ravens come, their long toes scratching on the prayer walls.

The sun refracts from the white glaze of the mountains, chills the air. Old Sonam, who lives alone in the hamlet up the hill, was on the mountain before day, gathering the summer's dung to dry and store as cooking fuel; what I took for lumpish matter straightens on the sky as the sun rises, setting her gaunt silhouette afire.

Eleven sheep are visible on the Somdo slope above the monastery, six rams together and a group of ewes and young; though the bands begin to draw near to one another and sniff urine traces, there is no real sign of rut. From our lookout above Sonam's house, three more groups—six, fourteen, and twenty-six—can be seen on the westward slopes, across Black River.

Unable to hold the scope on the restless animals, GS calls out to me to shift the binoculars from the band of fourteen to the group of six sheep, directly across the river from our lookout. "Why are those sheep running?" he demands, and a moment later hollers, "Wolves!" All six sheep are springing for the cliffs, but a pair of wolves coming straight downhill are cutting off the rearmost animal as it bounds across a stretch of snow toward the ledges. In the hard light, the blue-gray creature seems far too swift to catch, yet the streaming wolves gain ground on the hard snow. Then they are whisking through the matted juniper and down over steepening rocks, and it appears that the bharal will be cut off and bowled over, down the mountain, but at the last moment it scoots free and gains a narrow ledge where no wolf can follow.

In the frozen air, the whole mountain is taut; the silence rings. The sheep's flanks quake, and the wolves are panting; otherwise, all is still, as if the arrangement of pale shapes held the world together. Then I breathe, and the mountain breathes, setting the world in motion once again.

Briefly, the wolves gaze about, then make their way up the mountainside in the unhurried gait that may carry them fifty miles in a single day. Two pack mates join them, and in high yak pasture the four pause to romp and roll in dung. Two of these were not among the five seen yesterday, and we recall that the old woman had seen seven. Then they trot onward, disappearing behind a ridge of snow. The band of fourteen sheep high on this ridge gives a brief run of alarm, then forms a line on a high point to stare down at the wolves and watch them go. Before long, all are browsing once again, including the six that were chased onto the precipice.

Turning to speak, we just shake our heads and grin. "It was worth walking five weeks just to see that," GS sighs at last. "That was the most exciting wolf hunt I ever saw." And a little later, exhilarated still, he wonders aloud if I remember "that rainy afternoon in the Serengeti when we watched wild dogs make a zebra kill in that strange storm light on the plain, and all those thousands of animals running?" I nod. I am still excited by the wolves seen so close yesterday, and to see them again, to watch them hunt blue sheep in such fashion, flying down across the cliffs within sight of our tents at Shey Gompa—what happiness!

After years of studying the carnivores, GS has become fascinated by the Caprini—the sheep and the goats—which have the attraction of inhabiting the remote high mountains that he loves. And among the Caprini, this "blue sheep" is a most peculiar species, which is one reason we have come so far to see it. It is presumed that the sheep and goats branched off from a common ancestor among the Rupicaprini, the so-called goat-antelopes, which are thought[7] to have evolved somewhere south of the Himalaya; this generalized ancestor may have resembled the small goat-antelope called the goral, which we saw last month in the dry canyon of the Bheri. Besides the six species of true goat (*Capra*) and the six of true sheep (*Ovis*), the Caprini include three species of tahr (*Hemitragus*), the aoudad or Barbary sheep (*Ammotragus*), and the bharal or Himalayan blue sheep (*Pseudois*), all of which exhibit characters of both sheep and goat. The tahrs, which in their morphology and behavior appear to be intermediate between goat-antelopes and true goats, are classified as goats, and the sheeplike aoudad is mostly goat as well. *Pseudois,* too, looks very like a sheep; it recalls the Rocky Mountain sheep, not only in its general aspect but in type of habitat—rolling upland in the vicinity of cliffs. Certain specimens, GS says, possess the interdigital glands on all four feet which were thought to be a diagnostic character of *Ovis,* and the species lacks the strong smell, beard, and knee calluses that are found in *Capra.* Nevertheless, GS considers it more goat than sheep, and hopes to establish this beyond all doubt by observation of its behavior in the rut.

Hunters' reports account for most of what is known of the wild goats and sheep of Asia, which may be why the classification of *Pseudois* is still disputed. Since the blue sheep is now rare in world collections, the one way to resolve the question is to observe the animal in its own inhospitable habitat—above timberline, as high as 18,000 feet, in the vicinity of cliffs—in one of the most remote ranges of any animal on earth: from Ladakh and Kashmir east across Tibet into northwest China, south to the Himalayan crest, and north to the Kuenlun and Altyn mountains. In Nepal, a few bharal are found on the western and southern flanks of Dhaulagiri (this is the population that we saw near the Jang Pass), as well as in the upper Arun

Valley, in the east, but most are found here in the northwest, near the Tibetan border.

This morning, through the telescope, I study blue sheep carefully for the first time. Like the Rocky Mountain sheep, they are short-legged, strong, broad-backed animals, quick and neat-footed, with gold demonic eyes. The thick-horned male is a handsome slaty blue, the white of his rump and belly set off by bold black face marks, chest, and flank stripe, and black anteriors on all four legs; the black flank stripes, like the horns, become heavier with age. The female is much smaller, with dull pelage and less contrast in the black, and her horns are spindly, as in female sheep. Those of the males, on the other hand, are heavy, curving upward, out, and back. Also, the basio-occipital bone at the base of the skull is goatlike, and so are the large dew claws and the prominent markings on the fore sides of the legs. In this confused situation, the rutting behavior will be a deciding factor, yet from the limited reports available, even the rutting is ambiguous. For example, the courting sheep rarely raises its tail above the horizontal, whereas the goat may arch it back onto its rump: perhaps for lack of the odorous tail-gland secretions of true goats that the arched tail may help disseminate, both tahr and bharal compromise by erecting the tail straight up into the air.

Although the male herds are still intact—this sociability of rams is a trait of Caprini—the males are mounting one another, as much to establish dominance as in sexuality; among many sheep and goats, the juvenile males and the females are quite similar in appearance, and tend to imitate the behavior of the other, so that rams may fail to differentiate between them, treating all of these subordinates alike.[8] A few are displaying the bizarre behavior (heretofore unreported) that GS calls "rump-rubbing," in which one male may rub his face against the hind end of another. In the vicinity of females, the male "kicks"—a loose twitch of the leg in her direction that appears to be a mounting preliminary and may also serve to display his handsome markings. Also, he thrusts his muzzle into her urine stream, as if to learn whether or not she is in estrus, and licks in agitation at his penis. But the blue sheep stops short of certain practices developed by the markhor of Pakistan and the wild goat (the ancestor of the domestic goat, ranging from Pakistan to Greece), both of which take their penises into their own mouths, urinate copiously, then spit on their own coats; the beard of the male goat is an adaptive character, a sort of urine sponge that perpetuates the fine funky smell for which the goats are known.

The itch of the rutting season has begun, and even the young animals play at butting and sparring, as if anxious not to miss the only lively time in the blue sheep's year. GS wonders at the scarcity of the young, concluding that a 50 percent mortality must occur in the first year, due as much to weakness or disease caused by poor range conditions as to predation by wolves and leopard. Perhaps one juvenile in three attains maturity, and this may suffice to sustain the herds, which must adjust numbers to the limited amount of habitat that remains snow-free all the year. This region of the Tibetan Plateau is a near desert of rock and barren slopes dominated by two thorn shrubs, *Caragana* and a bush honeysuckle, *Lonicera;* the blue sheep will eat small amounts of almost any growth, including the dry everlasting and the oily juniper, and the adaptations of the Caprini for hard, abrasive forage permit limited browsing of this thorny scrub as well. But excepting a few tufts among the thorns, almost all the native grasses that are its preferred food have been eradicated by the herds of yak and sheep and goats that are brought here from distant villages in summer, and the overgrazing has led already to erosion.

NOVEMBER 4

Condemned by cold to spend twelve hours in my sleeping bag each night, I find myself inclined to my Zen practice. Each morning before daybreak, I drag my down parka into my sleeping bag to warm it, then sit up in meditation posture and perform a sutra chanting service for perhaps forty-five minutes, including the sutra dedicated to Kannon or Avalokita, and the Heart Sutra (the "heart" of the mighty Prajna Paramita Sutra that lies at the base of Mahayana Buddhism). This morning service is lent dignity by a clay *ts'a ts'a* Buddha taken from the piles of these small icons that litter the stupas at Ring-mo—that it may be "B'on" seems of small importance. I place the figure outside the tent on an altar of flat stone, where it will receive the first of the eastern light, down the White river, and I sit bundled up just inside the flap, for at this hour the temperature is never more than −12° Centigrade. Sometimes I am joined for morning service by a hardy little bird that dwells in the brush piles on the roof of the pink stone house behind the tent. With flicking tail, it hunts among the dung chips near the Buddha; the bill is slim in a pale-gray head, and it has a rufous breast and a white belly. This is the robin accentor (*Prunella*).

Today Dawa is better, and the Sherpas will climb up to Black Pond to fetch down three more loads. Being dependent on their good will, we try to spare them where possible, and share things, and wait for them to volunteer—they always do—before making our requests, but theirs is a wearing job, and poorly paid, and were they less faithful, they could simply abandon us, as they have seen the porters do so often.

In days to come, they will bring in the remaining loads, one trip a day, and for all of this period, from the Cave Camp onward, they will be paid as porters as well as Sherpas. No matter that they are wasteful and careless, and neglect to bring goggles into the snow mountains, or even good winter clothes—their spirit is wonderful. These three, at least, have decent boots, but Gyaltsen, who was given money to buy boots in Kathmandu, spent it on something less crucial, and Tukten, as is the Sherpa habit, sold his boots after his last expedition and started this one barefoot; they will cross the Kang Pass in the cheap Oriental sneakers that were issued to the porters to get them across the ice crusts of Jang La.

We cross the bridge to the island in the river, then jump stones across the shallows to the farther side.

Sun and a high cirrus cast metallic light on the Black River, and in this light, Shey with its two stupas and its flags is emblematic on its barren bluff, in lonely silhouette against the snows. We watch the Sherpas descend the steep path from the bluff; they cross the bridge at cheerful speed, like boys. We shall track the bands of blue sheep on the western slopes, and hunt for sign of snow leopard along the cliffs; we shall also visit the red hermitage, known as Tsakang, and collect firewood.

Descending from steep snowfields under Crystal Mountain is a series of ridges that terminate in buttresses or points where the mountain falls away into Black River; between these ridges, each one higher than the next as the path goes north, lie deep ravines. Winding in and out of these ravines, the path follows the contour around the outer points, which like all eminences in the region are marked by prayer flags and a wall of prayer stones. In an hour we are opposite the red hermitage, which sits high against the cliff across the gorge: three huge Himalayan griffons turn and turn on the cold updrafts from Black River Canyon. The path continues round the point and into the ravine, which is still in shadow, and sheeted with ice and snow on this north exposure; here the incline is so steep that any misstep might be fatal. At the head of the ravine, the trail crosses an icy stream and climbs up to the hermitage, which is perched on a ledge against bright cliffs of blue and red. A smaller hermitage, more isolated still, sits on the corner of a precipice still farther north. Such locations are traditional for spiritual pursuit in the Tibetan region, "proudly isolated on the summits beaten by the wind, amidst wild landscapes, as if bidding defiance to invisible foes at the four corners of the horizon."[9]

Tsakang itself consists of four stone structures plastered to the rock wall, like nests of swifts. One is a cell with a single narrow window slot that looks out on a world of snow and sky, pure white, pure blue; another has crooked doors and windows of carved wood. A tiny potato plot has been constructed on a ledge, and sliced potatoes lie drying on a stone. By the cliff wall are stacks of dung and juniper for winter fuel, and water issues from a cave, dripping sonorously onto slate conduits that conduct it to a copper cauldron; in the cave a small stupa has been built in honor of the water.

This hermitage is a true gompa, which is not really a monastery but "a dwelling in the solitude,"[10] located wherever possible against a cliff that overlooks a lake or stream, and often inhabited by a solitary monk. Tsakang is bedecked with prayer flags, white and blue, and has an astonishing ornate balconied window painted in red and fire-orange, blue, and turquoise; carved Buddha stones adorn its sunny walls.

The hermitage is situated so that nothing may be seen but snow peaks rising to a shining sky; even Shey is hidden by the slopes above the village. The effect is so hallucinatory that GS, disturbed, is stirred to protest at the hermit's life, and solitary meditation: "You have to have *something* coming in!" But the point of meditation is to let everything go: "When your mind is empty like a valley or a canyon, then you will know the power of the Way."[11]

On a ledge, two bronze-skinned monks sit quietly, as if in wait. One is patching his wool boots, the other is curing a goat hide in a yellow mix of goat brains and rancid yak butter. Smiling, calm, they let our greetings wander; perhaps they live here under vows of silence. The boot-mender is a clear-faced youth, little more than twenty, while the other, curiously ageless, is a handsome cripple in strange rags of leather. When we say goodbye, the two figures bow slightly, smile again, and keep their silence.

A steep path climbs to the slope above the cliffs, where the only color is a lichen of unearthly yellow-green; all else is thorn and the shale of mountain desert. On the stones of a large stupa we eat discs of greasy dough that Phu-Tsering identifies as "pancakes"; on other days they are dry-dough chapatis, or "breads," made with green buckwheat flour, unleavened, unadorned—no matter. At supper in the cooking hut, the dull food is disheartening, but here in the mountain sun and wind, in the bright cold, whatever is at hand tastes pure and vital.

Leaving GS to observe the Tsakang sheep, I descend the trail again, to gather fuel. On my way I meet a wild-haired stranger, bound for the hermitage, it seems, since this trail leads nowhere else. Chanting, he comes up the mountain to the ridge point where I have paused to let him pass, and there slings down his basket, steps behind a boulder, squats, returns, and says aggressively, "*Timi kaha gami?*" (You where go?) "Shey Gompa," I say, and he repeats it: we both point at Somdo, to make sure. This wayfarer is clad in blackened sheepskins, with the usual assortment of beads and amulets, silver pouch, silver flint case, silver dagger. Demanding a smoke, he laughs loud in disbelief when I say that I have none, and raises his dagger toward my throat in demonstration of my fate, were he but given to low banditry. Without goodbyes, we go our separate ways.

Farther down, where the wolves chased the sheep, lie mats of recumbent juniper, and I cull the tough brush for dead branches. The juniper is the only firewood available, though a stunted birch lives in the deep ravines, beyond the reach of man. With the line I carry in my rucksack, I tie up a big bundle of faggots, and humping it onto my back, descend the mountain, cross the river, and climb the bluff to Shey. The monastery is lively, for as it turns out, the man on the trail is a member of a Saldang group that has come in pursuit of eleven yaks: the beasts had summered here, taken a liking to the place, and returned spontaneously of their own accord. Several animals are visible on the hillside, and others have made their way down to the river islands, where there is more grass.

The visitors crowd into our cook hut to watch the Sherpas unload the broken food baskets brought down from Kang La. These herders say that nine or ten wolves pass through Shey regularly on their hunting circuit, and that two or three snow leopards live along the river cliffs. They also say there is a police check post at Saldang, which makes it inadvisable for us to go there. One man has taken advantage of our absence to reach into my tent and pilfer a pair of drying socks, knocking over my B'on Buddha in the process; while they remain, someone must stay on guard all day. Jang-bu believes that the herders will report our presence to the police at Saldang, and since foreigners are not welcome in this remote region of Dolpo, we may have a visit in the next few days.

NOVEMBER 5

The snow stopped just at dark last evening; and soon the moon appeared, then stars. This morning the sky is clear: at dawn, the black and shaggy yaks stand motionless by the ice river.

For the first time since September, GS is entirely happy. Like myself, he is stunned by Shey, which has more than repaid the long, hard journey; he scribbles his data even while he eats. I keep thinking, How extraordinary!—knowing that this adjective is inadequate and somehow inaccurate, as well; it's not so much that what we have found here is extraordinary as that all has the immediate reality of that region of the mind where "mountains, wolves . . . snow and fire had realized their true being, or had their source."[12] And yet I grow uneasy every day, when dark clouds build in the north and south. At the Kang Pass and southward, it looks as if it is snowing. To waste time in worry that the snow will trap us makes me feel ashamed, all the more so since GS shows no concern. Yet this morning he said that the night view of those icy peaks over which we came was enough to scare him back into his sleeping bag, and of course he knows as well as I do that the monastery has no food to spare us, or not enough, at least, to get everyone through the winter.

In midafternoon, there comes a sudden hail. Soon the hail has turned to snow, and after dark, it is still snowing. Returning from Black Pond, Jang-bu reports that our track down from the Kang Pass has disappeared, and the Saldang people tell us that the trail to Samling, where we hoped to visit in the next few days, is blocked by drifts. As long as the Shey Pass to the east is open, one can cross over to Saldang in a single day, and

these people speak of a lower route from Saldang across to
Tarap and the Bheri River that usually is passable all winter.
However, we have no permit for the Tarap region, nor any wish
to spend a winter in the Tarap jail. GS speaks of "passing
the Tarap police post at night," but it would be difficult to
do this undetected by the dogs. Usually he refers obliquely to
the problem, and then when I take it up, will say offhandedly,
"Well, let's not dwell on it; let's just do our work, and see what
happens."

Toward midday, a wind comes from the southeast and the sky
thickens. It is heavy cold. Yesterday the Saldangs slaughtered a
yak and offered to sell us meat, but our shrunken funds cannot
absorb their bandit prices; another man offered rancid yak butter wrapped in skin, but we cannot afford this either. Now
some of the Saldangs have departed, fetching away meat and
potatoes on the backs of their renegade animals, and also one
of GS's two thermometers. Since the thermometer is part of his
professional equipment, he is naturally outraged, and has
threatened those who stayed behind with the Saldang police;
they have offended emissaries of His Majesty's Government in
Kathmandu, he says, here to explore the possibilities of a national park! Though this is true, it means nothing at all to these
wild, rude, long-haired men, so many centuries away across the
Himalaya.
    The man with bold earrings and mustache who offered us
butter is named Tundu, and his companion is a youth named
Tasi Fintso. Helped by Namu and Tasi Fintso, he loads yak
meat and potatoes on the four remaining yaks and *dzos* that
stand hobbled in front of the gompa. With their short noses
and short fluffy tails, yaks have an appealing air, but they are
shaggy brutes of a half-ton or better, with rude temperaments
to match. Tasi Fintso is gingerly in their presence, but Tundu is
firm and gentle with the balky animals, talking to them in a soft
no-nonsense way as he straps on pack saddles of wood and
leather, hoists cargo sacks of striped brown-and-white homespun, and lashes down the lot with braided rope. There is a
quiet in his actions that gives him a strong presence, and appar-

ently he is the headman here: he will bring the key to the gompa in five days or so, when he comes back from Saldang. Without a word, he leads his yaks away into the east, leaving behind his little girl, Chiring Doma, who sits on a blanket with Nyima Poti, eating potatoes in the sun. The gompa yard is windy and cold, yet Nyima Poti is naked, while her brother, Karma Chambel, is clad in a rag smock. In her dust and burlap, the red-cheeked Chiring Doma looks like a smiling potato given life. Once Tundu is gone, Namu resumes her work of spreading yak-dung fuel to dry along the prayer walls and abandoned houses.

NOVEMBER 6

The nights at Shey are rigid, under rigid stars; the fall of a wolf pad on the frozen path might be heard up and down the canyon. But a hard wind comes before the dawn to rattle the tent canvas, and this morning it is clear again, and colder. At daybreak, the White River, just below, is sheathed in ice, with scarcely a murmur from the stream beneath.

The two ravens come to tritons on the gompa roof. *Gorawk, gorawk,* they croak, and this is the name given to them by the Sherpas. Amidst the prayer flags and great horns of Tibetan argali, the gorawks greet first light with an odd musical double note—*a-ho*—that emerges as if by miracle from those ragged throats. Before sunrise every day, the great black birds are gone, like the last tatters of departing night.

The sun rising at the head of the White River brings a suffused glow to the tent canvas, and the robin accentor flits away across the frozen yard. At seven, there is breakfast in the cook hut—tea and porridge—and after breakfast on most days I watch sheep with GS, parting company with him after a while, when the sheep lie down, to go off on some expedition of my own. Often I scan the caves and ledges on the far side of Black River in the hope of leopard; I am alert for fossils, wolves, and birds. Sometimes I observe the sky and mountains, and sometimes I sit in meditation, doing my best to empty out my mind, to attain that state in which everything is "at rest, free, and immortal. . . . All things abided eternally as they were in their proper places . . . something infinite behind everything appeared."[13] (No Buddhist said this, but a seventeenth-century Briton.) And soon all sounds, and all one sees and feels, take on imminence, an immanence, as if the Universe were coming to attention, a Universe of which one is the center, a Universe that is not the same and yet not different from oneself, even from a scientific point of view: within man as within mountains there are many parts of hydrogen and oxygen, of calcium, phosphorus, potassium, and other elements. "You never enjoy the world aright, till the Sea itself flows in your veins, till you are clothed with the heavens, and crowned with the stars: and perceive yourself to be the sole heir of the whole world, and more than so, because men are in it who are every one sole heirs as well as you."[14]

I have a meditation place on Somdo mountain, a broken rock outcrop like an altar set into the hillside, protected from all but the south wind by shards of granite and dense thorn. In the full sun it is warm, and its rock crannies give shelter to small stunted plants that cling to this desert mountainside— dead red-brown stalks of a wild buckwheat (*Polygonum*), some shrubby cinquefoil, pale edelweiss, and everlasting, and even a few poor wisps of *Cannabis*. I arrange a rude rock seat as a lookout on the world, set out binoculars in case wild creatures should happen into view, then cross my legs and regulate my breath, until I scarcely breathe at all.

Now the mountains all around me take on life; the Crystal Mountain moves. Soon there comes the murmur of the torrent, from far away below under the ice: it seems impossible that I can hear this sound. Even in windlessness, the sound of rivers comes and goes and falls and rises, like the wind itself. An instinct comes to open outward by letting all life in, just as a flower fills with sun. To burst forth from this old husk and cast one's energy abroad, to fly. . . .

Although I am not conscious of emotion, the mind-opening brings a soft mist to my eyes. Then the mist passes, the cold wind clears my head, and body-mind comes and goes on the light air. A sun-filled Buddha. One day I shall meditate in falling snow.

I lower my gaze from the snow peaks to the glistening thorns, the snow patches, the lichens. Though I am blind to it, the Truth is near, in the reality of what I sit on—rocks. These hard rocks instruct my bones in what my brain could never grasp in the Heart Sutra, that "form is emptiness, and emptiness is form"—the Void, the emptiness of blue-black space, contained in everything. Sometimes when I meditate, the big rocks dance.

The secret of the mountains is that the mountains simply exist, as I do myself: the mountains exist simply, which I do not. The mountains have no "meaning," they *are* meaning; the mountains *are*. The sun is round. I ring with life, and the mountains ring, and when I can hear it, there is a ringing that we share. I understand all this, not in my mind but in my heart, knowing how meaningless it is to try to capture what cannot be expressed, knowing that mere words will remain when I read it all again, another day.

Toward four, the sun sets fires on the Crystal Mountain. I turn my collar up and put on gloves and go down to Somdo, where my tent has stored the last sun of the day. In the tent entrance, out of the wind, I drink hot tea and watch the darkness rise out of the earth. The sunset fills the deepening blues with holy rays and turns a twilight raven into the silver bird of night as it passes into the shadow of the mountain. Then the great hush falls, and cold descends. The temperature has already dropped well below freezing, and will drop twenty degrees more before the dawn.

At dark, I walk past lifeless houses to the cooking hut where Phu-Tsering will be baking a green loaf; the Sherpas have erected two stone tables, and in the evenings, the hut is almost cozy, warmed by the dung and smoking juniper in the clay oven.

As usual, GS is there ahead of me, recording data. Eyes watering, we read and write by kerosene lamp. We are glad to see each other, but we rarely speak more than a few words during a simple supper, usually rice of a poor bitter kind, with tomato or soy sauce, salt and pepper, sometimes accompanied by thin lentil soup. After supper I watch the fire for a time, until smoke from the sparking juniper closes my eyes. Bidding goodnight, I bend through the low doorway and go out under the stars and pick my way around the frozen walls to my cold tent, there to remain for twelve hours or more until first light. I read until near asphyxiated by my small wick candle in its flask of kerosene, then lie still for a long time in the very heart of the earth silence, exhilarated and excited as a child. I have yet to use the large packet of *Cannabis* that I gathered at Yamarkhar and dried along the way, to see me through long lightless evenings on this journey: I am high enough.

"Regard as one, this life, the next life, and the life between," wrote Milarepa. And sometimes I wonder into which life I have wandered, so still are the long nights here, and so cold.

NOVEMBER 7

High on the mountain, I come upon a herd of twenty-seven blue sheep that includes males and females of all ages; until today the Somdo rams formed their own herd.

At the sight of man, the bharal drift over a snow ridge toward the north. I trail this promising mixed party, hoping to make observations for GS, who is working near Tsakang. Eventually, the sheep lie down on a steep grassy slope that plunges toward the mouth of Black River Canyon, and I withdraw to a point where they cannot see me, letting them calm themselves before attempting to go closer.

For a long time I sit very still. To a nearby rock comes a black redstart, bobbing in spry agitation and flaring its rufous tail. Then choughs come squealing on the wind, lilting and dancing in a flock of fifty or more: the small black crows, in escadrilles, plummet from view, filling the silence with a rush of air.

In my parka I find a few wild walnuts from Rohagaon, and crack them open with a stone. From this point of mountain, I can see in four directions. Eastward, the White River comes down out of the snow—this is the direction of Saldang. To the south, the Black River canyon climbs into the Kanjirobas. To the west is the great pyramidal butte of Crystal Mountain, parting the wind that bears uneasy clouds down the blue sky. Northward, beyond Somdo mountain, on a hidden plateau above the canyons, lies the old B'on stronghold at Samling.

The Somdo herd has moved uphill, above 15,000 feet. Since the wind is from the south, bearing my scent, I traverse a half mile to the east before starting to climb; by the time the climb is finished, the wind has shifted to the north, and I can wriggle to a point not one hundred yards away from the nearest animal.

To be right among the sheep like this is stirring. I lie belly down, out of the wind, and the whole warm mountain, breathing as I breathe, seems to take me in. All the sheep but two are lying down, and four big rams a little uphill from the rest face me without alarm. The sun glows in the coarse hairs of their blue coats as they chew their cud, carved faces sweeping back to the huge cracked horns. These males are big and heavy, broad across the back, strong, handsome animals: although I am downwind of the herd, there is no smell at all.

One of the males senses me, for there is an elegant arch to his neck, and his eyes and ears are wide in that relaxed readiness that reminds me unaccountably of Tukten: what can our evil monk be doing now? The other sheep are dozing. Most of the young animals lie with their rumps downhill, in my direction (the reverse is true of the adults, which expect threats from below), and two sprawl out in an adolescent manner, heads laid back along their flanks. This is the morning lull, observed each day; they will not browse again for at least an hour. I back down behind the rise, to wait. An hour later, when I stalk them once again, they are just getting to their feet. A female squats to urinate, and a male thrusts his muzzle into the fluid and then into her vulva, upon which he extends his neck in seeming ecstasy and curls his upper lip, eyes closed, the better to savor his findings. Another ram follows a different female, and he, too, pokes his nose against her rump; a third turns his head along his flank as if to seek out his own penis, in the way of goats, then loses interest.

Now the animals begin to graze, twisting their necks to search out grass tufts under the bush honeysuckle; a few browse the small yellow-green leaves of the shrub itself. Led by a female—and in this mixed herd a female usually leads—they move downhill a little as they feed, until they disappear below the rise. When they reappear, they come directly toward the hummock where I lie. Suddenly the creatures are so close that I must lower the binoculars inch by inch so as not to flare them, drawing my chin deep into the thin growth of the mountain-side, hoping my brown hair may be seen as marmot. On they come, browsing a little, males sniffing ignominiously after the females, the two calves of the year bringing up the rear.

The lead female comes out of the hollow not ten yards up the hill, moving a little way eastward. Suddenly, she gets my scent and turns quickly to stare at my still form in the dust below. She does not move but simply stands, eyes round. In her tension, the black marks on her legs are fairly shivering; she is superb. Then the first ram comes to her, and he, too, scents me. In a jump, he whirls in my direction, and his tail shoots straight up in the air, and he stamps his right forefoot, venting a weird harsh high-pitched whinny—*chirr-r-rit*—more like a squirrel than any ungulate. (Later I described this carefully to GS—so far as we know, the first datum on the voice of the blue sheep.) Boldly this ram steps forward to investigate, and the rest follow, until the mountain blue is full of horned heads and sheep faces, sheep vibrations—I hold my breath as best I can. In nervousness, a few pretend to browse, and one male nips edgily at a yearling's rump, coming away with a silver tuft that shimmers in the sun. Unhurriedly, they move away, rounding the slope toward the east. Soon the heads of two females reappear, as if to make sure nothing is following. Then all are gone.

On the way down the mountain, I stop outside Old Sonam's yard in the upper village. In sooty rags and rough-spun boots, wearing the coral-colored beads of her lost girlhood, Sonam is sitting legs straight out in the dry dung, weaving a blanket on a crazy handloom rigged to rocks and sticks, bracing the whole with old twine soles pushed stiff against a stone. Her wool has a handsome and delicate pattern, for there is design in the eye of this old wild one. I admire her sudden grin, strong back, and grimy hide indifferent to the cold.

Once Sonam was an infant with red checks, like Sunny Poti. Now she works close in the last light, as cold descends under a faint half-moon. Soon night will come, and she will creep through her narrow door and eat a little barley; what does she dream of until daybreak, when she goes out on her endless quest for dung? Perhaps she knows better than to think at all, but goes simply about the business of survival, like the wolf; survival is her way of meditation. When I ask Jang-bu why Sonam lives alone all winter in the upper village when she might use an empty house near Namu, he seems astonished. "She has the habit of that place," he says.

NOVEMBER 8

Namu is setting mousetraps for GS, and he soon has a series of fluffy short-tailed mice, a set of voles, and a small shrew,[15] collected on the mountainside. Besides sheep and wolves, there is sign of weasel, Tibetan hare, and fox, but all of these stay out of sight, like the hibernating marmots; except for one glimpse of the hare, we have had to be content, so far, with a few droppings. This is also true of an unknown grouse—very likely, the Tibetan partridge. There is a small company of mountain birds— eagles, griffons, lammergeiers, choughs, hill pigeons, finches, redstarts, accentors, and larks—and also the hardy skinks of the sunny slopes, and an assortment of ants, bees, grasshoppers, and spiders.

I wonder about the populations of small creatures that live just over the White River. For more than a month, they have been locked under heavy snow, and ordinarily they must spend about four more months each year in hibernation than individuals of their own species that live here on the sunny side of the same valley. It seems to me that the resulting adaptations (or lack of them) across millennia, in otherwise identical populations of the same species, would make a fascinating study, and GS agrees.

Yesterday, more yaks appeared, and a belled pony led by Ongdi, brother of Namu and the owner of our cooking hut, who has come here with his daughter-in-law and sons. No doubt Ongdi has got word in Saldang that one of his houses has been occupied by outlanders, here to collect dead mice and wolf shit, and thought to turn this unhealthy situation to his own advantage. Impressed, perhaps, by the stone tables set up by the Sherpas, this sharp-eyed, shifty, and forever smiling fellow demands five rupees a day for his poor hut, but agrees to settle for one rupee if a pound of cheap tea is thrown in. Ongdi covets everything we have, he is possessed by the fury of acquisition: later this month, his sister says, this insatiable trader is off on a bartering expedition across eastern Dolpo to Jamoson and the Kali Gandaki, and even, perhaps, as far as Kathmandu. He has been to Kathmandu before, and is much celebrated in these parts on that account. In exchange for biscuit tins, plastic containers, and other treasures that would have been left behind in any case, had Ongdi not come, Phu-Tsering acquires a good stock of potatoes and some yak butter. Last night, we had butter on potatoes baked in coals—the first butter since Pokhara, and the closest thing to *haute cuisine* in weeks.

Sunrise, illuminating my thin tent, transforms it from an old refuse bag of brown plastic to a strange womblike balloon. True, it remains a wretched tent, stained, raggedy, and sagging, yet I find I have grown fond of it, for it is home. Each day I sweep out the heavy dust that comes creeping, blowing, seeping from the bottomless supply of dry dung in the yard. One understands better the local indifference to cleanliness when one is shrouded with dust within moments of each washing: I am grained with filth.

By the prayer wall, in an early shaft of sun, Namu is gathering her dried yak chips, tossing them back over her shoulder into her wide-mouthed wicker basket; these chips are precious, and her brother Ongdi, when he leaves, will lug some with him over the east mountains to Saldang, where fuel is still more scarce than it is here. Yak dung burns with a hot, clear flame that is almost without smoke, and in these mountain deserts above tree line, it is worth its weight in almost anything.

This morning Ongdi's young son, Tema Tende, in his own unfathomable rhythm, is pounding stolidly on a hide drum, and the hollow sound resounds in the mountain air.

BUM-bum-bum, BUM-BUM-BUM, bum.

With his older son, Karma Dorje, and Karma Dorje's pretty child wife, Tende Samnug, Ongdi packs potatoes, meat, and barley on his yaks for trade in Saldang, together with a small crude chest of drawers. They will be accompanied to Saldang by Jang-bu, who is to inquire about food, police, and the trail to Tarap, in case the Kang Pass should be closed down by snow.

When Ongdi isn't looking, Tende Samnug slips me four potatoes as a gift: the gift is spontaneous and simple-hearted, and she stands there smiling in the pleasure of it, round-eyed and red-cheeked in the sun. Meanwhile Ongdi is entreating me to part with the only kerosene lantern that we have; should he return in a week or two, when our kerosene is gone, it shall be his. Karma Dorje, another smiler, is also begging me for something, and so we chatter back and forth in the greatest animation, although "Saldang" is the only word in the entire conversation that is comprehended by both sides.

Watching sheep early this morning, GS and I agreed upon a plan. I shall leave Shey on November 18, assuming that Tukten and Gyaltsen have arrived; otherwise we must assume that one of the many imaginable mishaps has occurred. Even if Tukten fails to come, I shall leave as planned, accompanied by Jang-bu on the first part of the journey. We shall go out by way of Saldang, over the eastern mountains, hoping to meet the missing Sherpas on that route. If not, Jang-bu will find a porter for me in Saldang, as GS wants him back as soon as possible. I feel better for having settled this, and now the whole subject can be put aside.

NOVEMBER 9

From the path that leads beyond Tsakang, along the precipices of the Black River Canyon, there is a stirring prospect of the great cliffs and escarpments, marching northward toward the point where this Yeju-Kangju flows into the great Karnali River. The path is no more than a ledge in many places and, on the northward face of each ravine, is covered by glare ice and crusted snow. Even on the southward face, the path is narrow, and concentrating hard on every step, I come upon what looks like a big pug mark. Because it is faint, and because GS is too far ahead to summon back, and because until now we have found no trace of leopard, I keep quiet; the mark will be there still when we return. And just at this moment, looking up, I see that GS has paused on the path ahead. When I come up, he points at a distinct cat scrape and print. The print is faded, but at least we know that the snow leopard is here.

Mostly we spend the day apart, meeting over the clay oven for breakfast and supper, but whenever we act like social animals, the impulse has brought luck. A little farther on there is another scrape, and then another, and GS, looking ahead to where the path turns the cliff corner into the next ravine, says, "There ought to be a leopard scat out on that next point—it's just the sort of place they choose." And there it is, all but glowing in the path, right beneath the prayer stones of the stupa— the Jewel in the Heart of the Lotus, I think, unaccountably, and nod at my friend, impressed. "Isn't that something?" GS says, "To be so delighted with a pile of crap?" He gathers the dropping into one of the plastic bags that he keeps with him for this purpose and tucks it away into his rucksack with our lunch.

Though the sign is probably a week old, we are already scanning the sunny ledges and open caves on both sides of the river that we have studied for so many days in vain.

On the ledge path we find two more scats and a half dozen scrapes, as well as melted cat prints in the snow on the north face of the ravines. Perhaps this creature is not resident but comes through on a hunting circuit, as the wolves do: the wolves have been missing now for near a week. On the other hand, this labyrinth of caves and ledges is fine haunt for leopard, out of the way of its enemy, the wolf, and handy to a herd of bharal that is resident on the ridge above and often wanders down close to these cliffs. Perhaps, in the days left to us, we shall never see the snow leopard but it seems certain that the leopard will see us.

Across the next ravine is the second hermitage, of earth red decorated in blue-gray and white. It lacks stacked brush or other sign of life, and its white prayer flags are worn to wisps by wind. In the cliffs nearby are smoke-roofed caves and the ruins of cells that must have sheltered anchorites of former times; perhaps their food was brought them from Tsakang. This small gompa, half-covering a walled-up cave, is tucked into an outer corner of a cliff that falls into Black Canyon, and like Tsakang it faces south, up the Black River. Because the points of the Shey stupas are just visible, its situation is less hallucinatory than the pure blue-and-white prospect at Tsakang, but the sheer drop of a thousand feet into the gorge, the torrent's roar, the wind, and the high walls darkening the sky all around make its situation more disturbing. The hermitage lies on the last part of a pilgrim's path that climbs from Black River and circles round the Crystal Mountain, striking Black Canyon once again on the north side of this point and returning to Shey by way of Tsakang; but most of the path is lost beneath the snows.

Taking shelter on the sunny step, leaning back into the warmth of the wooden door, I eat a green disc of Phu-Tsering's buckwheat bread that looks and tastes like a lichened stone mandala from the prayer walls. Blue sheep have littered this small dooryard with their dung, a human hand has painted a sun and moon above the lintel, yet in this forlorn place, here at the edge of things, the stony bread, the dung and painted moon, the lonely tattering of flags worn to transparence by the wind seem as illusory as sanity itself. The deep muttering of boulders in Black River—why am I uneasy? To swallow the torrent, sun, and wind, to fill one's breath with the plenitude of being . . . and yet . . . I draw back from that sound, which seems to echo the dread rumble of the universe.

Today GS is stumbling on the ledges. He speculates about atmospheric ions that affect depression, as in the mistral winds of southern France (there are recent speculations[16] that negative ions, which seem to be positive in their effect on animals and plants, may be somehow related to *prana,* the "life energy"), and we agree that one is clumsy when depressed, but he feels that his own stumbling is a sign of incipient sickness, a cold coming on or the like. Perhaps he is right, perhaps I imagine things, but earlier on this same ledge, as if impelled, my boots sought out the loose stones and snow-hidden ice, and I felt dull and heavy and afraid; there was a power in the air, a random menace. On the return, an oppression has lifted, I am light and quick. Things go better when my left foot is on the outside edge, as it is now, but this cannot account for the sudden limberness, the pleasure in skirting the same abyss that two hours ago filled me with dread. Not that I cease to pay attention; on the contrary, it is the precise bite and feel and sound of every step that fills me with life. Sun rays glance from snow pinnacles above and the black choughs dance in their escadrilles over the void, and dark and light interpenetrate the path, in the all-pervading presence of the Present.

NOVEMBER 10

The high stone wall of the compound of this house separates my tent from the others. Therefore it is vulnerable to theft, which is not unheard of in these parts, and I keep a sharp eye on two wool traders, filthier than most, who came yesterday from Saldang, bearing no wool or other evidence of honest trade. The first I saw on my way home from the west side of the river, eating barleycorns in Namu's yard; the second paid an uninvited visit to my tent, poking his head straight through the flap to feast his eyes upon the contents—a larcenous overture if there ever was one, so thought I. The tent is so small that in effect one wears it, and the abrupt intrusion of another head—and a strange, wolfish, dirty head at that—put our faces much too close together for my liking. That this head was not withdrawn upon discovering that the tent was occupied was, I suppose, an evidence of innocence, but all the same I made sign to it, not cordially, that it take leave at once. At this point the head spoke for the first time. In English, very gently, it inquired, "I go?" I was astounded. Then it vanished, after offering a smile that transfigured what had seemed to me a sly, distempered face, not a charming smile but a smile truly blessed in its wholehearted acceptance—approval, even—of the world and all its ways.

I opened the tent flap to call after him, but did not know what to say; the man waved goodbye to me and my bad manners and vanished from the yard.

I soon discovered that the other wool trader, the one who was eating barleycorns in Namu's yard, has a fine smile, too, though this man lacks the seraphic air of his companion. At supper, I decided not to talk about these smiles in the face of GS's stern conviction, shared by Phu-Tsering, that the two were temple looters who would cheerfully make off with our last lentil. It was agreed that the wood door to the cooking hut should be locked, lest they steal poor Dawa blind in his thick sleep; tomorrow the Sherpas would keep watch until this unsavory pair had slunk away.

Now it is morning, and all precautions have been foolish, since the wool traders departed at first light, up the Black River toward the Kang Pass. I am sorry about this, as I wished to make up for my lack of trust by wishing them Godspeed in a warm way. In truth, they are our benefactors, for if they cross over the Kang La, they will reopen the trail in the high snows for Tukten and Gyaltsen, who might arrive this very day at Ring-mo. Learning that two men had crossed the Kang Pass in recent days, the Sherpas would feel inspired to do the same.

Namu takes tea with us this morning, bringing roast barley-corns, which give a welcome character to the gray porridge. She vouches for the traders, telling us that they had come through here last year from their home on the Bheri River. Formerly they traded into Bhot, or B'od, which she pronounces "Po." The Land of Po. Traditionally, the central provinces of U and Thang are known to Tibetans as "B'od," which has been translated as "native place," or "home": eastern Tibet is known as Khams, and western Tibet was composed formerly of small kingdoms such as Lo (Mustang) and Dol. I think of Tsurton-Wang-Gay— like Milarepa, a disciple of Marpa—who came from the Land of Dol; if, as may be, the ancient Dol and Dol Po are the same, then the oldest prayer stones deep in the stone field west of the gompa might have been carved in the days of the eleventh century when Tsurton-Wang-Gay walked these mountains, and Milarepa's skin was turning green due to subsistence on the nettles near his cave. Perhaps it was just such light-fingered fellows as our visitors from Saldang that Milarepa had in mind when he referred to "those lawless folk, the Yepo and Yemo of Dol."[17]

This morning I go up on Somdo mountain to observe twelve rams that so far show no interest in the females; they remain on the horizon, under the snows. After two hours of hard climbing, I am higher than Black Pond, and the whole canyon of the Black River, ascending toward the Kang Pass, lies exposed to view. Beyond the Kang soars a resplendent wall of white that dominates the sky to the southwest; it is the great ice wall of Kanjiroba, a rampart of crystalline escarpments and white-winged cornices, well over 20,000 feet in height. Here there is only a light air from the east, but the high wind on Kanjiroba is blowing clouds of a fine snow from points and pinnacles that turn into transparency against the blue.

Two black specks of life twitch on the whiteness. The wool traders are nearing the Black Pond and by early afternoon might reach the pass; perhaps they will sleep tonight at Cave Camp and be safe at Ring-mo late tomorrow. For some reason, the sight of the two figures on the waste brings to mind Ongdi the Trader, then the Kathmandu of my first visit in 1961, in winter, when the old bazaars were thronged with mountain folk come down to trade. That year, the refugee Tibetans were numerous in the Nepal Valley, bartering their precious religious objects in order to survive: most were indistinguishable from Bhotes like Ongdi, down out of the hills in beads and braids to trade their wool and salt for knives and tea. In the Asan Bazaar I found the green bronze Akshobhya Buddha that became the center of a small altar in D's last room; Akshobhya is the "Imperturbable," being that aspect of Sakyamuni's nature that resisted the temptation of the demons under the *bodhi* tree at Gaya. The Buddha was placed on a throne of pine bark, a red berry in his lap and over his head a *bodhi* tree made from a bunch of pearly everlasting, very like this everlasting here on the slopes of Shey.

These days are luminous, as in those far October days in Tichu-Rong. There is no wisp of cloud—clear, clear, clear, clear. Although the shade is very cold throughout the day, and wind persists, the sun is hot—imagine a striped and shiny lizard above 15,000 feet, in deep November! For the first time in my life, I apprehend the pure heat of our star, piercing the frigid atmospheres of so many million miles of outer space.

Rock, and snow peaks all around, the sky, and great birds

and black rivers—what words are there to seize such ringing splendor? But again something arises in this ringing that is not quite bearable, a poised terror, as in the diamond ice that cracks the stone. The brain veers; the sun glints like a weapon. Then Black Canyon writhes and twists, and the Crystal Mountain looms as a castle of dread, and all the universe reverberates with horror. My head is the sorcerer's skull cup full of blood, and were I to turn, my eyes would see straight to the heart of chaos, the mutilation, bloody gore, and pain that is seen darkly in the bright eye of this lizard.

Then lunacy is gone, leaving an echo. The lizard is still there, one with its rock, flanks pulsing in the star heat that brings warmth to our common skin; eternity is not remote, it is here beside us.

My plan is to stalk the bharal rams from above and from the east, with the sun behind me; the light east wind will soon die out, as it does each morning in fair weather, giving way after a lull to a north wind that will not carry my scent. I climb to snow line at the east end of the ridge and wait for the wind to die.

Across the crest fly the Tibetan snow finches that until now I have only seen across the distance, blowing in flurries through the blue. The finches land among the rocks, accompanied by larks, then rise with faint tinklings as suddenly as they have come, circling the summit in the morning light in showers of white wings, and bounding away into the north.

In a shift of wind, it is so still that melt trickles can be heard from beneath the snow: the whole world rests. I work west along the ridge, peering down over mixed scree and snow until a strange outcrop of horn crescents comes in view. The bharal are wary, watching the lower mountain: the nearest horns are perhaps two hundred yards to westward and below. Crouching, I make my way in stealth to a rock clump within stoning distance of my quarry. There I indulge myself in a silent chortle of self-satisfaction, at which, in instant retribution, there falls upon my ears the hollow drumming of wild hooves upon the mountain.

The sheep move west and north around the summit, and I

follow. This time I arrive safe at my vantage point, and keep stern watch as consenting males push, shove, lick, sniff, and mount upon their colleagues. But soon there comes a familiar *chirr-it, chirr-it, chirr-it,* so very like a scolding rodent that I search among the grass tufts for a marmot. More than one bharal is snorting in alarm, and in seconds the band is off again at a scattering gallop on the gravel, leaving me dumbfounded, for I am well hidden, and I have not stirred.

Perhaps I underestimate my smell.

A golden eagle, with shrill peeping, glides down along the snows almost at eye level; the deep voice that would better suit this noble bird would not carry very far in so much emptiness. Soon afterward, wild pigeons pass on snapping blue-gray wings—the Turkestan hill pigeon that replaces the snow pigeon here on the Tibetan Plateau. In the frozen air, pigeons and eagle are superb, but they do not console me for the loss of my sheep, which I track over the ridge to the northern buttes; there the fresh prints in the snow lead down an incline so steep and icy that neither man nor wolf would care to follow. But the sheep have led me to the only point in all this landscape from which one might see those two pale buildings, far away on a plateau to the north and east. This view is my first and last in my present incarnation of the old B'on monastery called Samling, for the deep gorge of Black Canyon is impassable, and the way over the mountains blocked by snow.

Jang-bu returns this afternoon with great good news. It is true that the track from Saldang across to Tarap remains open almost all winter; one has only to cross the Shey Pass to Saldang. And a yak trail from Saldang to Murwa, that pretty village below Ring-mo, under the great falls, stays open longer than the Kang. In this season many people from Saldang leave for Murwa and the Bheri in search of winter work; some go as laborers and porters, some hire out their yaks on the main route between Tarakot and Jumla, and others transport wool and salt for trade. At present they dance and drink their *chang,* in preparation for the winter exodus, but no doubt some few will be left by the time we need them for the outward journey.

While in Saldang, Jang-bu talked to the two wool traders who later passed through Shey, and it turns out that these men whom we treated so inhospitably were carrying Jang-bu's messages to Tukten and Gyaltsen. There are no police at Saldang, Jang-bu says: there are "many temples," and a lama from Shey is there, just as reported. But the true Lama of Shey—and we realize now that Namu was protecting him—the *tulku,* or incarnate lama, whom I was so anxious to find, is none other than the crippled monk who was curing the goat skin in yak butter and brains, up at Tsakang.

NOVEMBER 11

In the east, at dark, bright Mars appears, and soon the full moon follows the sun's path, east to west across a blue-black sky. I am always restless in the time of the full moon, a common lunatic, and move about the frozen monastery, moon-watching. Rising over the White River, the moon illuminates the ghostly prayer flag blowing so softly on the roof of the still hut, and seems to kindle the stacked brushwood; on its altar stone my small clay Buddha stirs. The snow across the river glows, and the rocks and peaks, the serpentine black stream, the snows, sky, stars, the firmament—all ring like the bell of Dorje-Chang. *Now!* Here is the secret! *Now!*

At daybreak, when the blue-black turns to silver in the east, the moon sets with the darkness in the west. On frozen sun rays, fourteen pigeons come to pick about the yard, pale blue-gray birds with a broad white band across the tail that fills with light as they flutter down upon the rigid walls. Like all wild things at Crystal Mountain, the hill pigeons are tame, and do not fly as I draw near, but cock their gentle dovelike heads to see me better.

I climb the mountain with the sun, and find the mixed herd high up on the slope; I try angling toward them, then away again, zigzagging as I climb. For some reason, this seems to reassure them, for after watching me awhile, and perhaps concluding that I am not to be taken seriously, they go on about their business, which this morning is unusually dull. I keep on climbing. Far below, the torrent, freed from daybreak ice, carries gray scree down out of the mountains.

In hope of seeing the snow leopard, I have made a wind shelter and lookout on this mountain, just at snow line, that faces north over the Black Canyon all the way to the pale terraces below Samling. From here, the Tsakang mountainsides across Black River are in view, and the cliff caves, too, and the slopes between ravines, so that most of the blue sheep in this region may be seen should they be set upon by wolf or leopard. (GS estimates a population of 175 to 200 animals on the mountainsides in the near vicinity of Shey.) Unlike the wolves, the leopard cannot eat everything at once, and may remain in the vicinity of its kill for several days. Therefore our best hope is to see the griffons gather, and the choughs and ravens, and the lammergeier.

The Himalayan griffon, buff and brown, is almost the size of the great lammergeier; its graceful turns against the peaks inspire the Tibetans, who, like the vanished Aryans of the Vedas, revere the wind and sky. Blue and white are the celestial colors of the B'on sky god, who is seen as an embodiment of space and light, and creatures of the upper air become B'on symbols— the griffon, the mythical garuda, and the dragon. For Buddhist Tibetans, prayer flags and wind-bells confide spiritual longings to the winds, and the red kites that dance on holidays over the old brown city of Kathmandu are of Tibetan origin as well. There is also a custom called "air burial," in which the body of the deceased is set out on a wild crag such as this one, to be rended and devoured by the wild beasts; when only the bones are left, these are broken and ground down to powder, then mixed into lumps of dough, to be set out again for passing birds. Thus all is returned into the elements, death into life.

Against the faces of the canyon, shadows of griffons turn. Perhaps the Somdo raptors think that this queer lump on the landscape—the motionless form of a man in meditation—is the defunct celebrant in an air burial, for a young eagle, plumage burnished a heraldic bronzy-black, draws near with its high peeping, and a lammergeier, approaching from behind, descends with a sudden rush of feathers, sweeping so close past my head that I feel the break of air. This whisper of the shroud gives me

a start, and my sudden jump flares the dark bird, causing it to
take four deep slow strokes—the only movement of the wings
that I was ever to observe in this great sailer that sweeps up and
down the Himalayan canyons, the cold air ringing in its golden
head.

Dark, light, dark: a raptor, scimitar-winged, under the sun
peak—I know, I know. In such a light, one might hope to see
the shadow of that bird upon the sky.

The ground whirls with its own energy, not in an alarming
way but in slow spiral, and at these altitudes, in this vast space
and silence, that energy pours through me, joining my body
with the sun until small silver breaths of cold, clear air, no
longer mine, are lost in the mineral breathing of the mountain.
A white down feather, sun-filled, dances before me on the
wind: alighting nowhere, it balances on a shining thorn, goes
spinning on. Between this white feather, sheep dung, light, and
the fleeting aggregate of atoms that is "I," there is no particle
of difference. There is a mountain opposite, but this "I" is opposite nothing, opposed to nothing.

I grow into these mountains like a moss. I am bewitched.
The blinding snow peaks and the clarion air, the sound of earth
and heaven in the silence, the requiem birds, the mythic beasts,
the flags, great horns, and old carved stones, the rough-hewn
Tartars in their braids and homespun boots, the silver ice in the
black river, the Kang, the Crystal Mountain. Also, I love the common miracles—the murmur of my friends at evening, the clay
fires of smudgy juniper, the coarse dull food, the hardship and
simplicity, the contentment of doing one thing at a time: when
I take my blue tin cup into my hand, that is all I do. We have
had no news of modern times since late September, and will
have none until December, and gradually my mind has cleared
itself, and wind and sun pour through my head, as through a
bell. Though we talk little here, I am never lonely; I am returned
into myself.

Having got here at last, I do not wish to leave the Crystal
Mountain. I am in pain about it, truly, so much so that I have
to smile, or I might weep. I think of D and how she would
smile, too. In another life—this isn't what I know, but how I

feel—these mountains were my home; there is a rising of forgotten knowledge, like a spring from hidden aquifers under the earth. To glimpse one's own true nature is a kind of homegoing, to a place East of the Sun, West of the Moon—the homegoing that needs no home, like that waterfall on the upper Suli Gad that turns to mist before touching the earth and rises once again into the sky.

NOVEMBER 12

Tukten and Gyaltsen came yesterday evening, a day ahead of the most optimistic schedule. They had good weather all the way and no snow at all on the low passes between Tibrikot and Jumla; they met the wool traders at Ring-mo, and someone led them to the Kang Pass. But according to Gyaltsen, who got here first, and burst out with his side of the story, there had been bad trouble on the journey. At Jumla, Tukten, very drunk, had hatched a plan to make off into India with the money that was sure to be found in our mail; the ensuing series of disputes between them had ended in Ring-mo in a violent fight the day before.

Gyaltsen is young, excitable, and upset, but he is no liar; the Sherpas have warned us about Tukten all along. Still, the story is unclear, and the mail has arrived safely. When Tukten comes, he is as open-faced and calm as ever, and says nothing against Gyaltsen, but includes his erstwhile traveling companion in a general attitude of friendliness. I admire Tukten for making no effort to defend himself, and even Jang-bu, who is Gyaltsen's friend and the one most suspicious of Tukten from the start, is soon laughing at his stories, entirely disarmed. Thief or no, I am happy and relieved to see him, as I am counting on this man for the outward journey.

My letters I put away unopened, in my pack; they will not be read until I get to Jumla or Kathmandu. Today is the twelfth, and I leave on the eighteenth; even if the letters bring bad news, I could leave no earlier than the fifteenth, since Tukten and Gyaltsen have traveled hard, and must have rest. And good news, too, would be intrusive, spoiling this chance to live moment by moment in the present by stirring up the past, the future, and encouraging delusions of continuity and permanence just when I am trying to let go, to blow away, like that white down feather on the mountain.

Yesterday a circumambulating wolf left a whole circle of tracks around the prayer wall across the river, at the foot of the trail that climbs around the mountains to Tsakang, and this morning, on the trail itself, there are prints of leopard. As if seeking protection, the blue sheep feed close by the hermitage, where I go with Jang-bu to call on the Lama of Shey.

When we arrive, the Lama is inside chanting sutras, but his attendant sits outside, still cutting and sorting the small store of potatoes; he is an aspirant monk, or *trapa,* whose clear gaze makes him look much younger than he is. His name is Takla, he is twenty-two years old, and he comes from the great northern plain of Tibet.

On the sunny ledge, under the bright blue window of the gompa, we listen to the murmurs of the Lama and contemplate the prospect of the snows. Soon the mountains stir, then shift and vibrate—how vital these rocks seem, against blue sky! If only they would fly apart, consume us in a fire of white light. But I am not ready, and resist, in fear of losing my death grip on the world, on all that provides the illusion of security. The same fear—of loss of control, of "insanity," far worse than the fear of death—can occur with the hallucinogenic drugs: familiar things, losing the form assigned to them, begin to spin, and the center does not hold, because we search for it outside instead of in.

When the Lama appears, he seems glad of our visit, though we lack the gift of a *kata,* or ceremonial white scarf, that is customary on such occasions. He is an imposing man with the long hawk nose and carved cheekbones of a Plains Indian; his skin is a dark reddish copper, his teeth are white, his long black hair is tied up in a braid, and he wears an old leather jacket with brass buttons, patched with burlap homespun of strange colors. When talking, he sits with legs crossed, barefoot, but puts on ancient laceless shoes when he moves around; in the doorway behind him hangs a wolf skin that he wears about his waist, indoors, to warm his back. Now he relates his history to Jang-bu, whose halting translation is more or less as follows:

Karma Tupjuk was born fifty-two years ago of Tibetan parents in the region of Manang, a Tibetan town on the northern slopes of Annapurna. At this time, the Lama of Shey, Tuptok Sang Hisay, had been dead for several years, and as he had been a *tulku*—that is, the reincarnation of his predecessor—the people of Dolpo were on the lookout for the new *tulku*, who usually turns up within a few years of the death, not as the same flesh and blood, but in the way that a live flame is passed to a new candle. Those sent in search turned up eventually at Takang, in Manang, near the pilgrim shrine at Muktinath, where water, air, and earth burn in strange fire. Hearing of a boy who claimed to be the *tulku*, the searchers put him to such tests as the unhesitating selection of the dead man's personal effects—cups, clothes, religious objects, and the like—from a series of nearly identical objects belonging to others. When Tupjuk had satisfied them that he was indeed the *tulku* whom they sought, they declared him such, and took him away to Shey, but since he was only eight years old, he returned each year to Manang for religious instruction from his brother, the Lama Pamawongal.

Belief in the *tulku* principle is a relatively recent tradition, made retroactive: thus, the Dalai Lamas, who did not exist until the sixteenth century, are considered to be *tulkus* of Chenresigs. Karma Tupjuk is regarded as the true reincarnation of certain great lamas of the Kagyu lineage, from the Indian sage Tilopa to the Lama Marpa, and from Marpa through nine centuries to Tuptok Sang Hisay. Like Milarepa and many other Kagyu-Karma-pas, he has chosen a hermit's life of solitary meditation, which being the "Short Path" to true knowledge is therefore the supreme form of existence. But to renounce the world in this way requires the ultimate discipline, as well as exceptional power and inner resources, and my admiration is mingled with regret that, by comparison, my own dedication is halfhearted and too late.

Long ago, Karma Tupjuk retreated to Tsakang, where he expects to pass the remainder of his life. Until ten years ago, he liked to walk around the mountain, but since that time he has become crippled by what appears to be arthritis, and moves painfully on twisted legs on two crutch canes. Even so, he seems cheerful, open, natural, and strong, and as he talks, he smiles at Crystal Mountain, which sails on the western sky over our heads.

The monastery must be very old, the Lama thinks, much older than the present buildings, to judge from the age and number of the prayer stones; most of the prayer flags in the Dolpo region are printed on ancient wood blocks kept at Shey. A thousand years ago, the old scripts say, a great yogin named Drutob Senge Yeshe[18] arrived here on a flying snow leopard to convert to Buddhism a wild folk ruled by a dread mountain god. Aided by snake-beings, the mountain god resisted this conversion, but the snow leopard reproduced itself one hundred and eight times, and the mountain god was overcome. Drutob Senge Yeshe made the mountain god a Protector of the Dharma and transformed an undistinguished summit into this crystal mountain that is sacred throughout all of Dolpo and beyond.

The Lama displays the long horn of a Tibetan antelope, which he brought back years ago from the northern plain of Tibet known as the Khang. The Sikkim stag whose antlers adorn Shey Gompa is also a creature of the Khang, he says, as is a certain "horselike" animal—presumably the wild ass. As for the argali (*Ovis ammon:* the best-known race is the Marco Polo sheep), such animals were here just a few years ago—he points at the Somdo mountainsides above the village. I wanted to bellow all this news across the valleys to GS. *Sao,* as the snow leopard calls itself, he has seen often on these trails below Tsakang, which got its name from the red color of its clay. The smaller hermitage, on the cliffs farther north, is called Dölma-jang or the Green Tara—"goddess of girls," Jang-bu informs me. (The Green Tara is an honorary name of the Nepali princess who, with another wife, the White Tara, made a Buddhist of Sron Tsan Gampo, the great seventh-century king of Tibet.) A solitary *trapa* lives at Dölma-jang, but he has gone away to beg for food. Dölma-jang, which hides the meditation cave of

Drutob Senge Yeshe, is thought to be the oldest building in the region. Last year a fine statue of the Green Tara was stolen from that hermitage by wandering Kham-pas, which helps to explain why the people at Shey were so wary of our presence.

Rising painfully, the Lama hobbles out upon a stone platform that overhangs the cliff and squats to urinate through a neat triangular hole, into the ravine; as if to enjoy this small shift in his view, he gazes cheerfully about him, his *tulku* pee drop sparkling in the sun upon the stone.

Presently we are led into the gompa, through small dark rooms full of barley, oil, red peppers, and the like, all given to Karma Tupjuk by his people. The lamasery owns farmland at Saldang, worked by sharecroppers who bring it half the produce, but most of its tea and yak butter and *tsampa* come as offerings. Karma Tupjuk mounts a log ladder to a room on the second floor that contains a brazier and some large copper pots and urns. He removes the top from a canister of water, laying it down on a pile of dung chips while rinsing his hands. Then he enters the little prayer room that looks out over the snows through its bright blue window. On the walls of the prayer room hang two fine *thankas,* or cloth paintings, and the altar wall has figures in both brass and bronze of Karma-pa, the founder of this subsect, as well as Dorje-Chang, Sakyamuni, and Chen-resigs. Surprisingly, a large statue of Padma Sambhava occupies the very center of the altar, which is heaped with offerings of highly colored cakes, wax-paper flowers, and brass goblets full of barley grains. On both sides are shelves of ancient scrolls, or "books," as well as *thankas* (the old *thankas* on the wall are in poor repair, and these rolled-up ones must be even more decrepit). The walls all around are crowded with frescoes and religious paintings, and each corner is cluttered with old treasures, all but lost in musty darkness. Lighting incense, the Lama opens a small trunk and takes out sacramental cakes, which he presents in silence, with a smile.

NOVEMBER 13

The last fortnight has been clear and warm, day after day, but early this morning there were wisps of cloud which could mean a change in weather. On these last mornings, just an hour after sunrise, sun and moon are in perfect equilibrium above the snows to east and west. High cirrus in the north, seen yesterday, foretold a drop in temperature: it is $-11°$ Centigrade this morning. The wind on Somdo mountain has a hard bite in it, and the lizards have withdrawn into the earth.

From sunrise to sundown I move with the Shey herd, which has been joined in recent days by the band of rams. The herd is up at snow line, to the eastward; this Somdo summit must be close to 17,000 feet. Climbing, I traverse the slopes with my zigzag technique, stopping and stooping and otherwise signaling to the browsing sheep that I am but a harmless dung-seeker, like other *Homo sapiens* of their acquaintance. By the time I arrive at snow line they have started to lie down; I reach a lookout knoll perhaps 150 yards away. The animals will feed again in the midmorning, then rest through the noon lull, then feed intermittently until sundown.

A little past ten, the sheep begin to browse, at the same time paying close attention to the other animals. Though now and then two females chase each other, the activity is mostly among the males—male mounting male, and rampant rump-rubbing, and some mild shoving. There is a "pairing" that becomes apparent when one spends the entire day with a single group: the males that test each other, shove, mount, butt, and rub, also seem to feed and rest together, and furthermore, are very like in size of horn, development of black display markings, and dominance position in the herd; these trial confrontations and approaches are almost never between mismatched pairs.

Nibbling the snow patches and pawing up dust before settling gracefully, bent foreknees first, in the warm sun of a hollow, out of the wind, the animals have let me come so close that I can admire their orange eyes and the delicate techniques of horn-tip scratching, as well as the bizarre activities centered upon the hindquarters of both sexes: at this early stage in the progress of the rut, the recipients of rump-rub and urine-check pay little heed or none to their admirers. Meanwhile, the yearlings scamper prettily to stay out of the reach of itching adults. There has been no real fighting or advanced sexual display of the sort that is beginning to be seen in the western herds, although occasionally a male will approach a female slowly, his extended neck held low, in what GS calls "low-stretch" behavior, an overture to copulation. Since the Somdo herd has grown so used to me that I can observe it comfortably, without binoculars, it is a pity that I must leave before full rut.

Toward noon there comes cold wind from the southeast, quite disagreeable on this bare scree slope without cover, and getting chilled, I ease the herd downhill and to the westward, simply by crowding it a little, on the lookout for a rock or tussock shelter. The herd pauses for an hour or more on a flat ridge while I lie back snugly against my rucksack in a dense clump of honeysuckle, just above: directly below lies the Crystal Monastery, with the home mountains all around, the sky, and as the sheep browse, I chew dry bread, in this wonderful immersion in pure sheep-ness.

In midafternoon, in a series of exciting flurries, I move the sheep farther downhill again to where GS, on his return from the Tsakang slopes, might study them without making a long climb. Then Old Sonam, out hunting dung, scares the herd back toward the east. The animals are flighty now, and so I stalk them with more care, rounding the mountain and crawling upwind to a tussock within sixty yards of the small rise where they stand at attention, staring the wrong way. Now and then, a head turns in my direction; I stay motionless, and they do not flare. The creatures are so very tense that even the heavy horns bristle with life. No muscle moves. For minute after minute I watch the roughing of their coats by the mountain wind.

Thinking to move them back toward the west, I sit up slowly, and all turn to look. But the contrary beasts, having fled so often for no reason, confound me once again. With a man popping up almost on top of them, they now relax a little, and begin to feed, as if the suspense of not knowing where I was had been what bothered them. They even start to lie down again. Cold and fed up with their lack of behavior, abandoning all hope of witnessing goatish outrages unknown to science, I shoo them rudely toward the village. This time they run a quarter mile, straight to a rock outcrop just east of the first houses.

I descend the mountain to the Saldang path, turn west toward Shey. Already the path lies in twilight shadow, but the rocks on which the blue sheep stand, not thirty yards above, are in full sun. And now these creatures give a wild sunset display, the early rut that I had waited for all day. Old males spring off their rocks to challenge other males, and chase them off, and young males do as much for the females and young, and even the females butt at one another. Unlike the true sheep, which forges straight ahead, the bharal, in its confrontations, rears up and runs on the hind legs before crashing down into the impact, as true goats do—just the sort of evidence that GS has come so far to find. The whole herd of thirty-one joins in the melee, and in their quick springs from rock to rock, the goat in them is plain. Then one kicks loose a large stone from the crest, scattering the animals below, and in an instant, the whole herd is still.

Gold-eyed horned heads peer down out of the Himalayan blue as, in the silence, a last pebble bounces down the slope and comes to rest just at my feet.

The bharal await me with the calm regard of ages.

Have you seen us now? Have you perceived us?

The sun is retreating up the mountain, and still the creatures stand transfixed on their monument of rock.

Quickly I walk into the monastery to tell GS he can study his *Pseudois* by poking his head out of his tent. But a note says that in the hope of photographing the snow leopard he will sleep tonight across the river near the Tsakang trail: with a creature as wary as this leopard, there is no place for two.

If all else fails, GS will send Jang-bu to Saldang to buy an old goat as leopard bait. I long to see the snow leopard, yet to glimpse it by camera flash, at night, crouched on a bait, is not to see it. If the snow leopard should manifest itself, then I am ready to see the snow leopard. If not, then somehow (and I don't understand this instinct, even now) I am not ready to perceive it, in the same way that I am not ready to resolve my *koan;* and in the not-seeing, I am content. I think I must be disappointed, having come so far, and yet I do not feel that way. I am disappointed, and also, I am not disappointed. That the snow leopard *is,* that it is here, that its frosty eyes watch us from the mountain—that is enough.

At supper the Sherpas, in good spirits, include me as best they can in their conversation, but after a while I bury myself in these notes, so that they can talk comfortably among themselves. Usually this means listening to Tukten, who holds the others rapt for hours at a time with that deep soft voice of his, his guru's hands extended in a hypnotizing way over the flames. I love to watch our evil monk with his yellow Mongol eyes and feral ears, and it is rare that I look at him when he isn't watching me. One day I will ask this yellow-eyed Tukten if, in some other incarnation, he has not been a snow leopard, or an old blue sheep on the slopes of Shey; he would be at no loss for an answer. At supper, he regards me with that Bodhisattva smile that would shine impartially on rape or resurrection—this is the gaze that he shares with the wild animals.

NOVEMBER 14

Crossing Black River, I climb the west slope trail, out of the night canyon, into the sun. In the matted juniper is a small busy bird, the Tibetan tit-warbler, blue-gray with a rufous cap, and an insistent call note, *t-sip:* what can it be insisting on, so near the winter?

On this bright morning, under the old moon, leopard prints are fresh as petals on the trail. But perhaps two hundred yards short of the trip line to GS's camera, the tracks appear to end, as if the cat had jumped aside into the juniper; the two prints closer to the trip line had been made the day before. Beyond the next cairn, where the path rounds the ridge high above the river and enters the steep snow-covered ravine below Tsakang, more fresh tracks are visible in the snow, as if the snow leopard had cut across the ridge to avoid the trip line, and resumed the path higher up, in this next ravine. Close by one print is an imprint of lost ages, a fernlike fossil brachiopod in a broken stone.

From Tsakang comes the weird thump of a *damaru,* or prayer drum, sometimes constructed of two human skulls; this instrument and the *kangling* trumpet, carved from the human thigh bone, are used in Tantrism to deepen meditation, not through the encouragement of morbid thoughts but as reminders that our time on earth is fleeting. Or perhaps this is the hollow echo of the cavern water, dripping down into the copper canister; I cannot be sure. But the extraordinary sound brings the wild landscape to attention: somewhere on this mountainside the leopard listens.

High on the ridge above Tsakang, I see a blue spot where GS is tracking; I come up with him in the next hour. "It fooled me," he calls by way of greeting. "Turned up the valley just be-low the trip line, then over the ridge, not one hundred yards from where I was lying, and down onto the path again—typical." He shifts his binoculars to the Tsakang herd, which has now been joined by the smaller bands of the west slope. "I've lost the trail now, but that leopard is right here right this minute, watching us." His words are borne out by the sheep, which break into short skittish runs as the wind makes its midmorning shift, then flee the rock and thorn of this bare ridge, plunging across deep crusted snow with hollow booming blows, in flight to a point high up on the Crystal Mountain. Blue sheep do not run from man like that even when driven.

The snow leopard is a strong presence; its vertical pupils and small stilled breaths are no more than a snow cock's glide away. GS murmurs, "Unless it moves, we are not going to see it, not even on the snow—these creatures are really something." With our binoculars, we study the barren ridge face, foot by foot. Then he says, "You know something? We've seen so much, maybe it's better if there are some things that we *don't* see." He seems startled by his own remark, and I wonder if he means this as I take it—that we have been spared the desolation of success, the doubt: is this *really* what we came so far to see?

When I say, "That was the haiku-writer speaking," he knows just what I mean, and we both laugh. GS strikes me as much less dogmatic, more open to the unexplained than he was two months ago. In Kathmandu, he might have been suspicious of this haiku, written on our journey by himself:

> Cloud-men beneath loads.
> A dark line of tracks in snow.
> Suddenly nothing.

Because his sheep, spooked by the leopard, have fled to the high snows, GS accompanies me on my last visit to Tsakang. There we are met by Jang-bu, who has come as an interpreter, and by Tukten, who alone among the Sherpas has curiosity enough to cross the river and climb up to Tsakang of his own accord. Even that "gay and lovable fellow," as GS once said of

Phu-Tsering, "hasn't the slightest curiosity about what I am doing; he'll stand behind me for two hours while I'm looking and taking notes and not ask a single question."

Once again, the Lama of Shey lets us wait on the stone terrace, but this time—for we are here by invitation—the aspirant monk Takla has prepared sun-dried green yak cheese in a coarse powder, with *tsampa* and buttered tea, called *so-cha,* served in blue china cups in the mountain sun. The sharp green cheese and bitter tea, flavored with salt and rancid yak butter, give character to the *tsampa,* and in the cool air, this hermit's meal is very very good.

Takla lays out red-striped carpeting for us to sit upon, and eventually the Lama comes, wrapped in his wolf skin. Jang-bu seems wary in the Lama's presence, whereas Tukten is calm and easy and at the same time deferential; for the first time since I have known him, indoors or out, he doffs his raffish cap, revealing a monk's tonsure of close-cropped hair. Tukten does most of the translation as we show the Lama pictures from our books and talk animatedly for several hours. Lama Tupjuk asks about Tibetan lamas in America, and I tell him about Chögyam Trungpa, Rinpoche (*rinpoche,* or "precious one," signifies a high lama), of his own Karma-pa sect, who left Tibet at the age of thirteen and now teaches in Vermont and Colorado. For GS, he repeats what he had told me about the snow leopard and the argali, pointing across Black River at the slopes of Somdo.

Horns high, flanks taut, the blue sheep have begun a slow descent off the Crystal Mountain, in a beautiful curved line etched on the snow. The leopard is gone—perhaps they saw it go. Through binoculars, now and again, a ram can be seen to rear up wildly as if dancing on the snow, then run forward on hind legs and descend again, to crash its horns against those of a rival.

In the high sun, snows shift and flow, bathing the mind in diamond light. Tupjuk Rinpoche speaks now of the snow leopard, which he has seen often from his ledge, and has watched carefully, to judge from the accuracy of all his observations: he knows that it cries most frequently in mating time, in spring, and which caves and ledges it inhabits, and how it makes its scrape and defecation.

Before we leave, I show him the plum pit inscribed with the sutra to Chen-resigs that was given me by Soen Roshi, and promise to send him my wicker camp stool from the tea stall on the Yamdi River. The Lama gives me a white prayer flag—*lung-p'ar,* he calls it, "wind pictures"—printed with both script and images from the old wood blocks at Shey; among the Buddhist symbols is an image of Nurpu Khonday Pung-jun, the great god of mountains and rivers, who was here, says the Lama, long before the B'on-pos and the Buddhists: presumably this was the god who was vanquished by Drutob Senge Yeshe and his hundred and eight snow leopards. Nurpu is now a Protector of the Dharma, and his image on flags such as this one is often placed on bridges and the cairns in the high passes, as an aid to travelers. The Lama folds it with greatest concentration, and presents it with the blessing of his smile.

The Lama of the Crystal Monastery appears to be a very happy man, and yet I wonder how he feels about his isolation in the silences of Tsakang, which he has not left in eight years now and, because of his legs, may never leave again. Since Jang-bu seems uncomfortable with the Lama or with himself or perhaps with us, I tell him not to inquire on this point if it seems to him impertinent, but after a moment Jang-bu does so. And this holy man of great directness and simplicity, big white teeth shining, laughs out loud in an infectious way at Jang-bu's question. Indicating his twisted legs without a trace of self-pity or bitterness, as if they belonged to all of us, he casts his arms wide to the sky and the snow mountains, the high sun and dancing sheep, and cries, "Of course I am happy here! It's wonderful! *Especially* when I have no choice!"

In its wholehearted acceptance of *what is,* this is just what Soen Roshi might have said: I feel as if he had struck me in the chest. I thank him, bow, go softly down the mountain: under my parka, the folded prayer flag glows. Butter tea and wind pictures, the Crystal Mountain, and blue sheep dancing on the snow—it's quite enough!

Have you seen the snow leopard?

No! Isn't that wonderful?

NOVEMBER 15

All morning the moon hangs frozen on the sky, and the wind-bell rings unheard on the hard east wind. The robin accentor has perished, or fled south across the mountains, since it no longer turns up in my yard. To the cook hut, in the bitter cold, comes Namu with a blanket wrapped around her head, to take a cup of tea: ordinarily, her wild black hair blows free. The days are shorter now. The sun is gone by midafternoon, when this primordial woman fills the mountain dusk with her wild cries, calling her black *dzo*, scaring off wolves.

I climb early to the northwest ridge of Somdo mountain, from where I can watch all the trails, scan all the valleys of the western slopes, beyond Black River: if the snow leopard is abroad, then I may see it, and if it makes a kill, I shall see birds. GS has crossed the river early to look for more fresh sign: he tries not to let the leopard interfere with his study of blue sheep, but the great cats have a strong hold on him, and the snow leopard is the least known of them all. It is wonderful how the presence of this creature draws the whole landscape to a point, from the glint of light on the old horns of a sheep to the ring of a pebble on the frozen ground.

Since it is too cold to sit in one position, I roam up and down the ridge, scanning the west walls every little while, and keeping an eye on the blue sheep of Somdo, which seem well behind the Tsakang herd in the progress of the rut. On this slope there are many fossils, mostly spiraled ammonites, and in the river lie wild rocks of great beauty. I love wild rocks, I covet them, but they are too big to carry away over the passes. Perhaps I shall take a few shards of broken prayer stones; the river rocks will stay where they belong.

With the wind and cold, a restlessness has come, and I find myself hoarding my last chocolate for the journey back across the mountains—forever getting-ready-for-life instead of living it each day. This restlessness is intensified by the presence of the extra Sherpas, who can do little besides use up precious food; they sleep and sit around, waiting to go.

Like heralds of the outside world, Tukten and Gyaltsen arrived with the full moon. Now the moon is waning, and the fine lunar clarity of life at Shey swiftly diminishes. Exciting days have occurred since their arrival, and yet a kind of power is winding down, a spell is broken.

And so I, too, prepare to go, though I try hard to remain. The part of me that is bothered by the unopened letters in my rucksack, that longs to see my children, to drink wine, make love, be clean and comfortable again—that part is already facing south, over the mountains. This makes me sad, and so I stare about me, trying to etch into this journal the sense of Shey that is so precious, aware that all such effort is in vain; the beauty of this place must be cheerfully abandoned, like the wild rocks in the bright water of its streams. Frustration at the paltriness of words drives me to write, but there is more of Shey in a single sheep hair, in one withered sprig of everlasting, than in all these notes; to strive for permanence in what I think I have perceived is to miss the point.

Near my lookout, I find a place to meditate, out of the wind, a hollow on the ridge where snow has melted. My brain soon clears in the cold mountain air, and I feel better. Wind, blowing grasses, sun: the dying grass, the notes of southbound birds in the mountain sky are no more fleeting than the rock itself, no more so and no less—all is the same. The mountain withdraws into its stillness, my body dissolves into the sunlight, tears fall that have nothing to do with "I." What it is that brings them on, I do not know.

In other days, I understood mountains differently, seeing in them something that abides. Even when approached respectfully (to challenge peaks as mountaineers do is another matter) they appalled me with their "permanence," with that awful and irrefutable *rock*-ness that seemed to intensify my sense of my own transience. Perhaps this dread of transience explains our greed for the few gobbets of raw experience in modern life, why violence is libidinous, why lust devours us, why soldiers choose not to forget their days of horror: we cling to such extreme moments, in which we seem to die, yet are reborn. In sexual abandon as in danger we are impelled, however briefly, into that vital present in which we do not stand apart from life, we *are* life, our being fills us; in ecstasy with another being, loneliness falls away into eternity. But in other days, such union was attainable through simple awe.

My foot slips on a narrow ledge: in that split second, as needles of fear pierce heart and temples, eternity intersects with present time. Thought and action are not different, and stone, air, ice, sun, fear, and self are one. What is exhilarating is to extend this acute awareness into ordinary moments, in the moment-by-moment experiencing of the lammergeier and the wolf, which, finding themselves at the center of things, have no need for any secret of true being. In this very breath that we take now lies the secret that all great teachers try to tell us, what one lama refers to as "the precision and openness and intelligence of the present."[19] The purpose of meditation practice is not enlightenment; it is to pay attention even at unextraordinary times, to be of the present, nothing-but-the-present, to bear this mindfulness of *now* into each event of ordinary life. To be anywhere else is "to paint eyeballs on chaos."[20] When I watch blue sheep, I must watch blue sheep, not be thinking about sex, danger, or the present, for this present—even while I think of it—is gone.

NOVEMBER 16

The snow leopard has been hunting in the night, for part of the Tsakang herd has fled off toward the north, taking shelter in the yard of Dölma-jang, and the rest have crossed the ridges to the west; from Somdo, a calligraphic track up Crystal Mountain can be seen that disappears at the white rim, into blue sky. Having dispersed the Tsakang herds, the leopard crossed over the Black River—or perhaps a second leopard has arrived—for here on Somdo, the big herd is also scattered, with males and females reverting to their separate bands. As we climb the broad mountainsides above the village, a lone band of nine male animals is in sight.

Not a thousand feet above our tents at Shey, on the path that I walked yesterday, a leopard has made its scrape right in my boot print, as if in sign that I am not to leave. The leopard may still be present on this slope, for the rams are skittish. Even so, the rut is near, activity is constant, and GS scribbles in his notebook. "Oh, there's a penis-lick!" he cries. "A beauty!" The onanism is mingled here and there with fighting, especially among the older rams, which rear repeatedly on their hind legs; remarkably, another rears at the same instant, and the two run forward like trained partners, coming down together with a crash of heads. For most creatures, such an encounter would be fatal, but bharal are equipped with some two inches of parietal bone between the horns, together with a cushion of air space in the sinuses, thick woolly head hair, and strong necks to absorb the shock, and the horns themselves, on the impact side, are very thick and heavy. Why nature should devote so many centuries—thousands, probably—to the natural selection of these characters that favor head-on collisions over brains is a good question, although speaking for myself in these searching days, less brains and a good head-on collision might be just the answer.

Watching blue sheep in the sun and windlessness is pleasant, and reminds us that this pleasantness must end. We discuss logistics briefly, and also the implications of our journey, and our great good fortune. Last night at supper, GS remarked that this was one of the best trips he had ever made, "tough enough so that we feel we have really accomplished something, but not so tough that it wiped us out entirely." I feel the same.

This morning, expressing his relief that such good bharal data have come in, GS refers again to his dread of failure, of the satisfaction that his peers might take in his first mistake, and after two months I feel I know him well enough to point out how often this refrain occurs in his conversation, and how baseless his apprehension seems to be: no matter how badly he might fail on any expedition, his abilities and good reputation are beyond dispute. GS recognizes his mild paranoia, and discusses it quite frankly as he stands there, observing the blue sheep's world through his faithful spotting scope; he is more open and relaxed each day. When I say so, he looks doubtful, and I quote his remark about the snow leopard: "Maybe it's better if there are some things that we *don't* see." He nods grudgingly, as if in disapproval, but later he resists the implications of his repeated observation at Tsakang that mountains move. "Well," he mutters, "from a certain point of view, I mean, geologically, of course, the Himalaya is still rising, and then there is a downward movement due to erosion—" I interrupt him. "That's not what you meant," I say. "Not at Tsakang." Still squinting into the telescope, my partner grins.

GS feels that our journey has had the quality of adventure because we depend entirely on ourselves; that this is an old-fashioned expedition in the sense that we are completely out of touch with our own world, with our own century, for that matter—no vehicles, no doctor, and no radio, far less airdrops or support teams or other such accoutrements of the modern "expedition." "This is the way I like it," GS says. "You haven't got the whole goddamned society backing you up, you're on your own: you have to take responsibility for your mistakes, you can't blame the organization. And inevitably, you make mistakes— you just hope they aren't too serious." I like it, too, for the same reasons, and also because the penalty for error makes me mindful as I walk among these mountains, heeding the echo of my step on the frozen earth.

At midmorning, when the blue sheep have settled for their rest, we walk a long eastward traverse, then west again, hoping to jump the leopard from a gully. On the stony ground, the few prints are indistinct, with nothing fresh enough to indicate where the creature might be lying. If this is the Tsakang cat, then it is hungry, and there is a chance that it will kill tonight. Since it will stay close enough to guard its kill from the lammergeiers and griffons, this is my last hope of seeing it.

With the herds scattered, it appears unlikely that full rut will get under way in the next fortnight; if the leopard is gone, it is not apt to return again in the next week. And so I have put aside my doubts about departing here the day after tomorrow, and have asked Tukten to obtain stores and a few utensils from Phu-Tsering for the outward journey. We can take little, for the camp is running short; in Saldang, perhaps, some *tsampa* and potatoes can be obtained.

GS feels that I make too much of Tukten's spiritual propensities and, like Jang-bu, warns me to beware of him. On both points he is probably right. Still, I am glad that Tukten will be with me, for unlike all but the head Sherpa, he anticipates problems and deals with them unasked. Gyaltsen has no wish to travel on in life with Tukten, preferring to remain at Shey with Jang-bu; Dawa will go out with us instead. Dawa's morale has been uncertain since his two bouts of snow blindness, and as a rule he appears happiest when by himself: I hear him singing every time he passes my stone wall, bound down to the White River to fetch water. He rarely joins the other Sherpas at the fire, preferring to sit back in the shadows by the wall; though they like him, the others tease him and order him about, and he smiles shyly, as if grateful that they don't pretend he isn't there.

NOVEMBER 17

Last night, the snow leopard left tracks just outside the monastery, on the Saldang path that I shall take tomorrow; like the scrape found yesterday over my bootprint, it is hard not to read this as a sign. Then the cat recrossed the Black River—either that, or there are two leopards in the region, as we think. Followed or preceded by a solitary wolf—perhaps the same elusive beast that circled the prayer wall here last week—this leopard or another has prowled the Tsakang trail, and on my last day here, as the sun rises from the ice horizon, we climb the westward slopes in hopes of locating a kill. Part of the main bharal herd has come back across the snows to graze warily just above Tsakang, and another band—many animals are still missing—steps daintily along the ledges of the cliff below the hermitage, the sunrise bright on their white knees. The only other time the bharal have been seen on the steep cliff face was the morning they were chased there by the wolves, but they may have come here of their own accord, since a few are licking alkali salts from the icicles in the small caves, and others are nibbling at stunted barberry in the crannies.

A young ram tries halfheartedly to mount a ewe, but it now appears that it will be the first days of December before the females come fully into estrus and the height of the rut occurs. After all these weeks of itch and foreplay, only a few dominant males will take part in copulation, which will last but a few seconds at each encounter.

GS is satisfied that the bharal is neither sheep nor goat but a creature perhaps very close to the ancestral goatlike animal of about twenty million years ago from which *Ovis* and *Capra* evolved. ("The behavioral evidence," he wrote later, "confirms the morphological evidence that bharal are basically goats. Many of the sheep-like traits of bharal can be ascribed to convergent evolution, the result of the species having settled in a habitat which is usually occupied by sheep. . . . The species has straddled an evolutionary fence, and if it had to make a choice of whether to become an *Ovis* or a *Capra* it could become either with only minor alterations. Like the aoudad, the bharal probably split early from the ancestral goat stock. If I had to design a hypothetical precursor from which the sheep and goat lines diverged, it would in many ways resemble a bharal in appearance and behavior.")[21]

GS continues up the valley to the herd near snow line, while I return slowly down the ridges, wishing to spend most of this last day on the home mountain. At each stupa on the canyon points, the prayer stones are lit by fire-colored lichens; in the shine of thorn and old carved stones, the print of leopard and thick scent of juniper, I am filled with longing. I turn to look back at Tsakang, at the precipices and deep shadows of Black Canyon, at the dark mountain that presides over Samling, which I shall never see. Above the snowfields to the west, the Crystal Mountain thrusts bare rock into the blue; to the south is the sinuous black torrent that comes down from Kang La, the Pass of Snows. And there on the low cliff above the rivers, silhouetted on the snow, is the village that its own people call Somdo, white prayer flags flying black on the morning sun.

On the river islands, winter ice has stilled the prayer wheels, but under the bridge the water is deep, gray, and swift, hurrying away west to the great Karnali. On the bluff, I pay my last respects to the white stupas and make a bow to bright-blue Dorje-Chang. I would enter and give the *mani* wheels a spin, and send OM MANI PADME HUM to the ten directions, but Ongdi the Trader has turned up again and locked the doors, in the hope of realizing a small gain by charging us admission. Accompanying Ongdi on this trip is the owner of the yard where my tent is pitched; he has no wish to charge me rent, merely goes about the walls adjusting prayer stones, in dour sign that

I must treat his dung heaps with respect. This dung extends from one wall to the other, my tent is pitched in it, for all I know it may be centuries deep. Yet the householder points at a stone-like coprolith frozen in the dung in the yard corner, and I am existentially embarrassed: there is no way to explain that this phenomenon of dung-on-dung occurred but once, in dire straits of night emergency and bitter cold. No, really, I am mortally offended, with no earthly target for my wrath: what has this dismal lump to do with those transparent states high on the mountain?

The stranger and I stand shoulder to shoulder, glaring downward in the wind and silence, as if the *dorje* lay before us, the adamantine diamond, ready to deliver up some Tantric teaching: *Take care, O Pilgrim, lest you discriminate against the so-called lower functions, for these, too, contain the inherent miracle of being. Did not one of the great masters attain enlightenment upon hearing the splash of his own turd into the water? Even transparency, O Pilgrim, may be a hindrance if one clings to it. One must not linger on the Crystal Mountain—*

Enough! I am not far enough along the path to perceive the Absolute in my own dung—yours, maybe, but not mine. Shit is shit, as Zen would say, or rather, *Shit!* I boot this trace of my swift passage through the world out of the yard. Then I thank the man for his hospitality and show him a rock that contains a pretty fossil, but having no idea what I require of him, he is indifferent to my thanks and stones.

Slowly I pass along the field of prayer stones to the picturesque low door of Crystal Monastery, with its old prayer wheels, one of copper, one of wood, inset in the walls on either side. Over the door is a small Buddha of worn stone, bright-painted in the reds and blues of earth and sky. Unless Tundu comes this afternoon, bringing the key, I shall never pass through this small door into Shey Gompa. The entrance stupas and Lama Tupjuk's chapel at Tsakang have given me a clue to the interior, and tomorrow, with luck, I shall visit the temple at Namgung, five hours hence across the eastern mountains, which is also a Karma-

Kagyu gompa. All the same, it seems too bad not to have seen the inside of the Crystal Monastery, having traveled so far to such a destination.

(Not long after my departure, Tundu's wife turned up with the key to the monastery, demanding one hundred rupees to open the door. GS ignored her, and on the eve of his departure, she let him enter for five rupees. According to his notes and floor plan, Shey Gompa contains a number of fine bronze Buddhas, hanging drums, old swords and muzzle loaders from the bandit days, and the heavy printing blocks that made the "wind pictures" given me by Lama Tupjuk. Otherwise, the gompa differs mostly in its large size from others in the region, excepting one bizarre and unaccountable detail: on a hanging cloth, with a wolf, Tibetan wild asses, and an owl, there is a picture of a female yeti.

This drawing at the Crystal Monastery is more curious than first appears. Pictures of yeti have been reported to exist in remote lamaseries, but they are in fact extremely rare; the only other I have ever heard of in Nepal is found at Tengboche Monastery, under Mount Everest. That such a drawing should exist well to the west of where yetis have been heretofore reported deepens the enigma of that sunny morning in the forests of the Suli Gad, and the strange dark shape that sprang behind a boulder.)

I climb to my old lookout, happy and sad in the dim instinct that these mountains are my home. But "only the Awakened Ones remember their many births and deaths,"[22] and I can hear no whisperings of other lives. Doubtless I have "home" confused with childhood, and Shey with its flags and beasts and snowy fastnesses with some Dark Ages place of forgotten fairy tales, where the atmosphere of myth made life heroic.

In the longing that starts one on the path is a kind of homesickness, and some way, on this journey, I have started home. Homegoing is the purpose of my practice, of my mountain meditation and my daybreak chanting, of my *koan*: All the peaks are covered with snow—why is this one bare? To resolve that illogical question would mean to burst apart, let fall all preconceptions and supports. But I am not ready to let go, and so I shall not resolve my *koan*, or see the snow leopard, that is to say, *perceive* it. I shall not see it because I am not ready.

I meditate for the last time on this mountain that is bare, though others all around are white with snow. Like the bare peak of the *koan*, this one is not different from myself. I know this mountain because I am this mountain, I can feel it breathing at this moment, as its grass tops stray against the snows. If the snow leopard should leap from the rock above and manifest itself before me—S-A-A-O!—then in that moment of pure fright, *out of my wits,* I might truly perceive it, and be free.

the way home

O servant, where dost thou seek me?
Lo! I am beside thee.
I am neither in the temple nor in the mosque,
neither am I in rites and ceremonies
nor in yoga nor in renunciation.
If thou art a true seeker, thou shalt at once see me.
Thou shalt meet me in a moment's time.

Songs of Kabir (trans. R. Tagore)

Do not be amazed by the true dragon.

DOGEN ZENJI
Fukanzazenji

NOVEMBER 18

At daybreak, with Tukten and Dawa, I walk up the White River toward the sun. We are accompanied by GS, who will go as far as the eastern pass on a blue-sheep survey, and by Jang-bu and Gyaltsen, off to Saldang to buy a goat. Frustrated by the snow leopard, GS is resorting to live bait, which if nothing else will provide the camp with meat; should wolves appear, the goat won't be set out, for wolves leave nothing.

(A week after my departure, two snow leopards traveling together skirted Shey Gompa. A goat was staked out, and GS slept near it for two nights, but the snow leopards vanished from the region; the goat was butchered and consumed by human beings. One goat leg was presented to Lama Tupjuk together with a pair of Phu-Tsering's trousers: Jang-bu wished to offer up his boots but was forbidden to do so by GS, who had to get his expedition out over the mountains.)

Phu-Tsering will stay behind, and I shall miss him. Last evening he astonished us with a sheaf of lively drawings—airplanes, the heads of girls, peculiar European scenes—one of which was made away with by our landlord, Ongdi, no doubt with an eye to sale or barter. Taking leave of Phu-Tsering this morning, I asked if I might call on him in Khumbu should I ever visit the lamaseries of eastern Nepal, and this good friend and merry cook, as upset as myself, cried, "Thank you!"

Not one hundred yards outside the village are three sets of fresh wolf tracks; the silver beasts had skirted the frozen dwellings, under the waning moon. On the slopes above, the big rams of the Somdo herd stand motionless against the snow line. I walk backward for a little way, watching as the transparent flags of Crystal Monastery withdraw into the Somdo mountain . . . *OM!* I set my rucksack and stride onward. In an icy brook, a spray of fossil pectens is set in a dark-gray stone shaped like a mountain. The stone is very beautiful, the scallop rays sparkling with rime. I return it to the stream, and keep on going.

A prayer wall on a rise is a haunt of wolves, and all around it in the snow are fresh wolf prints and yellow stains. The track turns northward, climbing the rocky bed of a tributary stream, and at the head of a long gradual ascent, a bowl of bright-blue sky appears between white walls. These portals shift and sink away as we draw near, it is no pass but only an illusion. Instead there is a slippery steep climb up ice and scree, between deep drifts. The air is thin, and stopping every little way to rest, I gaze over a world of purest white, without animal track or sound or passing bird.

On the summit of this eastern pass, at 16,000 feet, stands a great cairn, built up by stones of the travelers of centuries. Ahead, broad lunar landscapes, dry and brown, stretch away into Tibet. In this mountain desert, sere and bare as a world above the clouds, only the crests of the highest peaks are white. The spires and ravines of the Himalaya have rounded into mountains and deep valleys, and off to the east, beyond the mountains, is a vast pale region—Mustang, the old Kingdom of Lo.

Soon Tukten and Dawa rise from the banks of snow and cast their loads down on the cairn, and now there appear the boyish heads of Jang-bu and Gyaltsen. The Sherpas are impressed by the immense horizons, spreading away in a great circle of the world, and for some minutes look about them without speaking. Where we have come from, the north faces of the Himalayan ramparts (not often seen by Westerners) rise in ice towers of shining white; that human life could persist in such a place seems unimaginable, and yet we know, or think we know, that Shey Gompa is down in those lost ravines, under Crystal Mountain.

It is time to go. GS shakes hands with Tukten and Dawa, whom he will not see again, and the four Sherpas set off down the north slope, in single file across the fields of snow.

I stay a little. In the still windlessness, George blurts out, "I'm sorry as hell to see you go," and I say that I'm sorry as hell to leave; I try to express inexpressible thanks as we shake hands. "I've been very very *moved* . . ." I say, and stop. Such words are only clutter, they do not say what I mean; I am moved from where I used to be, and can never go back.

Each is happy for the other that this expedition has worked out so very well. We have been on different journeys, and mostly we have worked alone, which suits us both, and even in the evenings, we talked little. I never shared with George the changes in my head, for fear he might imagine I'd gone crazy; and who knows what was going on in his! But we were always glad to meet at the day's end, which after two months of enforced companionship, in hard conditions, is enough.

For want of words, we shake hands once more, knowing that when we meet next, in the twentieth century, the screens of modern life will have formed again, and we may be as well defended as before. Then I set off across the northern snow. When I turn to wave, there is no longer a blue parka and brown face, only the black emblem of a man against the sun, as in a dream. Slowly, the figure raises its right arm. Again I head north, and there at my feet are fine fresh wolf tracks in the snow. I turn again to yell about the wolves, but the sky is empty. There is only snow, whirling around the ancient cairn in golden sparkles.

The trail descends into gray stony canyons. I have left my stave up at the pass; it is too far to climb back. The Sherpas are long since out of sight, but Tukten waits at the first place where there is a chance of a wrong turning; he does not draw attention to his thoughtfulness, he is simply there. While waiting, this interested man has found more wolf tracks, and points out that one set is much smaller than the other—a cub. Two herders met with farther down say there are many *jangu* here, and *sao* as well, preying on the domestic herds and also *na*; though wolves prey more heavily on livestock than do leopards, it was a *sao* that had made off with a goat just the night before. In the early afternoon, bharal appear, twenty or more, apparently drawn to the herds of sheep and goats above Namgung. These *na* of Namgung are harassed by a pair of hunters who kill them for a living; in all this region, only Shey is free of hunting, thanks to the presence there of Lama Tupjuk.

The village of Namgung is higher than Shey; it must be close to 16,000 feet. Namgung Gompa is a red stone structure built into the north wall of a gorge, and the Namgung villagers have carved out terrace fields on both sides of the Namgung torrent, which flows down to the Nam-Khong Valley. Leaving the others on the trail above, Jang-bu and I descend to the first house in the gorge, where we are driven back by a savage mastiff on a long thin chain; in this land without a tree, I regret bitterly the loss of my faithful stick. Emerging upon his roof, the householder is glaring down upon us with suspicion; making no effort to calm the maddened dog, he grooms his very long unbraided hair with an outlandish comb that resembles a small broom. But the man has the key to Namgung Gompa, under the gorge wall. The red-and-white of the gompa and its stupas is the only color in this barren landscape.

At the gompa, the log ladders climb to a small third-story room, lit by a dusty ray of light from one small window. The chapel is a litter of worn draperies, leather cases, hide drums, copper cauldrons, conch-shell ceremonial horns, painted wood boxes, wood-bound books, and terra-cotta figures of Karma-pa, Sakyamuni, and a bulge-eyed Padma Sambhava. A splendid bronze of Dorje-Chang on a platform above the center of the room seems to vibrate in the dusty light: I keep expecting it to speak, and can scarcely turn my back upon it.

Disturbed by the neglect and disrepair, I ask if there is a Lama of Namgung. At this, the temple-keeper identifies himself as "lama," although such lamas are mere sacristans by comparison with a true lama, far less a *tulku,* such as the Lama of Shey. Jang-bu tells me that his own father is a "lama," presumably a lay person of this sort. The man lights two butter lamps in demonstration of the ceremonial prerogatives of his office, but he admits that the temple is much neglected, and that the

more valuable *thankas* have already been removed. He is comb-
ing his long hair again when we take leave of him.

The trail winds down around mountain after mountain, in a
long slow descent toward Saldang. A second herd of blue sheep,
thirty-three or more, stands on a crag across the valley. Jang-bu
and Gyaltsen, dropping their Buddhist precepts with their
loads, vainly pursue a flock of Tibetan snow cocks with hurled
stones; then we go on again. Tukten carries food and cooking
gear, Dawa my backpack, Gyaltsen some trading articles such
as GS's old suitcase, to be bartered for the decoy goat, and
Jang-bu a load of juniper, since fuel in this mountain desert is
so scarce; as for myself, besides tent and bedroll, I lug a rucksack full of books and fossils. At dusk, after nine hours of hard
going, Saldang appears below, on a plateau high above the
Nam-Khong River.

Jang-bu made friends on his first visit to Saldang, and goes
straight to a house where we are welcome. The house has an
upper storeroom that is used also as a prayer room, almost as
large and considerably tidier than Namgung Gompa. There are
no icons, and but two or three poor *thankas* in the garish modern style, but the array of butter lamps and brass offering
bowls, the fine hide drum and other implements, testify to the
strong faith of the family. Our Namu, Chirjing, and her ancient
mother give me this room as a place to sleep, thereby trusting
me with their scarce winter stores; when visitors arrive, the old
lady secures the storeroom door with an iron lock so primitive
that, later in the evening, letting me back in, she opens it readily with a twig of wood.

In the storeroom corner stands a savage-looking spear that
Chirjing says was made here in Saldang; it dates from the time,
not more than thirty years ago, when bandit nomads from Tibet were descending on this region, killing and pillaging, until
at last the villagers took up arms to keep them off.

Tukten brings me tea on the open roof, and in the dying light,
I gaze out over the Nam-Khong Valley toward Tibet, known
here simply as *Byang*, the North. The eroded landscape, minced
to dust by the sharp hooves of sheep and goats, is a waste of

worn-out hills and deep gaunt gullies that is desert-brown for eight months of the year, and erosion continues even in the dearth of snow and rain, due to the endless freezing and thawing, cracking and quiet crumbling caused by the great range of temperature. With passing centuries, the rain clouds from the south no longer come; the soil is poor, the growing season brief, and even the old slow caravan trade in salt and wool to the south side of the Himalaya is dying, as cheaper supplies from India spread north. Eventually this town may be abandoned to the desert, like the old cities of western Tibet.

I ask Jang-bu to buy meat, and later our hostesses prepare the best meal we have eaten since September, a goat stew with potatoes, turnips, and a little rice, accompanied by many cups of barley *chang*. Jang-bu is my drinking companion; Dawa and Gyaltsen will not drink, and Tukten, despite his reputation, seems indifferent to it, though he takes a glass or two. The feast is held over a smoky fire of dung and twigs in the windowless main room on the ground floor, and afterward pretty Chirjing serves hot wheat bread with salt and a pat of butter. While we feed, more villagers come in, until the firelight is a circle of lively faces, young and old. I wonder if I have ever seen so many faces that I like in a single circle, and I go off happily to bed, my belly glowing. Soon Jang-bu calls me down again, for a man has brought the thin elegant lute known as the *danyen*, its stem carved as the long neck of a swan. Everyone is dancing. More villagers come, filling the smoky room with the companionable smells of human grease and coarse tobacco, and the old woman makes a fresh pot of *chang*, squishing the fermented barley through a wicker basket. One fetching, round-faced girl who looks somehow familiar brings a round-faced infant named Chiring Lamo, and while the young mother dances, our old woman holds the little girl in her lap. Infant and ancient are both heavily beaded, and the baby has a copper locket and a string of money cowries; the wizened visage and the pearly one wear identical expressions of wide-eyed childlike wonder, all the more affecting because the old head rests its chin upon the new. The infant's clean face looks transparent, and the ancient has a spiritual serenity that has gone transparent in old age. Soon Chiring Lamo stands and urinates on the dirt floor, gazing down with curiosity at her fat wet legs.

Laughing, the baby's mother dances, holding hands with cat-faced laughing Chirjing. The lute player, a dashing handsome fellow in short smock and boots, smiles at me wholeheartedly in welcome, as if I were his dearest friend on earth. Soon others come, including a man who appears to be Chirjing's suitor. Jang-bu is playing his harmonica, and Dawa and Gyaltsen laugh indiscriminately at all they see, but the only one of the Shey party who will dance is Tukten—Tukten Sherpa, cook and porter, alleged thief, bad drunk, old Gurkha, is a dancer, too, and dancing, he smiles and smiles. The dance is a short rhythmic step well suited to small spaces, and very like Eskimo igloo dances, even to the jet-black braids and red-bronze faces and the shuffle of the soft, mukluk-like boots. Soon the dancers begin singing, and Tukten joins them but not Dawa, who has an exceptional voice but is much too shy. The songs are melodious and wistful, and as in Dhorpatan I am reminded of the mountain *huainus* of the Andes. A Buddhist song has the modest title "Taking Flowers to the Lama," but there is also a song of older centuries, called "Highest Mountain": *"Even the highest mountain cannot keep me from reaching Nurpu!"* Or so Jang-bu translates it, watching to see if I will laugh at this longing reference to an ancient god.

We drink more *chang,* Jang-bu and I, as he tells me that all of Tukten's few belongings were stolen at Ring-mo during the return trip from Jumla; Tukten himself has never mentioned this. Jang-bu speaks again of how he was invited by the members of a Japanese mountaineering expedition to go to Japan and study agriculture. He is tempted by the idea, and certainly this handsome boy, with his harmonica, big finger rings, and flashing smile, is too sophisticated to devote his life to expeditions, though he is very good at this, even-tempered and adaptable and smart, and tough enough to move the porters when he has to—the B'on-pos were the only bunch that cowed him. However, he likes his wandering life, his *chang* and arak, and will never go.

I sit here as peaceful as a Buddha, and from across the fire, Tukten smiles as if I had held up the lotus. The dancing is over, and now this humble *tulku* of Kasapa is seated thigh to thigh with the bright-eyed ancient, delighting her with Tukten jokes while soothing the sleepy infant girl, who has crawled into his lap. There are no boundaries to this man, he loves us all.

NOVEMBER 19

I wake in happiness before first light, and do morning chanting in Chirjing's chapel until the sun softens the sky behind the mountains, and Tukten, unasked, brings me tea. Afterward, Jang-bu in his finger rings and Gyaltsen in his schoolboy knickers come to say goodbye. I thank Jang-bu especially for his good grace in asking so many stupid questions on my behalf and tease Gyaltsen one last time about my boots. Then I take leave of Chirjing and her mother, saying how honored I have been to sleep in a temple of the Buddha. Tears in her eyes, the old lady takes my hand and bangs her head against my chest in blessing, saying something like, *"Tuchi churochi,"* which seems to mean, "Thank you very much," or perhaps it is *"Tashi shok!"*—"May these blessings prevail!"—or even (I hope not) *"Tanga cheke,"* a small coin. Then I set out to explore Saldang.

Though the village lies at about the same altitude as Ringmo, perhaps 12,000 feet, it is utterly different in aspect. Ringmo is a Himalayan village below tree line, while Saldang belongs to the treeless deserts of the Tibetan Plateau. The village is scattered on an open slope that descends the sides of the Nam-Khong Valley to the river, and its houses are the desert gray-brown of this land, from which they crop up like eruptions. Drought and erosion have left a soil of hard-caked dust, yet the slopes have been terraced for marginal planting, made possible by snowmelt of spring and summer; the melt also supports small clumps of birch and willow planted near the houses and protected from famished livestock by stone walls. The branches are cropped for fodder, it is said, but this use must be very limited; one feels that the trees were brought here to relieve the extreme severity of the landscape. In late November, the starkness of Saldang is pointed up by the scarcity of its inhabitants; at least one member of every family, usually more, has gone off to the south or east, in search of work, and the beasts are gone, too, for want of grass or fodder. (In former times, the herds would have wintered on Tibetan plains, but now they must be taken south across the mountains.) In such barrenness, the neat aspect of houses, walls, and fields speaks for the strong spirit of these villagers, who constructed spears to drive off bandits, and can dance so merrily when their food is almost gone; the religious fervor here is represented by the many walls of heavy prayer stones, the stupas that rise like turrets on each barren knoll, and the strange rows of upright slabs, like gravestones, known as *obo,* which are characteristic of northern Tibet and Mongolia.

The landscape is mysterious, all contrast: in the clear, hard light, the shadow of a motionless horse has the force of omen. One day human beings will despair of grinding out subsistence on high cold plateaus, and the last of an old Tibetan culture will blow away among the stones and ruins.

I wander down the hill to Saldang Gompa. The temple is locked, since its lama is away in another village, but in a yellow building that abuts it are suspended two enormous cylindrical prayer wheels, perhaps four feet in diameter and ten feet high, brightly painted with such symbols as Asoka's wheel, the ceremonial conch, the orb of compassion, serpents, flowers, barley offerings, OM MANI PADME HUM. Saldang is a Sakya-pa gompa, and the Bodhisattvas Manjusri and Chen-resigs are celebrated here, together with the historical Buddha, Sakyamuni, and Maitreya, the Buddha to come. In the brilliant frescoes on the walls, the ubiquitous Padma Sambhava holds a *danyen* very like the one that was played last night by the dashing lutist of Saldang; the Lotus-Born is celebrating some celestial event with a blue Lord of Death, who one day will hold up a bright mirror from which we cannot hide, and weigh the white pebbles and the black in final balance.

Tukten has been acquiring a few supplies, and at midmorning he and Dawa meet me at the gompa. With them is the handsome

lutist, off to Kathmandu to seek his fortune: he will accompany
us as a porter-guide as far as Murwa. Karma, as he is called,
seems less spontaneous than he did last evening, over *chang* and
firelight; he tends to accost one with his charm. Happily this
charm is leavened by the unsophisticated smiles of his young
Tibetan wife, she who danced so joyfully the night before, and of
the infant Chiring Lamo, who sits atop her load like a smiling
Buddha—what good luck to have this Chiring Lamo in the party!
Besides the baby, the girl carries the family belongings, while
Karma will lighten the loads of the two Sherpas, Dawa especially:
although more cheerful now that he is on his way home, Dawa
seems listless, and is giving muted hints of obscure illness.

The trail ascends the river bank to a string of hamlets known
collectively as Namdo. In this region, temples and villages alike
have entrance stupas with bright well-made frescoes and mandalas, all of them in excellent repair. There are also imposing
prayer walls with inscribed scriptures and the wheel mantras
that Tukten calls *ling-po*. Beyond Namdo, on an isolated tower
of rock over the river, is a Nyingma temple called Sal Gompa
with a wonderful meditation chamber, surrounded by a covered gallery but itself wide open to the skies. Sal Gompa is very
well maintained by a tall woman of great presence who feels no
need to call herself a "lama"; a couch is ready for the Lama of
Saldang when he comes to stay. The statues at this Old Sect
temple are unexceptional, but the bright *thankas* there are del-
icately done, perhaps the best that we have seen, and we con-
gratulate the caretaker on the care taken with Sal Gompa, so
markedly in contrast to Namgung.
    The path continues up the western bank of the Nam-Khong,
passing two more gompas, one of which, on the far side of the
river, appears to be abandoned. The prayer walls on the river
path are much visited by wolves, but there is no sign of blue
sheep or of leopard. At one of the prayer walls, the girl sits
down in the sun and offers her breast to Chiring Lamo, sere-
naded the while by a crowd of chukar partridge that had flut-
tered off the holy stones into the gullies. The girl is wearing a
helmet of red wool, and suddenly I recognize that these red

cheeks and pretty smile belong to Tende Samnug, who wore
this red helmet on the day at Shey that she gave me four potatoes. Karma, of course, is Karma Dorje, son of Ongdi the
Trader; what I have taken for false charm was only his eager
overtures of recognition. That day at Shey, they had no baby
with them, and were all bundled up against the cold, but all the
same, I much regret that I did not recognize them until Tende
put on her red winter hat, or respond more warmly to their
claim of friendship at last night's fire. Soon this merry Tende
rises in a tinkle of small bells that dance from her sash and
from the gay striped apron worn by married women of Tibet;
and Karma, stepping jauntily along with his beautiful swan's-
head lute strapped to his pack, seems ready to smile at anything
at all. Like many Bhotes from Dolpo and Mustang, he calls
himself a "Gurung"—"Karma Dorje, *Gurung*," he insists. Being thought of as inferior by the Hindu tribes that rule Nepal,
some younger Bhotes seek in this way to raise their status, but
there is no real link between these people and the Gurung,
whose villages we passed in late September, along the southern
slopes of Annapurna.

At the small hamlet known as Tcha, we finish the day's journey. I protest at first: there is plenty of time to get to Raka, the
last settlement before the first of two high passes between here
and Murwa. But Karma says that the people of Raka are hostile Kami people, and when Tukten supports him, I give in; I remember too well the Kamis on the trek between Dhorpatan
and Yamarkhar, not to speak of the Kami people of Rohagaon.

In its narrow canyon, already in shadow, Tcha is a gloomy
place, and its people hide from us. It lies at the mouth of a tributary ravine, and up the hill across the river is Hrap Gompa,
now abandoned. In caravan come seventy yaks that are turned
loose to graze around Hrap Gompa; the herders are from Ny-
isal, bound southward for Rohagaon to find grazing. Now
heavy clouds appear over the canyon walls, shrouding the
mountains and bringing misgivings about GS, who will stay at
Shey into early December and may see the onset of real winter
weather.

NOVEMBER 20

A night wind in the Nam-Khong Canyon rattled my thin tent like a dry walnut leaf, but this morning the wind is moderate, and stars fill the wedge of blue-black sky that is visible above the enclosing walls: I set out before daybreak, to get warm. The canyon is bitter, bitter cold, as if winter were locked all the year in this dungeon of black stones and ice closed by sheer walls. It seems much colder than the coldest dawn at Shey, it is well below freezing, and there is no hope of sun before midmorning. At a turn in the canyon above Tcha are the heavy square tents of the nomads from the north; since I have no stick, and cannot find one in this treeless land, I am glad that my footsteps on the frozen sand are inaudible over the torrent, for there is no place to hide here from their dogs.

On a gravel bar is a gaunt cairn to the water demons, *klu,* who can be vengeful if neglected, Tukten says. Among the rocks move shadows, trollish shapes—a little old woman, much too old to be the mother of the two bundled children who are with her. In this wintry place, in the gray light, the little band has strayed from some Gothic tale. The shivering boy, not more than ten, carries a load that looks heavier than my own; the little woolen girl, still toddling, must be lifted across the frozen brooks that protrude like ice tongues from ravines in the east wall. The old woman is bent beneath a load of sheepskins; what she will get for them farther south can scarcely repay such a hard journey. She lifts gnarled fingers to her mouth, but I have no food: I make sign that she should ask food of the Sherpas when they come. They smile at me as best they can. Perhaps these cheerful children are brave orphans, perhaps they are abroad so early to avoid freezing to death for want of fuel. I go on to Raka, walking as hard as possible just to keep warm.

A yak herd goaded by wild boys descends the mountain to the huts at Raka. In a stone corral are more than one hundred yaks, which will carry these stacked bales of wool and salt into the south; the bales are guarded by big-headed mastiffs that lie quiet, dog eyes fixed upon the nearest dog. Long-haired men wearing short swords, striped cloaks, sashed short tunics, and wool boots lashed tight under the knee sit smoking by their fires. These men of the north are bold and colorful, but the denizens of Raka are brigands, "bad men," Karma Dorje says, who live all year in this dark canyon, as if hiding from the light. Pinch-faced as prisoners, they watch us pass.

Above Raka, the canyon narrows to a gorge, and the torrent veers from one wall to the other. Neither the Raka dwellers nor the nomads have bothered to make bridges, but in this season, after a long month without rain, the river is low. To cross and recross it dry-shod, we try to make steps by heaving heavy stones into the shallows, but the big stones are frozen hard into the gravel bars, and the small ones that are freed, when piled up high enough to protrude out of the torrent, are soon slicked over by a gloss of ice. We throw sand on the stones and extend hands and leap. But after three precarious crossings, the tactic is given up; it is tiring, and requires too much time. Instead we take off boots and socks, roll up our clothes as high as possible, and wade out barefoot, breaking through the skim of ice on both sides of the stream. The repeated crossings turn my feet to stone, and I curse Karma: how much simpler it would have been to pass Raka yesterday afternoon, make these crossings in the warmth of day, and camp beyond, where the gorge opens out into high valley. As it is, the three hours of good light wasted yesterday at Tcha have condemned us to a long hard day with a high pass at the end of it. But throughout, Tende laughs and chatters, and her gay spirit eases my annoyance with her husband, whose manner is just as light, though not so fetching. He leads in the bridge-building and testing, and when inevitably he slips, and soaks his clothes, he laughs, a gallant minstrel after all. Tukten is also cheerful and resourceful, but

Dawa stands there oxlike, and I must call out to him time and again to come and help us. Seemingly, he is not present, he is stumbling and apathetic. At one point, sliding his load across wet ice, he places its cover uppermost, thereby soaking my exposed sleeping bag below. Of late, this instinct for the inept move has been unerring, and no amount of remonstrance does any good.

On the far side of the Raka gorge, cold sun shafts burst from easterly ravines: one ravine, so Tukten says, leads down to Tarap. The northern slopes are green with thorny growth, but there are no cliffs here, and no sign of blue sheep. The river must dance with fine white-water torrents in the spring, for the canyon ascends steeply to an open valley, where a broad black gravel bed, windswept, without life, comes down out of the snows. Here we turn south, toward the Himalaya.

In this stretch, the going is easy, and Tende, taking Karma's load, removes her boots and goes on barefoot, leaving Chiring Lamo to her husband. Where the river turns, Karma stops to build a fire. Having no faith in his assertion that this Namdo Pass, though "very steep," is only an hour's climb above the riverbed, I take off my boots and wade a tributary stream and keep on going, hoping that my stern example will hurry this laggard in his midday meal.

Across the stream is a large stupa, and near the stupa is a cairn of ragged prayer flags and crude *mani* stones. Mixed with the stones in a jumbled heap are huge-horned skulls of the argali, one of which looks relatively fresh. The argali, long-legged and swift, does not depend on nearby cliff ledges for safety, and for the rest of the day I scan the thorny mountainsides for *Ovis ammon*.

Ahead, two herders turn twelve yaks loose among the thorns. They will not try the pass today, for one is collecting brush for firewood while the other guards his bales beside a cave. Not far beyond, the yak route turns off from the riverbed, starting a steep ascent into the snows. Already it is afternoon, and I have been walking steadily for seven hours, and it feels too late in a long day to start a hard climb to the Raka Pass. On the other hand, if we make camp this early every day, it will

take us five days instead of three to get to Murwa. I keep on going in the hope that Tukten will make the others follow.

Whoever opened up this track after the October blizzards
wanted badly to go south, for to judge from the signs, his hap-
less animals broke through the crust repeatedly into deep snow,
and made aimless furrows where they struck off on their own
before floundering back to join the others. Since then, however,
a number of caravans have crossed the pass. The broad yellow-
pocked track is strewn with dung, and the frozen dung offers
footholds on the ice. Excepting a vole avenue that leads from
one rock outcrop to another, there are no wild tracks to be
seen; the only life is a high flock of pale finches, crossing the
frozen sky toward the south.

The track mounts toward triangular snow peaks, the sun
falls. I climb hard to keep up with the light as it withdraws in
its great silence up the mountain; thus, I manage to stay warm
right to the summit, where the sun sinks into the crescent between peaks. Wind has blown some snow from the steep faces,
and black wing shapes of exposed rock fly on the whiteness.
The sky gleams, and the rigid peaks resound. The beauty of the
Namdo Pass opens the mind, for it is a true portal of the Himalaya, where the traveler passes from one world to another. I
have no idea of its name, but this one suits it: Nam-do means
"sky-stone."

I turn at the cairn to stare behind me. All around the northern hemisphere lies the brown waste of the Tibetan Plateau,
without a single sign, not one, of the human life in the shadows
of its canyons. (Here at the summit cairn, in the first week of
December, GS was overtaken by a snowstorm; he later described how a yakherder in his rough skins, in swirling snow,
planted a prayer flag on this cairn, where GS's altimeter read
17,500 feet.)

The sun is gone. From far below rises the cry of Chiring
Lamo, her infant voice the only life in the white waste. Considering the clouds of yesterday and last night's wind, we are
damned lucky that this fair weather has held. When Dawa's
head appears at last, I wave to him, then cross the saddle
quickly to the farther side, for it is dusk. Below is a great bowl

of snow, a mile or more in width, and beyond the snow bowl the head of the valley that descends to open mountainside where we might camp.

I hurry through cold shades, under the mountains. Strangely, the track emerges into sun, for this long valley, descending westward, opens out again upon the sky where the sun, setting, bathes the mountainsides in holy light.

Then Dawa comes, and we make camp on a tundra ridge. Tende comes next, haggard but smiling: she moves about in the cold dusk, crooning to Chiring Lamo, gathering up dry yak chips for a fire.

NOVEMBER 21

The camp is less than a thousand feet below the Namdo Pass, and so this morning there is biting cold, with no warmth in the frozen sun when it appears over the eastern rim. This canyon plunges eventually into a maelstrom of narrow, dark ravines that must emerge into that eastern arm of Phoksumdo that we saw on October 25, for there is the aura of a void between one spine of summits and the next where the turquoise lake of the great demoness lies hidden.

Despite the cold, Tende and Chiring Lamo sit near naked on a sheepskin by their daybreak fire, the child's head laid amongst the beads and amulets and cold silver on Tende's round brown breasts. But Dawa is sick this morning; through Tukten, he tells me that even before leaving Shey, he suffered from dysentery and internal bleeding. That last is worrisome; it might well lead to worse. Perhaps he should rest, but we cannot stay in this wild place between high passes. And of course it is only luck that he came out with us; had it not been for Gyaltsen's fear of Tukten, Dawa might have remained behind and died there, without ever speaking up, less out of fortitude than in that peasant apathy and fatalism that is so often taken for stupidity.

I give him something for his dysentery; it may kill him. In his weakened state, Dawa longs to be taken care of; it pleases him to be reminded that he must wear a snow mask, so as not to complicate his sickness with snow blindness. He stands before me in knee britches, big head hanging, like a huge disobedient child.

The yak route descends into night shadows, crossing the ice rivers of this canyon and emerging again on sunny mountainside. Here where sun and shadow meet, a flock of Himalayan snow cock sails away down the steep mountain. To the north and west, across the canyons, the thorn-scrub slopes are cut by cliffs, and soon blue sheep come into view, two far pale bands, one of nine, and the other of twenty-six. I search in vain for sign of the snow leopard.

Down in the shelter of a gully, a yak caravan is preparing to set out; two men strap last loads on the balky animals. Before long, there appears another caravan, this one bound north; having discharged its salt and wool, it is headed home with a cargo of grain, lumber, and variegated goods, its yaks rewarded for their toil with big red tassels on their packs and small orange ones decking out their ears. The dark shapes of the nomads glint with beads and earrings, amulets, and silver daggers; here are the Ch'ang Tartars of two thousand years ago. With their harsh cries and piercing whistles, naked beneath filthy skins of animals, these wild men bawling at rough beasts are fit inhabitants of such dark gorges; one can scarcely imagine them anywhere else. The Redfaced Devils are inquisitive, and look me over before speaking out in the converse of the pilgrim.

Where do you come from?

Shey Gompa.

Ah. Where are you going?

To the Bheri.

Ah.

And as the wary dogs skirt past, we nod, grimace, and resume our paths to separate destinies and graves.

Winding around beneath towers of rock that fall away into abyss after abyss, the path wanders randomly in all directions. In the cold shine of its ice, this waste between high passes is a realm of blind obliterating nature. The labyrinth is beautiful, yet my heart is touched by dread. I hurry on. At last the ledge trail straightens, headed south, and I reach the foot of the last climb to the pass just before noon. On a knoll, there is a prayer wall and a stock corral for those who come too late in the day to start the climb. Plainly, we shall not reach Murwa before nightfall, despite Karma's assurances to the contrary; we shall have to press hard just to cross the pass and descend far enough below the snows to find brushwood to keep warm. Lacking mountain lungs, I am slow in the steep places, and I start the climb at once, without waiting for the others to come up.

Looking back every little while as I ascend, I see that Karma, arriving at the prayer wall, sets out a sheepskin and lies down, while Tende, Dawa, and Tukten perch on rocks. No doubt Karma will build a fire here and delay everyone with a lengthy meal, thus assuring himself and his wife and child the miserable task, at the end of a long day, of setting up camp in cold and dark, for he is as lightheaded as he is lighthearted, and gives the day's end no more thought than anything else. Every piece of information that this smiling man has offered has been wrong: the climb to this pass, it is plain to see, is not only steeper but longer than the last one.

In the cold wind, the track is icy even at midday, yet one cannot wander to the side without plunging through the crust. The regular slow step that works best on steep mountainside is difficult; I slip and clamber. Far above, a train of yaks makes dark curves on the shining ice; soon a second herd overtakes me, the twine-soled herders strolling up the icy incline with hands clasped behind their backs, grunting and whistling at the heaving animals. Then black goats come clicking up the ice glaze, straight, straight up to the noon sky; the goat horns turn silver on the blue as, in the vertigo and brilliance of high sun, the white peak spins. The goatherd, clad from head to boots in blood-red wool, throws balls of snow to keep his beasts in line; crossing the sun, the balls dissolve in a pale fire.

Eventually the track arrives at the snowfields beneath the summit rim; I am exhausted. Across the whiteness sails a lammergeier, trailing its shadow on the snow, and the wing shadow draws me taut and sends me on. For two more hours I trudge and pant and climb and slip and climb and gasp, dull as any brute, while high above, the prayer flags fly on the westering sun, which turns the cold rocks igneous and the hard sky to white light. Flag shadows dance upon the white walls of the drifts as I enter the shadow of the peak, in an ice tunnel, toiling and heaving, eyes fixed stupidly upon the snow. Then I am in the sun once more, on the last of the high passes, removing my woolen cap to let the wind clear my head; I sink to my knees, exhilarated, spent, on a narrow spine between two worlds.

To the south and west, glowing in snow light and late sun, the great white Kanjirobas rise in haze, like mystical peaks that might vanish at each moment. The caravans are gone into the underworld. Far behind me and below, in the wastes where I have come from, my companions are black specks upon the snow. Still breathing hard, I listen to the wind in my own breath, the ringing silence, the snow fire and soaring rocks, the relentless tappeting of prayer flags, worn diaphanous, that cast wind pictures to the northern blue.

I have the universe all to myself. The universe has me all to itself.

Time resumes, there comes a change in mood. Under the pack, my back is sweating, and the hard wind chills me. Before I am rested, the cold drives me off the peak into a tortuous descent down sharp rock tumulus, hidden by greasy corn snow and glare ice, and my weak legs slip between the rocks as the pack's weight pitches me forward. A thousand feet down, this rockfall changes to a steep snow-patched trail along an icy stream. Toward dusk, in the painful going, I am overtaken by Tukten in his scanty clothes and sneakers. Tukten's indifference to cold and hardship is neither callous nor ascetic: what it seems to be is calm acceptance of everything that comes, and this is the source of that inner quiet that makes his nondescript presence so impressive. He agrees that Murwa is out of the question, and goes on down, still quick and light, to find fuel and a level place to camp.

The steep ravine descending from the pass comes out at last on sandy mountainside that drops into the upper canyon of the Murwa River. Dusk has fallen, and I keep my distance from two herders' fires for fear of the big dogs. Farther on, as darkness comes, I call out, "Tukten, *Tuk-ten*," but there is no answer. Then, below, I see him making a fire; the inspired man has found a stone shed by a waterfall.

Dawa turns up an hour later, and lies down in the shed without his supper. Every little while we call to Karma and his family, but another hour passes, the stars shine, and no one comes. This morning a yawning Karma had excused his reluctance to get up by saying we would arrive at Murwa in midafternoon. Doubtless it was this feckless minstrel who told Jang-bu, who told me, that "one hard day, one easy one" would take us from Saldang to Murwa: two hard days and one easy one are now behind us, and still we are not there. In his airy way, Jang-bu concluded that we could cross both passes in a single day, since neither one, so he was told, was as high or as arduous as the Shey Pass, not to speak of the Kang La. Being ignorant, I didn't argue, though I had to wonder why, if this were true, the wool traders, coming from Saldang, had chosen the Shey Pass–Kang La route over the other. Tonight I know. Because the icy north face of Kang La is too steep for yaks, the traveler must break his own trail in the snow; otherwise that route is much less strenuous than the Shey-Murwa route, in which three passes must be crossed. And the descent from the third pass up there, in snow conditions, is as wearing as the climb. I hate to think of Chiring Lamo in the ice and starlight, swaying along near-precipices on Tende's small and tired shoulders; these ledge trails should not be traveled in the night, without a moon.

However, I am too tired to act, or even think. I am already in my sleeping bag when this innocent family appears out of the darkness; hearing Tukten's voice, I end these notes and go to sleep.

NOVEMBER 22

Last night I was asleep by eight and slept soundly until four, when I awoke in a deep glow of well-being; I am over the high passes before winter, I am going home. Unaccountably, the joy expresses itself in a surge of gratitude to family and friends, who were so generous in those days of D's dying—so many sad and happy memories at once that lying there in the black cold I grow quite warm.

In D's last hour, Eido Roshi came; he had shaved his head. I held D's right hand, and the Roshi took her left, and we chanted over and over again our Buddhist vows. A little past midnight, effortlessly, D died.

I left the hospital just before daybreak. It was snowing. Walking through the silent streets, I remembered D's beloved Zen expression: "No snowflake ever falls in the wrong place." Even in this grim winter dawn, everything was as it should be, the snowflakes were falling without effort, all was calm and clear. In her book, she says:

> The flower fulfills its immanence, intelligence implicit in its un-
>   folding.
> There is a discipline.
> The flower grows without mistakes.
> A man must grow himself, until he understands the intelligence
>   of the flower.

To proceed as though you know nothing, not even your age, nor sex, nor how you look. To proceed as though you were made of gossamer . . . a mist that passes through and is passed through and retains its form. A mist that loses its form and still is. A mist that finally dissolves, particles scattered in the sun.[1]

Tukten brings tea and porridge to my tent, and is routing out the others as I set off down the valley. Dawa is staggering, but he is no malingerer; if he collapses, it is very serious, as there is no doctor in these mountains, and we cannot just abandon him in Murwa. In the hope that he can be helped along to Jumla, we have spread his load amongst ourselves, and Karma has agreed to go as porter as far south and west as Tibrikot, on the Bheri River. Fortunately, our supplies are much diminished, and I discard something every day: it suits my spirits to arrive at Jumla on the wind.

The upper Murwa is a broad canyon of juniper and lone black-lichened granites, scattered like monuments in a natural pasture that descends in gigantic steps; the river itself has cut a gorge along the east wall of the canyon.

It is still dark, the sun is far away. To the south, in a wedge of light where the canyon sides converge, the dawn is touching the pink pinnacles of the Kanjirobas. From high across the canyon comes the tinkle of yak bells, and a ghostly smoke arises from the granites: behind a windbreak of heaped sacks, two herders hunch like stone men at their fire, and behind these figures, OM MANI PADME HUM is carved in immense characters on a huge boulder.

ཨོཾ་མ་ཎི་པ་དྨེ་ཧཱུྃ

Thinking of a friend's note, received before leaving home, I smile: "I can hardly imagine all the strange and wonderful sights that you will see." At sunset yesterday afternoon, far overhead, a rock turret cast a huge semblance of my silhouette on the high walls. This morning, I find a great round rock split clean as an apple, and in the split as on an altar a stone orb has come to rest, placed so strikingly by elements and cataclysms that its perfection stops me in my tracks, in awe of the wild, murderous, and splendid power of the world.

I cross a bridge where the torrent swings from the east wall to the west, digging ever deeper into stone to form its gorge, and continue down the mountain in long bounds, carried on waves of gratitude and mirth. My life and work, my children, loves and friendships, past and present—all seem marvelous, full of marvels.

On a bluff above the river cliffs stands the yak herd first seen yesterday on the snow slopes of the pass, and below this place I see a forest, see each birch and fir. And still the path steeply descends even as the canyon opens out, and the cedar and fir of tree line turn to spruce and pine, until at last Murwa itself comes into view, deep down in morning shadows of the mountain.

At Murwa, crows replace the ravens, for it is four thousand feet lower than Shey. It is as picturesque as I remember it, a grouping of orderly farms behind stone walls set in patterns on an open slope, under the great wall to the northwest that dams Phoksumdo Lake; the slope ends abruptly at the river cliffs where the Murwa torrent strikes the waterfalls below Phoksumdo.

Because Dawa is sick and we are all sore and tired after crossing three high passes in four days, the rest of this day will be spent at Murwa, where camp is set up below the spruce forest, by an abandoned farm. In a stock corral nearby are the bright strange tents of a Japanese mountain-climbing expedition, returning from a climb of Kanjiroba. The red tents bring on confused feelings—the re-entry into the twentieth century comes too fast. Still, it is good that the Japanese are here, for the expedition leader is a doctor. But for this improbable encounter, Dawa would have had no help before reaching Jumla. He does not realize how lucky he is, but Tukten does. "Nepali doctors," Tukten says, with a shrug and a sad smile: all the good Nepali doctors leave the country. Our kind benefactor gives Dawa a good going-over, and doses him with bright blue pills that Dawa, miserable though he is, will have to be prodded to ingest four times a day. The doctor thinks he has dysentery, highly contagious, and has pressed preventive dosages on all the rest of us, refusing any payment for his generosity. How we have avoided Dawa's dread disease until this moment is a mystery, since camp procedure is casual, to say the least. I have long since avoided looking at the way our food is handled, and the hands that handle it, since my own would be no better; ironically, until his morale disintegrated, Dawa was much the cleanest of the Sherpas, and the only one I ever saw to bathe.

From the maps of the mountaineering expedition, and from Anu, its head Sherpa (a neighbor and friend of Tukten, from Solu Khumbu, near Namche Bazaar), I learn that the peak of Kanjiroba with the precipitous glacier face like a huge ice waterfall—the one I admired from Cave Camp and again from the summit of Somdo mountain, behind Shey—is called Kang Jeralba, the Snows of Jeralba, which is another way of saying Kanjiroba; the true Kanjiroba is farther west, up the Phoksumdo River. Although theirs is the second climb of Kanjiroba, which is more than 23,000 feet high, the route of ascent was a new one, and therefore they may claim that they have conquered it.

As to names and locations of the passes we have crossed, the map is vague. Where the "Namdo Pass" should be is a pass called Lang-mu Shey, or "Long Pass in Shey Region"—a good description of the pass between Shey and Saldang. Yesterday's pass is located correctly and is known as Bugu La; it is 16,575 feet in altitude. According to Anu Sherpa, "Bugu" refers to a struggle that took place between a mountain god—Nurpu, perhaps?—and a demon who wished to kill him: at Murwa, the god vanquished the demon, who perished in this torrent beneath the falls.

I am grateful to the mountaineers, but the bright tents and foreign faces, like the mail at Shey, are an intrusion, and the high spirits of the upper Murwa die away. Sunlight will not come until late morning and will be gone not long thereafter: the world is dark. Two hours ago, it might have struck me as quite wonderful that the sun will never touch this tent, where its worshiper awaits its warmth, to wash; now I allow this to become a source of anger, and such foolishness annoys me all the more—have I learned *nothing*? Imperturbable, Tukten observes me; I glare coldly. That crazy joy, that transport, which made me feel as I ran down the mountain that I might jump out of my skin, leap free of gravity, as I do so often these days in my dreams—was that no more than pure relief at crossing the last high pass? If so, how sad it seems to celebrate the end of precious days at Crystal Mountain. Perhaps I left too soon; perhaps a great chance has been wasted; had I stayed at Shey until December, the snow leopard might have shown itself at last. These doubts fill me with despair. In worrying about the future, I despoil the present; in my escape, I leave a true freedom behind.

To an evergreen grove on the cliffs above the Suli Gad, below the village, I take this notebook and a few chapatis, desperate to get away from humankind. Not that I have talked much in this silent time, for in my party, only Tukten speaks a little English, and we have long since exhausted our few subjects; Tukten and I communicate much better without speaking. One of these Japanese has some English, too, but neither of us wishes to take advantage of it; the mountaineers must be as sorry as myself to meet a foreigner in such strange country.

The ponderous water rush, the peaks, the concord of brown habitations of worn stone are very soothing: I sit on sunny lichens, hidden from the wind, feeling much better. Above the falls, the rampart that contains Lake-by-the-Forest fills the sky. Up there, a month ago, a young girl gave me cheese from a wood flagon, and men on silvered saddles, cantering by, called out that the snow was much too deep to cross Kang La.

In early afternoon, the sun is pierced by the snow pinnacle to westward, and I rise, stiff and old, and return to camp. It is very cold. The fields are stubble, and the people stand huddled on the path, waiting for winter. A cold wind blows up dust in whirlwinds, so violent and choking that I move my tent into an empty shed beneath the abandoned farm. Then down off Bugu La come strangers from the north: they invade the house and drive their *dzo* into a stall behind my tent, uprooting the tent stays in the process. Resurrecting the tent, I lie awake most of the night, wondering what sort of cud this beast is chewing.

The Murwa people are denouncing what they call "the tiger," which last night killed a young yak above the village. Tomorrow I leave the snow peaks and descend the Suli Gad, and the last hope of seeing the snow leopard will be gone.

NOVEMBER 23

I wake refreshed and lie awhile, listening to the great rush of the falls. Dawa is better already, I can hear him singing. At daybreak, as I leave our camp, Karma gives me a spruce stave that he cut yesterday as a surprise present: his joy in his own generosity is so infectious that I laugh aloud. Tende is warming Chiring Lamo's bottom over the fire, and Tukten is cooking the neck of the yak—killed by the snow leopard—which he acquired from the new friends he has made here. Tukten is cook on this expedition as well as everything else, and on this outward journey will be paid as a head Sherpa, provided he does not mention this to Dawa.

At the Murwa stupa I place upon the wall my shards of prayer stone, on an impulse not to carry them away from Dolpo. Officially, the whole Suli Gad Valley lies in Dolpo, just as Dolpo, geopolitically, lies in Nepal. But it is here at the head of the river, under the snow peaks and the waterfall that thunders down out of the magic lake, that I shall pass from one world to another.

Already this place seems far away, although I am still here. In Rohagaon, the next village to the south, there are no prayer walls, and Masta takes the place of Nurpu; below Rohagaon lie the villages of the Bheri Valley, and the first scent of Hindu attars from the plains of the great Ganga that bears away all whisper of Sh'ang-Sh'ung into the sea.

In the winter canyon of the Suli, all has changed. Where banks of berries shone before, lone small red leaves still cling to the withered bushes; the green lichens on the stones have turned to

THE SNOW LEOPARD

gold. The moon bear's nest has been ripped down, perhaps for fuel, and the falling leaves have left exposed the ravaged canyon sides charred by man's fires.

In the autumnal melancholy I remember France, in the years that I lived there, still in love with my first wife. One day in Paris, I met Deborah Love, whom I was to marry ten years later. And now, in different ways, those life-filled creatures are both gone. I hurry with the river.

All my life, I have hurried down between these walls, the sun crossing high over my head, voice swept away in the din of this green flood. The river, and life going, the excruciating sun: why do I hurry?

The sun reveals itself, pouring out of a ravine. In an icy stream, I wash away the Murwa dust, and brush my teeth, and deck my cap with a rock dove feather found along the trail. Below, the Suli Gorge is deep and dark again; at this time of the year, there must be parts of it that never see the sun.

Toward noon, the trail climbs up out of the gorge onto the mountainside. In October, when I stared behind me at the snow peaks, this prospect struck me as one of the loveliest in all my lifetime, and I had thought to enjoy it even more on the return journey, in a slow descent into the valleys. Instead I feel driven, and my pace is urgent. Even the narrow trails no longer slow me, I am hardened to all but the worst of them. The season is turning rapidly from near winter to late autumn, and down the mountainside, fresh green bamboo appears along the river.

On a grassy lookout high over the green torrent, I eat one of Tukten's blackish "breads," then keep on going. Probably it would be best to wait for Tukten; I cannot. I keep on going, high on all the oxygen of lower altitudes, up and down and up and down the stony path that drops to the river and climbs up the steep canyon sides and drops again. The wind cave is passed, and the upside-down falls, but the stone demon— doubtless he who lost the epic struggle with the mountain god at Bugu La and was cast down into the Suli Gad ravines—is lost in the shifting lights of the swift river. I thought I remembered just the place, but the stone is gone.

The valley woods shelter herdsmen and their fires, and near

the hut, a big corral has been set up for yaks, dogs, goats, and human beings in rough skins and pigtails. In the chill air, the dark-skinned northerners sit stripped to the waist, amidst semi-circles of striped wool sacks that mark out each encampment. One gesticulates; he knows me, for he points and cries, "Shey Gompa!" I am told to stay, and so I do for an hour or more, skirting the half-wild wolf-eyed dogs as I stroll in curiosity about the camp. It is early afternoon, the sun here is already gone, and since Tukten and the others are so late, it seems sensible to remain here with the herdsmen. But I am too restless, I cannot wait here in this gorge when sun still shines on the trail along the mountain; abruptly I rise and, watched by impassive Tartar faces, set out without goodbyes toward the south.

At the only brook on this dry mountainside is a small meadow where it is level enough to pitch a tent; surely Tukten will catch up with me before I reach this place, in midafternoon. But he does not, and anyway, the meadow swarms with men and beasts; I drink cold water from the brook and hurry on. Now I am certain that Tukten is not coming, and disturbed about what might have happened—was Dawa too sick to travel after all? Did Chiring Lamo fall into the fire? Has Tukten borne out all the warnings of his doubtful character, and made off to India with my gear? I carry my notes, binoculars, and sleeping bag, with a change of clothes; he is welcome to the rest.

Still, it grows late, and I have neither food nor fuel, and there is no flat place for a fire, except this narrow path along steep mountainside, exposed to wind. I must go to Rohagaon, although I cannot reach it before dark. Yesterday, in the spirit of discarding, I threw away my cache of marijuana; today I want it for the first time since I gathered it at Yamarkhar, for I am worn out after ten hours on the steep sides of the Suli Gad, and have no heart for Rohagaon's denizens and dogs. And this thought of *Cannabis* has scarcely occurred when a small withered specimen turns up, just off the trail. I chew up a mouthful on the spot, and thus fortified, march ahead. An hour later, when the cairn to Masta looms on the corner of the mountain, I am all set for this dog-ridden hole, thumping the path with my new spruce stave, not to be trifled with by man or beast.

The dogs are still chained, as it turns out, but the school hut where I hoped to stay is already occupied by a wool trader who displays small enthusiasm for my company. On the roofs above, the somber townsmen gather. The children of Rohagaon now fall silent, and the dogs: all look down from the walls above, as if on the point of carrying out some dreadful judgment. Who is this tall, outlandish figure, come in out of the darkness without porters? For in the dark, they do not know me from the month before. *"Aloo, aloo!"* I cry, making weird hunger signals, as if this might identify me with mankind, and after a while they understand that I am trying to say, "Potatoes!" There are no *aloo*, it appears, only small *anda* laid by the gaunt chickens, which a filthy man of suppurating eye cooks for me in a skillet that his woman has wiped first on her black rags. I think of the kind Japanese doctor and his earnest warnings about boiling all food and drink, no matter what, and hope that by now I have absorbed sufficient germs to fight off everything. Another inhabitant, luring me to his low chamber, persuades me to buy a brass cup of his alcohol, which looks and smells like a pink gasoline; this stuff, I think, might disinfect the eggs. My host is teacher at the school: he calls me "my dear brother"—a Hindu habit he has picked up in the lowlands—and tries out other English, too, which I praise lavishly in a successful effort to usurp his bed. Safe from the dogs and the night cold, my belly placated by *anda, Cannabis,* and pink lightning, I lie back in near-spiritual bliss: why in hell do I work so hard at meditation? Someone once said that God offers man the choice between repose and truth: he cannot have both. I have scarcely decided on a lifetime of repose when the dogs set up a terrific row, and everyone rushes forth into the night.

The faithful Tukten has arrived in the pitch-dark, along trails that I don't care for much even in daylight. Dawa and the rest, says he, will no doubt turn up shortly, as indeed they do, with Chiring Lamo crying. While arranging for roof, firewood, and water, Tukten makes a place for me at the family hearth of Infected Eye, where I witness cooking rites so simple and certain in their movements that I sit marveling upon my goat skin, scarcely breathing. The cooking is done by the woman in black rags while Infected Eye lies glowering against the wall; the slow deft handling of burning twigs as *tsampa* and dried pumpkin squash are cooked on a brazier, the breadmaking, the murmuring, the love and food extended to the children without waste words or motion, the tenderness toward the sick husband—all has the pace and dignity of sacrament. Earlier, to impress his fellow villagers, Infected Eye had shouted senselessly at his woman, hurling my rupee note into her face; here by his hearth, where no one can be fooled, he is soft-spoken, humble, full of pain, and this good woman and his children tuck him up against the earthen wall in blankets, laying the infant in beside him. Under the black rags, filth, and brassy earrings of the valleys, she is young: I had thought her a crone. Now she eats the children's leavings—and that only—and sighs and yawns and spreads herself a mat beside her husband. Remarkably, all this takes place as if my own big unfamiliar presence were not there, though I sit here like a Buddha by the hearth. For some time, I have been utterly still, and the children look right through me; it is very strange. Perhaps I have grown invisible at last.

NOVEMBER 24

In the entrance of the dwelling of Infected Eye, I slept last night on a soft bed of dust a half-inch deep. The mad dog of Roha-gaon, chained outside, barked all night in vain, for I was too tired to be bothered by his uproar. Only in the early night, when he first woke me, did I go out and threaten him with my stick. This incensed him to the gargling point; he fairly tore his chain out of the wall. Carried away by drunkenness and mirth, I pissed on him, thereby wreaking my revenge for that night-marish October night as well as this one. And on the wings of this cowardly act, perpetrated by the light of a darkling moon, I went in the greatest peace and satisfaction to my rest.

At dawn, the family's sighed complaints came through the earthen wall, and then the father hobbled out into the light to hawk and piss and spit into the daybreak. Soon his woman went off around the mountain to fetch water, and perhaps squat at the path edge, gazing south at the dawn snow peaks on the far side of the Bheri, and letting who knows what manner of lorn thought pass through her head.

Even before sunrise, the air feels warmer; I can scarcely see my breath in the mountain air. A flight of rock doves, leaving its roost in a ravine below Rohagaon, opens out in the morning sun over the valley in a burst of blue-silver wings.

I pass the rock where the Tamangs cracked small walnuts, then the wild walnut wood, now stark and bare. The yellow is gone and the rich humus smell; and the brook that trickles through the wood, muted a month ago by heavy leaf fall, is now insistent, hastening away down the steep mountain to the Suli. There is only a silent company of gray trunks, dulled

mosses, stumps, and straying leaves, and the whispering small
birds of winter. But farther down the valley, the abandoned village, so empty-eyed and still in early autumn, has been brought
to life by voices of man, dog, and rooster, for its slopes are winter pasture now for the yak herds from the north.

From the village, a southward path quits the main trail, descending through rocks and shining olives to a bridge on the
green river. The portals of the bridge are carved in grotesque
figures, yellow and red. Awaiting the others, I stand on the hot
planks in the noon sun, overtaken by a vague despair. In this
river runs the Kang La stream, by way of Phoksumdo River
and the lake, and also the torrent down from Bugu La, and the
branch that falls from the B'on village at Pung-mo; the Suli carries turquoise from Phoksumdo, and crystals of diamond blue
down from Kang La.

Another hour passes; no one comes. Beside myself, I go on
across the bridge and climb the bluff. A half mile below, the jade
water of the snow peaks disappears into the gray roil of the
Bheri River, which will bear it southward into lowland muds.

The track follows the Bheri westward in a long, gradual climb
to the horizon, arriving at a village in a forest. In the cedars of
Roman, a fitful wind whips the mean rags on the shrines, and
phallic spouts jut from red effigies at the village fountains, and
west of the village stand wild cairns and tall red poles. From
fields below, a troupe of curltailed monkey demons gazes upward, heads afire in the dying light. Then the sun is gone behind the mountains.

I have a headache, and feel very strange. The whole day has
been muddied by a raging in my head caused by the tardiness
of my companions, who were two hours behind me at the
bridge—an echo of that grotesque rage at Murwa, where for
want of unfrozen air in which to bathe, I vilified the sun that
dodged my tent. I seem to have lost all resilience, not to mention
sense of humor—can this be dread of the return to lowland life?

Walking along the Bheri hills this afternoon, I remembered
how careful one must be not to talk too much, or move
abruptly, after a silent week of Zen retreat, and also the precarious coming down from highs on the hallucinogens; it is crucial

to emerge gradually from such a chrysalis, drying new wings in the sun's quiet, like a butterfly, to avoid a sudden tearing of the spirit. Certainly this has been a silent time, and a hallucinatory inner journey, too, and now there is this sudden loss of altitude. Whatever the reason, I am coming down too fast—too fast for what? And if I am coming down too fast, why do I hurry? Far from celebrating my great journey, I feel mutilated, murderous: I am in a fury of dark energies, with no control at all on my short temper.

Thus, when a Hindu of Roman, knocking small children aside, pushes his scabby head into my tent and glares about in stupid incredulity, yelling inchoate questions at my face out of a bad mouth with a rotting lip, I lunge at him and shove him bodily out of my sight, lashing the tent flap and yelling incomprehensibly myself: I do not have the medicine he needs, and anyway there is no cure for him, no cure for me. How can he know, poor stinking bastard, that it is not his offensiveness that offends me, the pus and the bad breath of him—no, it is his very flesh, no different from my own. In his damnable need, he returns me to our common plight, this pit of longing into which, having failed in my poor leap, I sink again.

"Expect nothing," Eido Roshi had warned me on the day I left. And I had meant to go lightly into the light and silence of the Himalaya, without ambition of attainment. Now I am spent. The path I followed breathlessly has faded among stones; in spiritual ambition, I have neglected my children and done myself harm, and there is no way back. Nor has anything changed; I am still beset by the same old lusts and ego and emotions, the endless nagging details and irritations—that aching gap between what I know and what I am. I have lost the flow of things and gone awry, sticking out from the unwinding spiral of my life like a bent spring. For all the exhilaration, splendor, and "success" of the journey to the Crystal Mountain, a great chance has been missed and I have failed. I will perform the motions of parenthood, my work, my friendships, my Zen practice, but all hopes, acts, and travels have been blighted. I look forward to nothing.

NOVEMBER 25

Today Karma and his family will go as far as Tibrikot, where they will turn down the Bheri trade routes toward the south. In the soft mist of the foothills, Karma is singing; last night, looking out across the Bheri Valley from this roof, he played his lute for the first time since the dancing at Saldang. At sunrise, I bid goodbye to this dashing minstrel, and to Tende where she lies with Chiring Lamo, lazing naked in warm sheepskins, baring herself in a charming way to wave.

At Raka it was dead of winter, at Murwa near winter, in Rohagaon the deep autumn; in the valley that leads down to Tibrikot, the walnut trees are still in leaf, and green ferns grow among the copper ones along the watercourses, and I meet a hoopoe; swallows and butterflies flit through the warm air. And so I travel against time, in the weary light of dying summer.

Not having to wait for Karma and his family, the Sherpas catch me before I get to Tibrikot, which lies on the east-west route between Tarakot and Jumla and is by repute the great trade center of this region. A large red Hindu temple stands on a knoll over the river, for Brahmins and Chetris have come up the Bheri River to this mighty bend among the mountains, and two small Hindu *dukhan* that adjoin each other are the first shops I have seen since leaving Pokhara. We obtain a few crucial supplies—salt, sugar, matches, soap—but since neither shop has candles, kerosene, or flashlight batteries, our evenings will continue to be lightless. Rice and flour are lacking, too, so that we must continue to subsist on lentils, scavenging *aloo* or *anda* where we may. There is so little to be had in Tibrikot that

we are done with the great trade center in a few minutes, taking the westward route on a long gradual ascent up the Bal-
ansuro River, under the snow peaks. Between here and Jumla,
we must cross two passes, but both are low, so Tukten says,
and we expect no trouble. Northward, there is a trail over the
peaks to the B'on village of Pung-mo, above Phoksumdo, but
this has been closed for winter by the snows.

Is today Thanksgiving?

Remembering the depression of my first descent from
Tarakot into the Bheri Canyon, I have convinced myself that
sudden loss of altitude is the main clue to my veering moods. A
change is taking place, some painful growth, as in a snake during the shedding of its skin—dull, irritable, without appetite,
dragging about the stale shreds of a former life, near-blinded by
the old dead scale on the new eye. It is difficult to adjust because I do not know who is adjusting; I am no longer that old
person and not yet the new.

Already the not-looking-forward, the without-hope-ness
takes on a subtle attraction, as if I had glimpsed the secret of
these mountains, still half-understood. With the past evapo-
rated, the future pointless, and all expectation worn away, I
begin to experience that *now* that is spoken of by the great
teachers.

To the repentant thief upon the cross, the soft Jesus of the
modern Bible holds out hope of Heaven: "Today thou art with
me in Paradise." But in older translations, as Soen Roshi points
out, there is no "today," no suggestion of the future. In the
Russian translation, for example, the meaning is "right here
now." Thus, Jesus declares, "You are in Paradise right now"—
how much more vital! There is no hope anywhere but in this
moment, in the karmic terms laid down by one's own life. This
very day is an aspect of nirvana, which is not different from
samsara but, rather, a subtle alchemy, the transformation of
dark mud into the pure, white blossom of the lotus.

"Of course I enjoy this life! It's wonderful! *Especially* when I
have no choice!"

And perhaps this is what Tukten knows—that the journey to
Dolpo, step by step and day by day, is the Jewel in the Heart of

the Lotus, the Tao, the Way, the Path, but no more so than small events of days at home. The teaching offered us by Lama Tupjuk, with the snow leopard watching from the rocks and the Crystal Mountain flying on the sky, was not, as I had thought that day, the enlightened wisdom of one man but a splendid utterance of the divine in all mankind.

We climb onward, toward the sky, and with every step my spirits rise. As I walk along, my stave striking the ground, I leave the tragic sense of things behind; I begin to smile, infused with a sense of my own foolishness, with an acceptance of the failures of this journey as well as of its wonders, acceptance of all that I might meet upon my path. I know that this transcendence will be fleeting, but while it lasts, I spring along the path as if set free; so light do I feel that I might be back in the celestial snows.

This clear and silent light of the Himalaya is intensified by the lack of smoke and noise. The myriad high peaks, piercing the atmosphere, let pass a light of heaven—the light on stones that makes them ring, the sun roaring and the silverness that flows in lichens and the wings of crows, the silverness in the round tinkle of a pony's bell, and in the scent of snows.

The world turns, and the silver light takes on an unholy shine. It pierces small figures high up on the slopes, the peasants of fateful, demon-ridden ages, stiff two-legged effigies of men, harassing the accursed brutes that drag the dull wood blade. *E-ughaa!* Grunting and bellowing, man turns beast with the cruel ring through the nostrils, back again, turn again, back again, century upon century, in the grim plod that drags the harrow through the stony soil. And the lump woman, bent to earth one row ahead, hacking at stones with the crude mattock—step, hoe, step, hoe, step, hoe—*Whut!* She flinches as the twig goad whips, stinging the hard flanks of the beasts. *Whut! E-ughaa!*

Whut!

Below the track, an old woman in wild black rags flails barley heaps on the flat roof of her hut; the wood blade cuts the mountain sky as she rears to strike. Under a walnut tree, a hangman's limb, a black cow awaits the dusk; its bell is still.

The trail climbs through a gorge to Kalibon, which Tukten tells me has been occupied by Kham-pas for many, many years, long before "Nepal and Tibet were not the same." No doubt in some sense this is true, a Tukten truth: and by "Kham-pas" Tukten means not the nomad guerrillas, but plain folk of Khams, in eastern Tibet, who have come to Nepal more recently than the Sherpas and are thought of as slightly inferior on that account. As in the Hindu villages, these Kham-pas take no chances with the local demons, and have decked out their stupa as a cairn to Masta. They are hospitable people, eager to be of help, and Tukten obtains some shelled wild walnuts, green buckwheat flour, and potatoes, while I wash in the sun and take my tea, and, led by the children of this village, stroll out happily onto the eastern ridge. In the warm sunset, there is a view of the Dhaulagiris that we never had while skirting those massifs, and when Tukten comes, he points with pride to Churen Himal and Great Dhaulagiri, the mountaineers' Dhaulagiri One, to which he once accompanied an expedition. A north wind streams across these peaks, carrying off great clouds of powdered snow, as if the spires had gone up in fire. From Kalibon one can almost see the region of Jang La—how long ago, in another life, those days now seem!

NOVEMBER 26

A moonless night. I lie with head out of the tent, watching the stars, which twitch a little, drift a little, in the blue-black sphere. This morning I am tired, though I slept well for eight hours. Usually six hours are enough, and yet I was dozing again at dawn when Dawa brought me tea, and I still feel sore and heavy when I rise.

Now that Dawa feels better, he seems a little spoiled by special treatment: for the first time, he is dodging work, taking advantage of the fact that Tukten does not mind. With Karma gone, I carry most of my own gear, and Tukten has inherited a heavy load; though much smaller than either of us, he refuses to share his load with me and asks no help from Dawa. From the beginning, this leopard-eyed saint has outworked and out-walked us all; not once have I seen him downhearted or tired, nor has he responded with sullenness or rudeness to my own evil temper of these recent days. On the steepest slopes, paus-ing to rest, he talks to whoever is at hand, his soft deep voice as soothing and pervasive as this southern wind. All animals and wayfarers are Tukten's friends, and listen to him carefully, yet he rarely speaks except when spoken to, and never seems to speak too much; without obtruding, he becomes the center of each situation, so naturally does he belong where the moment finds him.

The sun pours a fine golden mist into the Bheri Valley, warm-ing my back as I climb the trail through rhododendron wood and shining oak. A boy in a sky-colored cap overtakes me and is gone, leaving a strange shadow in the air. He makes me shiver; I don't want him to look back. I never had a sky-blue cap, I never saw his face, yet this boy who vanishes into the trees is the same as me.

The pass is no higher than 13,000 feet, and there is little snow. I am hobbled by a sharp pain in one knee, and favoring it excites some odd pains elsewhere, and so I am grateful that the descent on the far side is the most gradual path we have yet walked in Nepal, following round the forest rims of four wild valleys before emerging on a hogback ridge. From the ridge, the path turns steeply down to a pretty village with old prayer walls, by a river. This warm season is the season of a dream, not quite like any autumn I have known. I smell fresh frog mud at the rivulets, and sweet chicken dung in sunny heaps, out of the wind, and woodsmoke and the acid smell of rotting leaves—the smells of childhood morning days that tug my heart.

Crossing a bridge, the westward path climbs the length of a long valley; as we draw near, a low pass through the hills brims over with the setting sun. Since I am lame, Tukten and Dawa are ahead, and their humble shapes, bent under loads, rise up in silhouette on the solar fire; like faithful pilgrims at the gates of Heaven, they appear in halo, burn, and disappear.

I turn and, resting on my stave, gaze eastward, the last look in this life, perhaps, at the great Dhaulagiris and the Bheri. Then I cross the divide and slowly descend into the vale between low mountains.

A drum resounds from Sonrikot, across the valley. Hobbling now, I shall not reach there until after dark, but this much-used track is smooth and wide, and I make my way easily enough by the light of stars. The path follows an open mountainside, descends to a dark stream, and climbs again.

Coming up toward the lightless huts, I set myself for dogs. But there is Tukten's silhouette, and I am touched; he has watched me come across the valley, and now stands waiting on the track, as if taking the evening air.

"Good night, sah," he murmurs, as I approach; he takes my pack and leads me up into the village, where my tent is pitched already on a roof. The last tough neck meat from the yak killed by the snow leopard at Murwa is served up with some local turnips, and our *namu* brings fresh yogurt in a bright brass bowl.

In Sonrikot, as at Roman, the tent spikes are driven into a clay rooftop, in a friendly and informal atmosphere of prayer flags, pumpkin seeds, fuel, fodder, dog dung, and red peppers spread to dry. But unlike Roman, this is a mountain village where strangers are made welcome. According to Tukten, many of the people here are from the north, come for the grazing, or to hire out their yaks as pack animals on the Jumla trade route. This is the last Buddhist village we shall see, and even here, the faith is dying out; the prayer walls are ancient, and no one has added a new stone in many years. For this is the Kali Yuga, the Dark Age, when all the great faiths of mankind are on the wane.

NOVEMBER 27

Today my boots seek quiet footholds and avoid loose, skidding stones, wasting no energy on stumbles. I move lightly, and my knee is better, and climbing through oak forest and rhododendron, I soon arrive at a high ridge with a wide western prospect. This pass, like the one yesterday, must be less than 13,000 feet high—before man came, neither pass on this Jumla track was above tree line—but the wind is cold, and the path on the north side is icy and precipitous, twisting down into deep virgin forest. Strong resin and sharp needle smells fill the great evergreens, and a dark humus that brings minerals into the nostrils.

Just ahead, where a stream brings light into the forest, the Sherpas point. In the water shimmer, treading the iced-green moss on a fallen fir, an unfrightened furred creature, the size of a wolverine, crosses the sun shafts. The Sherpas are gleeful, eager as two boys; I am grinning, too. The red panda—this one is lustrous red-and-black—must be the loveliest of all forest animals in the Himalaya; with the wild tracts of the Suli Gorge behind us, I had given up all hope of seeing it. And it makes me happy that the Sherpas take such pleasure in it; the panda has brought the first smile to Dawa's face since the dancing party at Saldang.

Drawn together by this rare experience, talking and laughing, we pause in the sunlight by the stream to share a piece of bread; it seems to occur to all three of us at once that our life together is almost at an end. The last pass is behind us, and a day and a half of gradual descent will bring us into Jumla.

————

Tonight we are camped on a birch island in the Zuwa River, since the canyon sides are much too steep to permit pitching a tent on the river shore; the air is dank and bitter cold, and the flood's roar is oppressive, drowning the voice and rushing it away. Earlier, I resisted Tukten's good advice that we make camp in open valley, some miles back; this river makes me restless, and I snapped at him that we would never reach Jumla by tomorrow evening if we made camp in early afternoon. (On other days I have complained when we make camp after dark instead of arriving in good light, in time to wash; the poor man must think I have gone crazy.) But at twilight it was plain that we would not make the huts at Muni, at the far end of Zuwa Gorge, which narrowed and grew dark as we went along: the island, reached by a fallen tree, was a last refuge.

Moving around trying to keep warm until a fire can be made, we wrest faggots from the frozen earth. I feel bad, all the more so because the Sherpas' clothing is inadequate, and Tukten's especially: what little he had was stolen at Ring-mo on his way back from Jumla. He is happy to wear whatever I can spare him, though not once has he asked for it: Tukten never seems to suffer—a true *repa*. At the fire, I make a special effort to be friendly, to acknowledge my stupidity in not deferring to his judgment—after all, he has been over this same route in the past month. But with this Tukten, all such effort is absurd; how can he forgive me, when he hadn't bothered with resentment in the first place?

Over supper, we discuss the yeti. Still under the sway of the sophisticated Jang-bu, Dawa giggles in embarrassment at talk of yeti, and the older Sherpa shifts upon his heels to look at him. Tukten says quietly, "I have heard the yeti," and cries out suddenly, "Kak-kak-kak KAI-ee!"—a wild laughing yelp, quite unlike anything I have ever heard, which echoes eerily off the walls of the cold canyon.

Stirring the embers, Tukten is silent for a while. Dawa stares at him, more startled than myself. According to Tukten, the yeti is an animal, but "more man-creature than monkey-creature." He has never seen one, but intends to turn quickly when he does and pretend he hasn't; the yeti never attacks men, but to see one is bad luck. Yetis were once common in the Khumbu region, but in the time of his grandfather, the people set out poisoned barley to keep yetis from raiding their crops, and killed them off—there were dead yetis everywhere, said Tukten's grandfather.[2]

Looking up, he gazes at me peacefully over the flame. Then he says something very strange: "I think the yeti is a Buddhist." When I ask him if he means a holy man, a hermit with strange powers, a *naljorpa*, he just shrugs, refusing with uncustomary stubbornness to explain further.

Tibetans claim to be descended from a monkey god who was an incarnation of Chen-resigs; he married a demoness who lusted after him, and they had six children with long hair and tails. However, he fed them sacred grains, and gradually the hair and tails grew shorter, then fell away entirely. According to the chronicles,[3] some had the virtues of their father while others had the vices of their mother, "yet all possessed strong bodies and courage," like the Tibetans of today. In a Sherpa version of this legend, a monkey converted to Buddhism lived as a hermit in the mountains, and was loved and married by a demoness; their offspring also had long hair and tails, and these were the *mi-teh kang-mi*, the "man-thing of the snows"—the yeti.

Sherpas also say[4] that yeti are the *dhauliyas*, or guardians, of Dölma (Tara), the feminine aspect of Chen-resigs. Many *dhauliyas* represent the animistic deities of pre-Buddhist religions, and supposedly there is "a great religious tradition which has for its focal point the mystery of the Sangbai-Dagpo, or Concealed Lords. This religion certainly antedates Lamaism, and is obsessed with the transmigration of the human soul into the bodies of the lower anthropoids. The Abominable Snowmen are revered by the adherents of this sect, and the heads, hands, and feet of deceased specimens find their way into their ritual. The effect of this animistic doctrine on Tibetan Buddhism should not be underestimated, and . . . motivates local people to protect these creatures from the quest of the Europeans."[5]

I gaze at Tukten, in hopes that he will say more, but he is

silent; in the firelight, his eyes are shining. There is power in the air, and Dawa feels it, too; Dawa and I exchange a glance, uneasy. A sorcerer sits on the far side of this night fire in the Zuwa Gorge. When I ask him to make the yeti cry again, he does so, holding my eyes with his, and not quite smiling.

"Kak-kak-kak KAI-ee!"

NOVEMBER 28

In the Zuwa Gorge, in gray darkness of dawn, a pack pony has got separated from its owner. Walleyed and wild as a horse of nightmare, it skids and dances on the sheet ice where the Zuwa overflows its banks, and there is no way to help it, or to reach it, even, since the ice sheets are so treacherous that I can barely stand upright. Several times the poor beast falls, kicking and lunging, skinny legs groping in the air. Finally, it attains dry ground and hobbles painfully into the forest. Uneasy, I continue on my way.

An hour's trek down the cold gorge brings me out at the police checkpoint under Muni, a fit entry to the lowland world we left behind two months ago at Pokhara. When the Sherpas come, the surly guards root through everything, even the rolled tents, on the lookout for stolen religious objects, so they say: they would doubtless confiscate valuable objects from a Tibetan or a Bhote, whether or not the man was the rightful owner. Even a bystander dares to pick through my belongings, and I snatch something from his hand with an oath for all to hear; at this, Tukten shakes his head in warning. When the man rides off on a horse, Tukten explains that this nosy fellow is a police official. (This same official was to turn up again at the next check post, closer to Jumla, and intervene there on behalf of the Westerner who had been so rude to him at Muni, commanding his minions to let us through at once. It is hard to adjust to the intricate hostile deference of Hindus, so many of whom—even the children—seem to be frowning.)

The fear-crazed pony on the ice was a grim portent, for beginning with the intrusions at the police post, the signs of approaching civilization come thick and fast—the litter of Chetri villages, ubiquitous police, dogs, human excrement, the hard blare of transistor radios, and finally Jumla, once a great kingdom of northwestern Nepal, now a frontier town littered all across the eroded hills on the far side of the river.

Excepting the half-day's rest at Murwa, we have been walking for eleven days. I am tired, and as filthy as I have ever been in life, which is saying a good deal. Although it is early afternoon, these villages on the south side of the river lie already in the mountain shadow; we must cross over to the farther bank and make camp in the sun, the better to celebrate our arrival with a wash. But Dawa will not keep up with us, he has no animation left, and Tukten is behaving oddly, causing needless delays and making foolish suggestions which are not foolish, only seem so, because I do not know what he is up to: plainly this man is in no rush at all to get to Jumla.

I have no wish to go to Jumla, either, since we may be here for days before air passage is available; a good campsite well outside that squalid town would suit me better. For want of destination, we wander onward, while Tukten suggests one bad site after another—this is as close as he has ever come to sullenness—until at last we reach a bridge where the Tila River joins the Zuwa. On the point is a pretty village called Dansango, upon which I see that the sun will shine until late afternoon because of a low saddle in the western mountains. The east end of the Jumla airport lies on a bluff just across the Tila, and Dansango is less than an hour's walk from town.

We camp at water's edge, beside an odd white shrine, in the court of which, out of the wind, the Sherpas build their fire. While the water heats, I read the mail that was brought to Shey by Tukten; there is no bad news, and I am glad that I put off the reading until now. I finish my wash and take sunset tea in the doorway of my tent, watching the rivers drink the light and the waters spiral round a strange black rock that lies downstream. In a meadow, ponies graze, and the low sun glows in the heavy guard hairs all around their bellies. Figures dark beneath their loads pass down the far bank of the river, rendered immortal by the streak of sunset upon their shoulders. The water turns black, and drops of spray jump up to catch the light as it leaves the valley. Then the sun is gone, the journey is done, the new moon rises.

NOVEMBER 29

Leaving Dawa to tend camp, Tukten and I climb to the plateau across the Tila and walk the last miles into Jumla, crossing the fields and descending through soiled, littered outskirts into the mud, smells, and offal of the town. Fortunately, we shall not be here long, for an airplane comes tomorrow at midday with mail and cargo, then carries workers down to the Nepalganj Road, on the Indian border, then returns here before proceeding to Bhairava and Kathmandu.

Once again we explain ourselves to the police, after which we change money at the bank, frequent a tea stall, and buy goat meat, rice, eggs, wizened oranges and apples, and some bootleg arak for the small celebration we shall have tonight. Tukten apparently made many friends during his visit, and knows just where to go to find some arak, which we receive in a soiled container at a private dwelling.

All morning I have been surprised by the number of people who approach Tukten to renew acquaintance, and address him with great warmth and respect; he never precipitates these encounters, and though he seems pleased at being hailed, he accepts the deference given him in a simple open way, in mild surprise.

What is perplexing is why Tukten did not hesitate to come to Jumla this morning despite his obvious reluctance yesterday afternoon. I ask him about Gyaltsen's charges—that, while in Jumla, he entertained a plan to steal our mail. Untroubled by the question, he reminds me that he never said anything against Gyaltsen, but let him do all the talking, telling his stories. He shrugs: not much happened except for that fight in Ring-mo.

Tukten smiles a little: "Gyaltsen hit me first." Tukten has no interest in defending himself further, and I am content to let the matter go.

The white crown of Great Kanjiroba, rising to 23,000 feet in the northeast, up the Tila Valley, is the one snow peak in sight: this was the peak climbed by the Japanese. Otherwise, the hills around are low and worn, sadly eroded by years of makeshift farming, and the town itself, with most of the vices and none of the virtues of the twentieth century, is depressing. I am happy to go back to Dansango, where the half-naked Dawa, having washed out all his clothes, walks about singing in the sunshine, so relieved is he that his hard journey is coming to an end.

Near the white shrine at the point of rivers, I spend a peaceful afternoon in meditation, letting my mind dissolve in the bright tumult where the rivers meet. At dark, I join Tukten and Dawa at the fire. Drinking our arak quietly, we talk little, feeling dull, content. I wonder if Tukten will drink heavily, but he does not.

I study this old soldier with the half-moon scar on his left cheekbone, the sad eyes and wild smile that light a face like an ancient Mongol mask. Away from the other Sherpas, Tukten and Dawa get on very well; not once have I heard a rancorous word between them, although they have to share the same small tent. Dawa defers to Tukten, as he should: throughout Dawa's illness and malingering, Tukten has been a true Bodhisattva, as courteous and gentle to the younger Sherpa as he is to me.

Coming down, coming down—a dream of falling, in a machine no longer in control. I manage my panic with deep breaths, go so far as to wish my fellow passengers good luck. At the point of crash, there comes a cosmic ringing, and, lulled by river sounds, I wonder if I am dead; I feel half in and half out of my body, fighting free, yet not ready to let go.

NOVEMBER 30

We are at the airport early, clean and rather shy with one another. Tukten has thrown away his cap and rags and looks refreshed in my spare jersey, for in Kathmandu I shall recommend him to the trekking outfitters as a sirdar or head Sherpa. I pay wages to the Sherpas for their months of faithful work, having Tukten explain to Dawa the when, where, and why of the accounting; then I take Tukten aside to pay him his promised bonus. They have no wish to question me or count their money, for fear of seeming impolite, and both are delighted with their tips. Presented with a receipt, Dawa takes special pleasure in drawing his own name for the first time in his life; the whole idea convulses him with laughter. As for Tukten, he seems pleased that I think him qualified to be a head Sherpa, and is willing to be interviewed in Kathmandu—less in hope of betterment, I feel, than out of courtesy to my ambitions for him.

A man on horseback, friend to Tukten, comes to make a parting gift of arak. Toward noon, a sound of motors falls out of the Kanjiroba skies; a flying machine is circling the new moon, and the whole town comes running to the airstrip. As the plane lands, the horses shy, and children run in the plane's dust; near the runway, two oblivious figures breaking the earth with their crude harrows move on and on and on, step after step. Then the plane roars away into the south, and excited crows swirl in the valley air.

Inspection by police is done with quickly because the inspector, too, turns out to be a friend of Tukten. When the plane returns, we are lifted up from Jumla and carried back east, in a matter of hours, over the dark canyons and white mountainsides that required so many long hard weeks to cross. Threading a high pass between peaks, the pilot, joking with the co-pilot, flies fifteen feet above the ground with one wing tip just yards away from the glinting ice, and the only one unfrightened by this idiotic trick is Dawa Sherpa, who smiles shyly, in awe.

The plane emerges from the snow peaks and drifts peacefully to the southeast, down along the white massifs of Dhaulagiri, past Annapurna and the clear cone of Machhapuchare and on south across the foothills to Bhairava, where the Kali Gandaki comes down out of the mountains into India. As the plane circles, its shadow falls on what must have been Lumbini, at the end of a raw new road over the mountains that is the gift of Buddhists from Japan: I call to Tukten to point out to Dawa the birthplace of the Buddha Sakyamuni. Dawa sighs.

Bhairava, on the Ganges Plain, is another name for Shiva the Destroyer. It is not far above sea level, and after two months at high altitudes, we gasp in its humidity and heat. Then the airplane is off again to the north and east, and the whole white rampart of the Himalaya is spread out, peak upon peak. As the plane circles Kathmandu, Tukten points to what he says is Everest, far away to eastward, great Lachi Kang where Milarepa died. However, I think that Tukten is mistaken. Lachi Kang is too far off to see.

At the trekking company, where we return our pots and tents, all praise of Tukten is in vain: he is known by bad reputation to the manager, who will have no part of him. Tukten, he says, is a loner who does not get on with the clannish Sherpa groups who make up the best expedition teams: unlike most Sherpas, he is an aggressive drinker, and his foul barracks language offends them. No doubt he is intelligent and able, no doubt he is excellent day by day, but sooner or later—the manager points sternly at the door, outside of which my friend awaits—that fellow will let you down when you most need him.

And Tukten has known the answer all along, having only assented to my great plans to be polite, for he smiles as I come out—not to make light of things, far less to save face, but to console me. "Plenty job, sah," Tukten says; he accepts his life, and will go on wandering until it ends.

Suddenly it is twilight, and our ways are parting. Shy Dawa, safely home with two months' pay, is happy and smiling; exhilarated by his flight through the thin air, he musters up some English, even looks me in the eye—"Goodbye, sahib!" But Tukten insists on escorting me to the door of my hotel, and is sorry that I will not let him pay the taxi. He wishes that I meet him three days hence at the great stupa at Bodhinath, four miles away, where he will stay briefly with his father's sister and renew himself as a good Buddhist before returning to Khundu, near Namche Bazaar, to pass the winter.

With hotel staff hissing at my elbow, I shake Tukten's hand under the portico, and it occurs to me to invite him in to supper. I know that this is sentimental, a show of democratic principles at his expense, for the caste-crazy staff will make things miserable for this soiled Sherpa in the jersey much too big for him. Even if they restrain themselves for the sake of their baksheesh, a friendship formed in mountain sun might be damaged in the sour light of the hotel. All true, all true, and yet that I feel too tired to transcend these difficulties upsets me very much. I let him go.

In the rear window of the cab, Tukten is ghostly; I stare after him as he withdraws into the dusk. It is not so much that this man and I are friends. Rather, there is a thread between us, like the black thread of a live nerve; there is something unfinished, and he knows it, too. Without ever attempting to speak about it, we perceive life in the same way, or rather, I perceive it in the way that Tukten lives it. In his life in the moment, in his freedom from attachments, in the simplicity of his everyday example, Tukten has taught me over and over, he is the teacher that I hoped to find: I used to say this to myself as a kind of instinctive joke, but now I wonder if it is not true. "When you are ready," Buddhists say, "the teacher will appear." In the way he watched me, in the way he smiled, he was awaiting me; had I been ready, he might have led me far enough along the path "to see the snow leopard."

Out of respect, I stand in the same place until Tukten is out of sight. The Hindus dart off with my backpack, sleeping bag, and rucksack, and for a moment I am all alone on the hotel steps. Off to the north, black clouds are shrouding the black mountains; it is snowing. I wonder if GS has left the Crystal Mountain. Here I am, safely returned over those peaks from a journey far more beautiful and strange than anything I had hoped for or imagined—how is it that this safe return brings such regret?

By mistake, all my November mail has been sent to Jumla: I stood right next to it this morning at the airstrip. India Airlines is on strike, and no one will say when a flight out of Nepal will be available. In my room-with-bath, anticipated for two months, the room is wintry and the bath has no hot water; for an hour, the unqualified crowd in and out while I stand fuming in my grimy long johns. Four or five line up at last for their baksheesh, and the plumber, whichever one is he, departs—gone until tomorrow, as I learn when it turns out that there is no more hot water than before. I force the door of the next room, usurp the bath: the hot water runs out as I soap. Stomping back to my own room, I discover that the hot water has turned up magically of its own accord. Feeling silly and quite suddenly exhausted, I sit down on the bed and begin to laugh, but I might just as easily weep. In the gaunt, brown face in the mirror—unseen since late September—the blue eyes in a monkish skull seem eerily clear, but this is the face of a man I do not know.

DECEMBER 1

On this day, for the first time since early November, the skies at Shey clouded over with "a grim wind," and on December 3, Jang-bu and two Saldang men left for Namdo with most of GS's gear. On December 5, as if to see him off, the frost-colored wolf and three of its pack mates appeared on Somdo mountain, and the following day GS and Phu-Tsering went out over Shey Pass to Namgung Gompa, and from there to Namdo, without passing by Saldang. From Namdo, where Jang-bu awaited them with porters, they went up the Nam-Khong River past Tcha and Raka, as far as the cairn of great argali skulls under Namdo Pass. The porters had promised to cross the pass that day, but now they refused to go until next morning. At six that afternoon, it began to snow. What follows are excerpts from GS's notes for December 8 and 9, 1973, which came in a letter from Kathmandu:

Dec. 8. Three inches of snow and still falling at 6 a.m. Porters of course beat it for home. Met a chap who said he'd guide us to pass. We have little choice but to go on. We threw away most food, all extra cooking gear, some of my specimens etc., etc., but our loads still awful. Guide fled after an hour. Weather getting worse and soon is a blizzard. We cannot see 100 feet, wind howling, snow flying horizontally and forming crust all over us. Once it cleared a little, and coming down slope toward us a caravan of 50 yaks in single file, moving black things in that white nothingness. One of most dramatic sights I have seen. Also they left us trail to follow for a little while. Then by luck a caravan of 6 yaks going *our* way came and took my suitcase. Still in the blizzard we crossed over the pass (alt. 17,500) and after an hour things cleared a little. Went on till dark, then stopped at a little cave.

Dec. 9. Yak chap said he would not go on for a couple of days until his yak has foraged. 6–8 inches of fresh snow on trail. He said he would carry one load to next pass for 60 rupees payable in advance. I was suspicious, but little choice. One hour out of camp he purposely fell and said he hurt his leg; the money was with his friend at camp. Sunny today and we have to push on. Jang-bu showed his annoyance by beating the hell out of the fellow. That cured the leg but he would not go to the pass. He suggested going down the khola to the lake. I did not like the idea, knowing what the canyons are like. But the sherpas wanted that route—and Gyaltsen had never bought himself boots with the boot money, I found out. He wore sneakers and it was very cold. I did not want frozen feet on my conscience. We forced our yak friend to carry the load down the canyon until at 2 p.m. he fled. But we got most of our money's worth. A hellish trip. Ice falls, slippery snow-covered rocks, 6" trails along ledges covered with snow with cliff above and below. Since I was heaviest, everyone felt it logical that I lead and test ice bridges as we crossed and recrossed stream. Logical but not always pleasant: once I fell in, getting soaked from chest on down, and got my feet wet several times. By evening had done most of canyon: at least we had big fire.

On December 10, the party emerged from the canyon onto the flats of Phoksumdo Lake's eastern arm that we had seen on October 25. Here a snow leopard—the only one ever seen on our expedition—jumped up ahead of GS in patchy snow, and the prints of a second animal were found nearby; since GS estimates a population of perhaps six for the whole Shey-Saldang-Phoksumdo region,[6] it pleases me to think that the two were breeding.

That day, GS's party climbed around the steep north end of the lake to our old Silver Birch Camp at Phoksumdo River. Leaving Jang-bu and Gyaltsen to follow with the gear, GS and Phu-Tsering set out next morning on a rapid march to Jumla, where they arrived on December 15, flying out two days later to Kathmandu. All this effort was in vain; GS's family had been unable to come to Kathmandu as planned, and because of the airline strike and other mishaps, he did not arrive home in Pakistan until three days after Christmas. Not long afterward, he had word from Nepal that because of a bloody skirmish between Kham-pas and Nepali troops near the Tibetan border north of Shey, the Land of Dolpo had been closed once again to the outside world.

On foot and bicycle, I wander the old city of Patan, across the river, where Tibetan refugees make copies of true ancient relics of the Land of B'od. I visit stupas, temples, and pagodas of the valley and climb the three hundred thirty steps to Swayambhunath where, it is said, the Buddha preached among the monkeys and the pines. In the Asan Bazaar I keep an eye out for Ongdi the Trader, and encounter instead the sheepish Dawa in a new red plastic jacket. From a thief I buy an antique image, in painted clay, of an eleven-faced Avalokita, head split apart in His great distress at the debased condition of mankind. I meet Pirim and Tulo Kansha, last seen as they skipped away with their goat and *chang* into the pine forests at Phoksumdo Lake; the Tamangs greet me with their fresh, wild smiles, as enchanted with their meager life as ever. Jostled by throngs of northern Bhotes down off the mountains, we stand there grinning and exclaiming, slapping one another on the shoulder for want of other means of communication. And then Pirim's English is all gone, we slap and grin again, and part as suddenly as we have met.

On the day appointed to meet Tukten, I pedal across the late-autumn landscapes of the Kathmandu Valley to the ancient shrine at Bodhinath; the painted eyes above the white dome of its stupa, peering over the brown rooftops, watch me come. Tradition says that Bodhinath's creation was blessed by Avalokita, and that it contains relics of Kasapa, he who smiled a Tukten smile when the Buddha held up the lotus flower in silent teaching. In former years, the shrine was visited by throngs of pilgrims from Tibet, and the colorful stupa is surrounded by a square of dwellings and small shops that sell brass Buddhas, icons, urns, and ritual daggers, beads of bone, stone, wood, and turquoise, incense, prayer wheels, cymbals, drums, and bells.

In one of these houses, Tukten said, he would be staying with his father's sister. Accosting inhabitants, calling his name, I walk my bicycle round and round the square, under the huge painted eyes, the nose like a great question mark, the wind-snapped pennants—Tukten? Tukten? But there is no answer, no one knows of Tukten Sherpa. Under the Bodhi Eye, I get on my bicycle again and return along gray December roads to Kathmandu.

Notes

PROLOGUE

1. George B. Schaller, *The Serengeti Lion* (Chicago: University of Chicago Press, 1972).
2. Lama Anagarika Govinda, *The Way of the White Clouds* (Boulder: Shambhala, 1971).
3. David Snellgrove, *Himalayan Pilgrimage* (Oxford: Cassirer, 1961).
4. Peter Matthiessen, *The Tree Where Man Was Born* (New York: E. P. Dutton, 1972).

I WESTWARD

1. George B. Schaller, *Mountain Monarchs* (Chicago: University of Chicago Press, 1977).
2. It has been suggested that the yogas were a kind of synthesis of Aryan physical austerity and the intricate psychic lore of the Dravidians. "The newly-settled nomads were striving to make themselves, body and will, tempered and taut like the bow and the bowstring—their favorite simile. They underwent intense tests and ordeals . . . sitting for long spans unwaveringly erect under midday sun surrounded by blazing fires. . . ." (Gerald Heard, *The Human Venture,* New York: Harper & Row, 1955). What was sought was a deflection of the vast forces of the Universe with *siddhis,* or powers cultivated through yogic mastery of body-mind—not the passive fatalism of which Eastern religions are so commonly accused but acceptance of each moment, resilience and serenity, calmness in action and intensity when calm. The yogi in seated meditation was called "the flame in the windless spot that does not flicker" (A. K. Coomaraswamy, *Buddha and the Gospel of Buddhism,* New York: Harper & Row, 1964).

3. Coomaraswamy, *Buddha and the Gospel of Buddhism.*

4. Altitudes in Nepal, based mostly on the nineteenth-century Survey of India directed by Sir George Everest and others, vary according to the map at hand, and in this book are regarded as approximate except where recorded by George Schaller's altimeter.

5. Heinrich Harter, *Seven Years in Tibet* (New York: E. P. Dutton, 1959); and Michel Peissel, *Mustang* (New York: E. P. Dutton, 1967). In 1974, the Kham-pas were finally subdued and resettled, following a major skirmish with Nepali troops that caused Dolpo to be closed once more to all outsiders.

6. (Tibetan) *Book of Golden Precepts,* ed. H. P. Blavatsky, quoted in W. Y. Evans-Wentz, *Tibetan Yoga and Secret Doctrines* (New York: Oxford University Press, 1967).

7. P'ang Chu-shih ("Layman P'ang").

8. William Blake, *The Marriage of Heaven and Hell.*

9. In Kenneth Grahame, *The Wind in the Willows.*

10. C. G. Jung, *Collected Works* (Princeton: The Bollingen Foundation, for the Princeton University Press, 1954); XVII, chap. 7.

11. Farid ud-Din Attar, *The Conference of the Birds: A Sufi Fable* (Boulder: Shambhala, 1971).

12. L. Austine Waddell, *The Buddhism of Tibet, or Lamaism* (London, 1895). *Dorje* (or *vajra*) is variously translated—thunderbolt, holy stone, the adamantine diamond—in effect, the distilled energy of the universe, cutting through everything without being affected.

13. Especially H. P. Blavatsky, various imaginative works, e.g., *The Secret Doctrine.*

14. Ma Tuan-lin, *Non-Chinese People of China* (ms. in Sterling Library, Yale University).

15. As quoted by A. David-Neel, *Magic and Mystery in Tibet* (New York: Penguin, 1971); See part II, 18.

16. Evans-Wentz, *Tibetan Yoga and Secret Doctrines.* See also George Gurdjieff, *Meetings with Remarkable Men* (New York: E. P. Dutton, 1969).

17. Mircea Eliade, *Shamanism: Archaic Techniques of Ecstasy* (Princeton: Princeton University Press, 1964).

18. Carlos Castaneda, *The Teachings of Don Juan* (Berkeley: University of California Press, 1968); *A Separate Reality* and *Journey to Ixtlan* (New York: Simon & Schuster, 1971, 1973). The "authenticity" of this shaman has been much debated, and the author has chosen to abet the obfuscation—no matter. If "Don Juan" is imaginary, then spurious ethnology becomes a great work of the imagination; whether borrowed or not, the teaching rings true.

19. It is not true, it is not true
  that we come to live here.
 We come only to sleep, only to dream.
     —Anon. Aztec

 Sometimes I go about in pity for myself,
  and all the while,
 A great wind carries me across the sky
     —Anon. Ojibwa

20. It is *baroka* to the Sufis: "Do you know why a Sheikh breathes into the ear of a newly born child? Of course you do not! You put it down to magic, primitive symbols representing life, but the practical reasons, the deadly serious business of nourishing the inner consciousness, passes you by." A Sufi sheikh, quoted in Rafael Lefort, *The Teachers of Gurdjieff* (Garden City, N.Y.: Doubleday, 1968).

21. See Benjamin Whorf, "An American Indian Model of the Universe," *International Journal of American Linguistics* 16, 1950.

22. Lao-tzu, the *Tao Te Ching*.

23. Rig Veda.

24. Werner Heisenberg, quoted by Lawrence LeShan in "How Can You Tell a Physicist from a Mystic?" *Intellectual Digest*, February 1972.

25. Lama Anagarika Govinda, *The Way of the White Clouds* (Boulder: Shambhala, 1971).

26. Evans-Wentz, *Tibetan Yoga and Secret Doctrines*.

27. Carl Sagan, in I. S. Shklovsky and Carl Sagan, *Intelligent Life in the Universe* (San Francisco: Holden-Day, 1966).

28. Harlow Shapley, *Beyond the Observatory* (New York: Charles Scribner's Sons, 1967).

II NORTHWARD

1. Deborah Love, *Annaghkeen* (New York: Random House, 1970).

2. Adapted from Trevor Leggett, *The Tiger's Cave* (London: Rider, 1964).

3. W. Y. Evans-Wentz, *Tibet's Great Yogi: Milarepa* (New York: Oxford University Press, 1969).

4. In the absence of a meaningful vocabulary, one must fall back on nebulous terms, on grandiose capital letters, and on Sanskrit. But Sanskrit terms are differently defined by Hindus and Buddhists, and even within Buddhism they blur and overlap a little, like snakes swallowing their tails in that ancient symbol of eternity:

samadhi (one-pointedness, unification) may lead to *sunyata* (transparency, void) which can open out in a sudden *satori* (glimpse) which may evolve into the *prajna* (transcendent wisdom) of *nirvana* (beyond delusion, beyond all nature, life, and death, beyond becoming) which might be seen as eternal *samadhi*. Thus the circle is complete, every state is conditioned by each of the others, and all are inherent in meditation, which is itself a realization of the Way.

5. Lawrence LeShan, in *The Medium, the Mystic, and the Physicist* (New York: Grossman, 1974), has suggested that some such plane or trancelike state in which one becomes a vehicle or "medium," beyond thought or feelings, laid open to the energies and *knowing* that circulate freely through the universe, may be the one on which telepathy, precognition, and even psychic healing are transmitted.

6. Richard M. Bucke, *Cosmic Consciousness* (Secaucus, N.J.: University Books, 1961).

7. W. Y. Evans-Wentz, *Tibetan Yoga and Secret Doctrines* (New York: Oxford University Press, 1967).

8. Translated by Shimano Eido Roshi.

9. See D. T. Suzuki, *Mysticism: Christian and Buddhist* (New York: Harper & Brothers, 1957).

10. Saint Francis de Sales called mystical experience the immediate experience of the love of God.

11. The Maha Ati, quoted by Chögyam Trungpa in *Mudra* (Boulder: Shambhala, 1972).

12. In Ivan Turgenev, *Virgin Soil*.

13. Maurice Herzog, *Annapurna* (New York: E. P. Dutton, 1953).

14. Evans-Wentz, *Tibetan Yoga and Secret Doctrines*.

15. Edward Cronin, "The Yeti," *Atlantic*, November 1975. See also E. Cronin, J. McNeely, H. Emery, "The Yeti—Not a Snowman," *Oryx*. May 1973.

16. John Napier, *Big Foot: The Yeti and Sasquatch in Myth and Reality* (New York: E. P. Dutton, 1973).

17. Mircea Eliade, *Images and Symbols* (New York: Sheed & Ward, 1961).

18. See David Snellgrove, *Himalayan Pilgrimage* (Oxford: Cassirer, 1961).

19. Ibid.

20. David Snellgrove, *The Nine Ways of B'on* (London: Oxford University Press, 1967).

21. John Blofeld, *The Tantric Mysticism of Tibet*. See also Lama Anagarika Govinda, "The Significance of Meditation in Buddhism," in *Main Currents of Modern Thought*. "The reflection is neither inside nor outside of the mirror, and thus 'things are freed from their "thing-ness," their isolation, without being deprived of their form; they are divested of their materiality without being dissolved'"—the mirror-teaching from the Atamsaka Sutra, attributed to Nagarjuna, an Indian sage of the first century A.D. who is also credited with the compilation of the Prajna Paramita Sutra, the fundamental text of Mahayana Buddhism.

22. See Snellgrove, *Himalayan Pilgrimage*.

23. A. David-Neel, *Magic and Mystery in Tibet* (New York: Penguin, 1971). See also Lama Anagarika Govinda, *The Way of the White Clouds* (Boulder: Shambhala, 1971), and Carlos Castaneda.

24. Quoted in Eliade, *Shamanism: Archaic Techniques of Ecstasy* (Princeton: Princeton University Press, 1964).

25. "The Sufis regard miracles as 'veils' intervening between the soul and God. The masters of Hindu spirituality urge their disciples to pay no attention to the *siddhis,* or psychic powers, which may come to them unsought, as a by-product of one-pointed contemplation." Aldous Huxley, *The Perennial Philosophy* (New York: Arno Press, 1970).

26. Sven Hedin, *Central Asia and Tibet*, vol. 1: *Towards the Holy City of Lhasa* (Westport, Conn.: Greenwood, 1968).

27. A. Henry Savage Landor, *In the Forbidden Land* (New York, 1899).

28. H. E. Richardson and David Snellgrove, *A Cultural History of Tibet* (London: Weidenfeld, 1968).

29. Snellgrove, *Himalayan Pilgrimage*.

30. See Gerald Heard, *The Human Venture* (New York: Harper & Row, 1955).

III AT CRYSTAL MOUNTAIN

1. David Snellgrove, *Himalayan Pilgrimage* (Oxford: Cassirer, 1961).

2. Lama Anagarika Govinda, *The Way of the White Clouds* (Boulder: Shambhala, 1971).

3. David Snellgrove, *Four Lamas of Dolpo,* (Cambridge, Mass.: Harvard University Press, 1967).

4. L. Austine Waddell, *The Buddhism of Tibet* (London, 1895).

5. H. E. Richardson, "The Karma-pa Sect: A Historical Note," *Journal of the Royal Anthropological Society,* October 1958.

6. George B. Schaller, "A Naturalist in South Asia," *New York Zoological Society Bulletin,* Spring 1971.

7. V. Geist, *Mountain Sheep* (Chicago: University of Chicago Press, 1971).

8. Ibid.

9. A. David-Neel, *Magic and Mystery in Tibet* (New York: Penguin, 1971).

10. Ibid.

11. Lao-tzu, the *Tao Te Ching.*

12. Malcolm Lowry, *Hear Us, O Lord from Heaven Thy Dwelling Place* (Philadelphia: Lippincott, 1961).

13. Thomas Traherne, *Centuries of Meditation.*

14. Ibid.

15. Respectively: Stoliczka's high mountain vole (*Alticola Stoliczkanus*), (unnamed) vole (*Pitymys irene*), (unnamed) shrew (*Sorex avaneus*).

16. See Robert Ornstein, *The Psychology of Consciousness* (New York: Grossman, 1973).

17. *The Hundred Thousand Songs of Milarepa* (Secaucus, N.J.: University Books, 1975).

18. Snellgrove, *Four Lamas of Dolpo.*

19. Chögyam Trungpa, *Cutting Through Spiritual Materialism* (Boulder: Shambhala, 1973).

20. Dogen Zenji, *Shobogenzo* (San Francisco: Japan Publications, 1977).

21. George B. Schaller (ms. in progress).

22. Bhagavad-Gita.

IV THE WAY HOME

1. Deborah Love, *Annaghkeen* (New York: Random House, 1970).

2. This story is a variation on a traditional account from Tukten's region.

3. Pawo Tsuk-lar-re Cho-chung III; cited in Sir Charles Bell, *Tibet: Past and Present* (London: Oxford University Press, 1969).

4. Swami Pranavananda, in *Journal of the Bombay Natural History Society* 54, 1956.

5. Yonah N. ibn Aharaon, in I. Sanderson, *The Abominable Snowman* (Radnor, Pa.: Chilton, 1961), p. 458. Perhaps *Sangbai-Dagpo* has been confused here with *Sa-bdag-po,* or "Earth-Master," a local earth-spirit who is much feared and respected but so far as I know

is not identified with the "man-thing of the snows." *Sanbahi' dag-po,* the "Concealed Lord," is a name given by exoteric cults to Dorje-Chang, the primordial Buddha of the Karma-Kagyu-pas. See L. Austine Waddell, *The Buddhism of Tibet* (London, 1895).

6. Dr. Schiller's recommendation to the Nepal government resulted in the creation of the 160-square-mile Shey Wildlife Reserve, which has not yet been given formal status as a national park. This is a pity, since evidence accumulates that the snow leopard may soon vanish from the country. A wildlife ecologist, Rodney Jackson, tells me that there may be fewer than 120 animals left in Nepal, most of them in the western region north of the Himalaya. In the winter of 1976–77, he conducted a snow leopard survey in the Lingo River region of Mugu, west of Dolpo (he had been re-fused permission to enter Dolpo, which was closed to foreigners early in 1974), and although he never saw a snow leopard, he found evidence of five in a study area of approximately two hun-dred square miles. In this region there is little grazing and there-fore no problem of leopard predation; also, the value of a leopard pelt to the hunter has been reduced to about ten dollars, due to the international import/export bans that are now taking effect. Yet the creatures are still hunted hard in Mugu, where the hunt-ing tradition is stronger than the waning Buddhism, and trade in musk deer pods—sold mostly in Jumla—is a crucial source of lo-cal income. For both deer and leopard, the hunting technique is the implanting of poison-tipped spears in likely places—in the case of the nomadic leopard, the trails that it follows habitually on its wide hunting circuit. Though both musk deer and snow leopard are protected by law, there is no enforcement. Of three local snow leopards, two were killed, the third wounded, during Jackson's stay; local hunters complained that only two years be-fore, they had managed to destroy six or seven.

Index